GILLIGAN

ALSO BY PAUL WILLIAMS

The Monk
Almost the Perfect Murder
Murder Inc.
Badfellas
Crime Wars
The Untouchables
Crimelords
Evil Empire
Gangland
Secret Love (ghostwriter)
The General

Paul Williams is Ireland's leading crime writer and one of its most respected journalists. For over three decades his courageous and groundbreaking investigative work has won him multiple awards. He is the author of eleven previous bestselling books and has also researched, written and presented a number of major TV crime series. His first book, *The General*, was adapted into the award-winning movie of the same name by John Boorman. He is a former presenter on Newstalk Breakfast and currently writes for the *Irish Independent*. Williams holds an MA in Criminology and is a registered member of the International Consortium of Investigative Journalists based in Washington, DC.

PAUL WILLIAMS

GILLIGAN

THE MOB BOSS WHO CHANGED
THE FACE OF ORGANIZED CRIME

ALLEN&UNWIN

First published in Great Britain and Ireland in 2021 by Allen & Unwin

This paperback edition published in Great Britain and Ireland in 2022 by Allen & Unwin

A CIP catalogue record for this book is available from the British Library.

Paperback ISBN 978 1 83895 491 8
E-Book ISBN 978 1 83895 490 1

Printed and bound by CPI Group (UK) Ltd, Croydon CR0 4YY

10 9 8 7 6 5 4 3 2 1

FSC
www.fsc.org

MIX
Paper from
responsible sources
FSC® C171272

CONTENTS

*Dedicated to the memory of Veronica Guerin
and journalists everywhere who have paid
the ultimate price for doing their jobs*

PROLOGUE

20 October 2020, Alicante, Costa Brava, Spain

The grandfather of organized crime had no intention of retiring from what criminals call 'the life' on his release from prison. Despite the fact that the sixty-eight-year-old pensioner had spent over seventeen years behind bars and had survived a near-fatal assassination attempt, it was clear that Ireland's Public Enemy Number One had not yet seen the error of his ways. The brutal mobster, who ordered the murder of a journalist to protect his once powerful criminal organization, was about to hit the international headlines again for all the wrong reasons.

The Spanish National Police like to put on a show when they swoop to arrest what they consider to be a major league godfather – to reassure the public that the good guys are cracking down on the scourge of organized crime. The cameras were all set when they stormed a villa in Torrevieja and busted the leader of a new Spanish-based Irish international drug and gun trafficking operation.

The most notorious and reviled gang boss in Irish criminal history was caught red-handed preparing a consignment of drugs. The raid was the culmination of several months of a joint international investigation, involving the Irish, UK and Spanish police, into the activities of a gang using the postal service to transport cannabis, prescription drugs and guns to the UK and Irish markets.

On the official Twitter account of the Policía Nacional the dramatic images show members of a heavily armed specialist weapons and tactics team (SWAT) piling through the front door after breaking it down. In the kitchen the camera zooms in on their elderly, white-haired target. He has been ordered at gunpoint to lie face down on the floor with his hands cuffed behind his back.

With his face covered with a Covid mask, he is then led to a seat by an officer while the search of the premises continues. He is in shock, looking down at the ground as he comes to terms with his latest predicament which is just about to get a whole lot worse.

On the video the action switches outside as the police make a dramatic discovery that will bring back memories of a shocking crime that took place almost a quarter of a century earlier – and increase the mobster's chances of getting an even longer stint behind bars this time.

In the garden of the house officers are shown digging up a gleaming silver .357 Magnum revolver. At a later press conference the Spanish police announce to the world that the handgun, an unusual Colt Python, is the same make and model as the weapon used in the execution of Veronica Guerin in 1996. They confirm: 'Spanish officers are working with the Irish police to determine if it's the same gun used to end her life.'

The hypothesis is that somehow the mobster has retained the weapon as a memento of the most egregious crime in his fifty-year career. Although he was not named in the police statement about the drug bust or gun find it was obvious who they were talking about.

In custody again, the investigation marked the opening of the latest chapter in the life of Ireland's most notorious gang boss – an evil criminal known as 'Gilligan'.

CHAPTER ONE

THE MAKING OF A MOBSTER

Special Criminal Court, Dublin, 15 March 2001

The old courthouse building in the centre of Dublin had been the venue for many noteworthy trials in Irish history since it opened its doors in 1797, including those of Irish freedom fighters Robert Emmet and Wolfe Tone. John Gilligan's trial on charges of murder, possession of firearms and running a multi-million-euro drugs empire was another landmark case. It had been one of the most high-profile trials in the history of organized crime. The three judges of the non-jury, anti-mafia and anti-terrorist court had sat through forty-three days of evidence.

John Gilligan sat in the raised dock looking down into the court chamber with his customary smirk on his face. He was the last member of his once powerful gang to face justice. The mobster, whose rapid ascent as the country's most powerful godfather ushered in a new era of violent organized crime in Ireland, had been tried in the special criminal court to prevent jury tampering.

On 15 March the judges returned to deliver their landmark verdict before a courtroom filled to capacity with police officers and the media. The judgment had been eagerly awaited as the trial gripped the nation. The courtroom was silent as the chairman, Mr Justice Diarmuid O'Donovan, stated:

> While this court has grave suspicions that John Gilligan was complicit in the murder of the late Veronica Guerin, the court has not been persuaded beyond all reasonable doubt by the evidence which has been adduced by the prosecution that that is so and, therefore, the court is required by law to acquit the accused on that charge.

Gilligan had successfully used his favourite weapons of intimidation and fear to beat the rap for the murder of investigative journalist Veronica Guerin. For the same reasons he had also been acquitted of importing large amounts of firearms and ammunition.

The gang boss looked jubilant as he was acquitted of one of the most shocking murders in Irish history. But the three judges wiped the smile off his face when he was convicted of running the biggest drug trafficking operation ever seen in Ireland.

Gilligan had to wait until after lunch to hear his fate on the eleven drug charges. He wasn't worried. He was confident that with the years he'd already served in prison awaiting trial he would be set free. The court, however, ensured that he would not be resuming his business anytime soon.

The diminutive mobster stood dumbfounded and ashen-faced in the dock as he was sentenced to twenty-eight years behind bars – the longest prison stretch ever handed down to a dope dealer.

Gilligan was taken into custody, leaving the court with a life sentence similar to the one he would have received had he been convicted of murder. The Irish State had shown its determination to put the country's most notorious and hated criminal out of circulation once and for all.

The conviction marked the denouement of a vast criminal conspiracy that had culminated in the journalist's murder in 1996 in an act of narco-terrorism which shocked the world. The assassination of the courageous young mother by a professional hit man had an unprecedented effect on the Irish public and caused a universal outpouring of revulsion, fear and anger. The national sentiment was symbolized by the wall of flowers in her memory which the ordinary citizens spontaneously erected at the gates of Dáil Éireann, expressing their outrage and demanding the government take action against mob bosses who considered themselves to be untouchable.

Gilligan had thrown down the gauntlet to the State with the implicit threat that anyone who interfered in his business was fair game regardless of who or what they were: politician, judge, cop, public servant or law-abiding citizen. He had gone far beyond the unofficial rules of engagement traditionally observed in the underworld.

The vast majority of criminals disapproved of the outrage, primarily because they could see it was bad for business and would have negative repercussions for all of them. They were right. The man who had brought a new level of organization to the business of crime would precipitate a fundamental reappraisal of the way international law enforcement and governments tackled the crime lords. The fightback would be spearheaded by the establishment of a revolutionary new body, the Criminal Assets Bureau (CAB), a unique innovation which became a template for similar units worldwide. The CAB would be given draconian powers to strike at the root of what criminality is all about – money.

In Gilligan's homeland in Ballyfermot, west Dublin, an elderly man watched the TV news report on the gangland trial which had captivated the nation. Gilligan's trial shone a rare light on the treacherous secret world of organized crime. It had laid bare a story that was both fascinating and shocking, involving intrigue, guns, drugs, violence, murder and money – eye-watering amounts of money. In just over two years Gilligan and his mob had conservatively profited to the tune of over €50 million in today's values, through the importation of cannabis worth over €250 million on the streets. And those figures did not include money from the sale and supply of other drugs including heroin, ecstasy and cocaine, or firearms. The prosecution had argued that Gilligan's motive for the murder of Veronica Guerin was 'the necessity of having to protect an evil empire'.

The TV footage showed a convoy of police and military vehicles whisking Gilligan off to Portlaoise Prison, the State's maximum-security detention centre. It was a scene that was more reminiscent of the aftermath of an Italian Mafia trial than an Irish one, reflecting the level of threat that he posed to civilized society. Against a cacophony of blaring sirens and clattering rotor blades from a police helicopter, several garda motorbike outriders, prison vans and jeeps carrying heavily armed soldiers raced through the streets of Dublin with the convoy's VIP – very important prisoner. Watching the spectacle on the TV screen the old man's mind wandered back in time to the Ballyfermot of 1960 and one of his first meetings with little John Gilligan.

He recalled being out for an evening stroll one night when he spotted a gaggle of excited little kids scurrying from cover at the edge of the golden wheat field that marked the border between the suburban sprawl and the countryside. It didn't take much deduction to work out that the little terrors were up to no good. They giggled and nervously glanced back into the vast field of wheat that was ready for harvesting.

The man shouted as he saw a single pillar of smoke rising up from the crop about 500 feet into the field. Within minutes the clouds of black smoke were blocking out the sun as flames destroyed the wheat. He recalled:

> I will never forget that day. Ever since the kids had moved out
> to the new council houses they were always messing in that

field lighting fires, but this was the worst I ever saw. It was pure devastation.

One of the watching children, eight-year-old John Gilligan, lived on his road and the old man remembers that the boy's face was full of excitement as fire engines rushed from the city to quell the inferno. When the fire threatened to spread to the nearby houses the boy laughed until tears streamed down his cheeks. This would not be the last time the eight-year-old caused panic and mayhem in his lifetime.

'When you look back you never think that an innocent kid like that would turn out to be such a gangster,' the elderly man reflected sombrely. 'I always thought that he was a grand kid who just dabbled in a bit of ducking and diving...but don't use my name, I wouldn't like the trouble,' he added cautiously.

The insistence on anonymity said a lot about little John Gilligan, the kid who had progressed from childish vandal and petty thief to international drug trafficker and boss of a dangerous criminal empire. Even old neighbours who had always liked and got on well with him and his family feared him. Despite being universally reviled by fellow criminals and law-abiding citizens alike, and safely locked away, a lot of people in 'Ballyer' still considered it safer to exercise discretion when it came to expressing their views on the mobster.

It was hardly surprising. Gilligan built his empire and fierce reputation through the use of fear and intimidation. It was how he had managed to escape a murder conviction. But the courts had ensured it was only a partial victory. He would have plenty of time to reflect on how he had ended up facing a rent-free, long-term stay at the pleasure of the State when he had gone to extraordinary lengths to avoid that exact outcome.

John Joseph Gilligan was born on 29 March 1952 in a rundown tenement in Dublin's north inner city. He was the fifth of eleven children, four boys and seven girls, born to Sally and John Gilligan, who both came from the area. Sally had been a factory worker until 1945 when it was her misfortune to marry John, a petty thief who also worked as a labourer at Dublin docks. John junior's arrival coincided with a period of mass migration in the 1950s as families were transplanted from the squalor of the inner-city slums to new sprawling corporation estates on the edge of the capital.

The governments of the day had done commendable work in accelerating slum clearance schemes to alleviate the hardship experienced by impoverished Dubliners for centuries. Unfortunately the new public housing projects that gobbled up the countryside in Ballyfermot, Cabra, Crumlin, Inchicore, Donnycarney, Glasnevin and Marino would sow the seeds of a whole new set of social problems.

Despite providing more living space, privacy and decent sanitation, the new peripheral estates had little else by way of social infrastructure. For many of the tenants this was a lonely, alien world, far removed from the cramped streets of Dublin's inner city. In the move to better living conditions, whole communities were uprooted and broken up.

The overall effect was a breakdown in social cohesion and an unravelling of the close bonds that had characterized the old neighbourhoods. The grinding poverty had also made the journey with them, with the new estates becoming unemployment black spots.

While the vast majority of people adapted and made decent lives for themselves, the gloomy estates also created criminogenic environments which would produce the armed robbers and drug traffickers of the future. It was on the streets of the inner city and the new suburban ghettos where the story of organized crime in Ireland began.

A new generation of young ruthless hoodlums emerged from the social ferment of the late 1960s and early 1970s and pioneered a new world called gangland. In the decades ahead the alumni of this underworld milieu would become household names – for all the wrong reasons.

John Gilligan was one of them.

Gilligan was a baby when his family was allocated number 5, Lough Conn Road, Ballyfermot, in 1952. It was a modest three-bedroom house with running water and toilet facilities. Although a vast improvement on the slums, the new homes were still relatively small for the large families sent to colonize them. In a society dominated by Catholic doctrine, contraception was both illegal and a mortal sin. It was better to create too many mouths to feed among the poorer classes than offend against the moral law.

Lough Conn Road was on the edge of the maze of concrete streets and lines of houses that marked the newly established border between the rural and urban. A few hundred feet away were wheat fields, stretching as far as the eye could see. The open fields were dubbed the 'Hollywood Hills' by the newcomers. A kid could ramble across the rustic expanses of Clondalkin, Palmerstown and Ronanstown, which, over the following decades, would also be gobbled up for homes in the voracious urban expansion around the capital.

Like most of their neighbours, the Gilligans arrived in Ballyfermot carrying all their worldly possessions in prams and carts. When the residents began moving in, the infrastructure was still incomplete and the bus service did not go as far as the estates, forcing them to walk the final part of the journey.

Sally Gilligan had a tough life and was left to make the move alone with her five children under the age of seven. Faced with her husband's indifference and abuse Sally had applied for one of the new houses in Ballyfermot herself. Unusually, she signed the paperwork, which, in a patriarchal era, was seen as the exclusive duty of the man.

John senior had little interest in the welfare of his young family. He was an alcoholic gambler and a professional thief with a penchant for violence. Small in physical stature, like his namesake son, he was regularly absent from home for long periods either because he was in jail or enjoying the life of a 'bachelor' crook in the inner city. He squandered his money on booze and racehorses, leaving his wife and children dependent on the charity of others.

Life in the Gilligans' new home was characterized by deprivation and physical abuse. When John senior turned up, he regularly beat his wife and children in drunken rages. A family member later described how the crook would send John junior down to the bookies to place bets on horses and wait for the results. When his son invariably returned home with bad news, his father rewarded him with a beating. The children didn't have toys like the other kids on the road and their father's self-centred profligacy meant they often went hungry.

Gilligan senior was despised as a bully and a thug who, whenever he was broke, had no compunction about breaking into his neighbours' homes to steal what little they had. The hallmark of his robberies was kicking in a lower door panel with the heel of his boot. One older detective who arrested him recalled how Gilligan couldn't understand how the police knew so much about him.

> Gilligan senior was one of our habitual thieves and he couldn't work out why we kept catching him. He often gave us information in return for dropping charges. His son obviously picked up a lot of his characteristics. He was a nasty, evil little man.

While the neighbours reviled John senior, his wife and children were popular in the area. A common theme running through the ethnographies of criminal figures is the perception of the mother as the only source of stability in their otherwise dysfunctional and chaotic lives. Sally Gilligan, like many of the mothers in their neighbourhood, was left to raise a gaggle of hungry children, often alone and penniless, while desperately trying to keep them out of criminality.

Locals would recall how Sally Gilligan insisted that her children were turned out clean and tidy in the best clothes they possessed. They were considered good, helpful neighbours. Gilligan junior's sisters were hard-working girls who helped babysit local children. One time when an elderly neighbour's wife died, Sally Gilligan ensured that her kids helped out the widower. A former resident recalled, 'You couldn't ask for better neighbours than the Gilligans.'

Whenever John senior was in prison the neighbours would warn their children against gossiping about it as an expression of respect and sympathy for his long-suffering wife. 'I remember my Da saying that that woman was too good for John Gilligan. She was a very quiet, pleasant woman. People didn't want to add to her misery,' a former neighbour explained.

As the children grew into their teens, they no longer tolerated their father's violent excesses, particularly him beating their mother. He was barred from the house until he had cleaned up his act. But by then the damage had already been done to the son who shared his name.

The backdrop of cruelty and turmoil experienced in childhood moulded the man John Gilligan would become. It taught him that violence and intimidation were the most effective tools in life. In his criminal career Gilligan was never known as someone who exercised pragmatism or reason to solve a dispute. He was widely regarded as a loud-mouthed bully, devoid of any class or style. With the subtlety of a bloodthirsty rottweiler marking his territory, his visceral response to any situation was to go on the attack, issuing sinister threats, and to never back down. However, the menacing side to his personality didn't manifest itself until he had reached young adulthood.

Those who knew Gilligan growing up described him as a pleasant young guy but otherwise quite unremarkable. Some of his contemporaries thought he was not very bright. Gilligan certainly wasn't a scholar. He attended the Mary Queen of Angels national school in Ballyfermot where his conduct was recorded as good. His teachers found him to be of low intelligence with learning difficulties. He spent more time 'mitching' (playing truant) than pursuing his education. He and his pals roamed around the wheat fields and rode the wild ponies and goats which wandered freely on the farms in the area.

Gilligan left school when he was twelve years old with no education and very few prospects for meaningful employment. But Gilligan's feral instincts and attention to detail more than compensated for a low IQ. Throughout his criminal career garda background reports on Gilligan classed him as 'cunning and violent'.

In 1966, at the age of fourteen, and at the insistence of his mother, Gilligan's uncle secured John junior a job as an apprentice seaman. He started with the state-owned B&I Line which had a passenger ferry and freight service operating between Ireland and the UK. It was the only legitimate job he would ever hold. His father also worked for the shipping line, having been employed as a result of who he knew rather than his ability to do an honest day's work. At this time in his life Gilligan junior had not yet come to the attention of the police and there are no indications that he had begun dabbling in crime. But that was about to change, thanks to his day job. Despite his mother's best attempts he began to follow in his father's footsteps.

Gilligan junior teamed up with one of his co-workers, John Traynor. Four years older than his diminutive pal, Traynor had been at sea since the age of fifteen and he helped to show his new friend the ropes. From Charlemont Street in the south inner city, and later nicknamed 'the Coach' by Veronica Guerin, Traynor was described as a clever, manipulative and duplicitous gangster who played on both sides of the tracks – with the criminals on one side and the cops on the other.

The Coach had a natural talent for organization and leadership. His smooth talk got him elected to the executive of the Seamen's Union which effectively ran the shipping company. From behind the protection of this position, Traynor and Gilligan worked together organizing the theft and resale of goods from containers on the ships. The duo also smuggled guns and other contraband from the UK on behalf of their shore-bound associates. It was a partnership that would endure for many years, with deadly consequences.

During the 1970s the B&I Line was, as a consequence of this corruption and mismanagement, being run aground. Successive governments had kept the ailing company afloat with taxpayers' money. They were told by management that nothing could be done as the company was in the grip of the unions. An internal investigation was launched which revealed that Traynor and the Gilligans, father and son, were part of a network of employees involved in a massive embezzlement racket on board.

A secret survey conducted among passengers illustrated the extent to which the company was being ripped off. On one sailing the manifest recorded 220 passengers, but a head count found that there were actually more than 700 people on board. The little cartel of corrupt workers had pocketed almost 500 fares in just one sailing.

In the early 1980s the then Minister for Transport, Jim Mitchell, reorganized the company and cleared out the fraudsters. By then Gilligan's seaman's record showed that he had been officially discharged in 1980 and that his conduct on the high seas had been rated 'very good' during thirty-six voyages around the world.

While on shore leave throughout the 1970s he began to get more deeply involved in crime. A year after joining B&I Gilligan had his first scrape with the law when he was convicted of larceny on 3 July 1967. Like many of his contemporaries his maiden crime was rather inauspicious – fifteen-year-old John was caught stealing a farmer's chickens in Rathfarnham, south Dublin.

On that occasion the District Court judge decided to give the teenager the benefit of the doubt and applied the Probation of Offenders Act (POA). The Act is intended as a slap on the wrist to a first-time offender and an incentive to guide their return to a law-abiding life. Practically every gangster who ever made his mark in Ireland has the POA letters typed alongside their first convictions. Gilligan's criminal record suggests that he may have actually heeded the warning for a while at least – or was just lucky and didn't get caught again. It would be another seven years before he next came before a judge.

John Gilligan was eighteen when he met the woman who would one day be described in court as his able 'partner in crime'. Geraldine Matilda Dunne from Kylemore Road in Lower Ballyfermot was fourteen when she first fell for the diminutive young thief in 1970. A former female friend recalled:

> Everyone wondered what Geraldine saw in him – the size of him
> – but she was mad about him. Everyone thought he was a bit of
> a gobshite and she was the real brains of the operation.

One of six children, Geraldine was born on 29 September 1956. Like her boyfriend, she dropped out of school when she was twelve. She was described by an old friend as a 'real live wire'. From the time she was a child she had a passion for horses. It wasn't unusual to see the feisty teenager galloping bareback on a piebald pony up Lough Conn Road to pick up her boyfriend for a date.

Geraldine worked in a factory making belts and buckles, and later as a basic line operative in a ladies' underwear factory in Ballyfermot. At lunchtime she would go with friends to see Gilligan, who invariably could be found lounging around the family home when on shore leave. She would ask her friends to tell her employer that she was sick and then spend the afternoon with John. After several sick days she lost her job, so she went to sea for three months with Gilligan, working in the kitchens of a merchant navy vessel.

In January 1974, at the age of seventeen, Geraldine discovered that she was pregnant. On 27 March, two days before Gilligan's twenty-second birthday, the couple got married in the Church of Our Lady of the Assumption in Ballyfermot. They later moved to live in a flat at the North Strand in Dublin. In September Geraldine gave birth to a daughter, Tracey. A month later Gilligan received his second ever conviction for which he received a six-month suspended sentence for larceny. A year later, in September 1975, the Gilligans had their second child, a son, Darren.

Unlike his father John Gilligan was very protective of his family and took his responsibilities seriously. He decided to knuckle down at his work and provide for them – he more or less gave up going to sea and began robbing full-time. The future drug baron made no secret of his belief that the only way to make money was through crime.

By the mid-seventies he was running with a group of other young criminals who would also make their mark in gangland history. Between them the brat pack ushered in a new era of violence as they became the first generation of organized crime in Ireland.

Among his associates were the Cunningham brothers, Michael, John and Fran, from Le Fanu Road in Ballyfermot. John and Michael were career armed robbers who gained notoriety when they kidnapped Jennifer Guinness, the wife of John Guinness, the millionaire chairman of the Guinness Mahon Bank. John Cunningham later became one of Europe's top drug traffickers working in partnership with another brat pack member, Christy Kinahan, the Dapper Don. Fran Cunningham, who was nicknamed the Lamb, preferred to spend his time in the fraud game, robbing banks with dud cheques and dodgy bank drafts. Also in the underworld brat pack was up-and-coming underworld heavy-hitter George Mitchell, who was destined to become a major international drug dealer known as the Penguin.

John Traynor introduced Gilligan to his closest friend from childhood, Martin Cahill. The former burglar from Hollyfield

Buildings in Rathmines was in the process of becoming one of the most prolific blaggers or armed robbers in the new gangland. His ability to mastermind some of the biggest heists in the history of the State would earn him the nickname 'the General'.

Gilligan was also associated with members of the Dunne family from Crumlin, the first truly professional armed robbery outfit in Dublin, who in turn introduced Martin Cahill and several other young hoods to the business.

This was the melting pot that produced hard cases like John Gilligan. Such was the homogeneous nature of the nascent organized crime scene that everyone worked together. Associates formed temporary collaborations and provided logistical backup for specific jobs. In the era before the underworld embraced the narcotics trade and wholesale greed and treachery poisoned relationships, there were no murderous gang feuds like those which became the norm from the 1990s onwards.

Disputes were generally settled with a fist fight – a 'straightener' – and the villains, despite their enmities, tended to respect each other's right to life. Murder was not such a casual affair when Gilligan started out in the age of the ODC – ordinary decent criminal.

———

The same year that Gilligan became a seaman, 1966, was to be the end of an age of innocence in a country where crime rates were still among the lowest in the world. The garda crime report for the year recorded that there had been six murders and seven cases of manslaughter which tended to be the result of crimes of passion, domestic disputes or rows over land. There were no armed robberies, with criminal activity confined to burglary, larceny and safe cracking. The Garda Commissioner of the day noted that 'no organized crimes of violence' had been recorded and the government was giving serious consideration to closing down prisons, where the daily average population was 300 inmates.

A few years later, however, a new era of violent crime had been declared. In April 1970 an unarmed garda, Dick Fallon, was shot dead during a robbery in Dublin. The killing was the work of the country's first armed robbery gang, a reckless quasi-republican collection of misfits called Saor Eire. Their inaugural operations took place in 1967 when the young Gilligan was still stealing chickens.

At the same time crimes related to the Troubles, which had flared up in Northern Ireland in 1969, were spilling over into the Republic where the Provisional IRA embarked on a deliberate campaign to destabilise the State and undermine its growing economy. From 1970 onwards the Provos unleashed mayhem, robbing banks, post offices and pay rolls throughout the country to fund their war with apparent impunity. They also carried out murders, kidnappings and bombings.

The sudden surge in serious crime threatened to overwhelm An Garda Síochána, a force which was untrained and ill-equipped to deal with it. On the streets uniformed and plainclothes officers were literally being outgunned by the robbers – the majority of detectives remained unarmed until the early eighties. Being held at gunpoint, pistol-whipped and shot at had become an occupational hazard for gardaí. Over the following years another eleven officers were murdered by Irish Republican Army (IRA) and Irish National Liberation Army (INLA) robbers. As a result the State poured most of its security resources into fighting subversion at the expense of other areas of policing.

And from the shadow of the shadow of the republican gunmen, Gilligan and his peers were watching and learning. The terrorists had opened their eyes to a whole new world of opportunity.

Commensurate with the unfolding law and order crisis was a dramatic upsurge in what gardaí classify as 'crime ordinary', or nonpolitical crime, as the former burglars and petty thieves joined in the chaos. The era of the armed robber was firmly established between 1972 and 1978. In that six-year period the number of recorded heists rocketed to over 200 per year and the amount of cash stolen increased fifteen-fold. In a society that operated primarily in cash there were plenty of easy pickings for everyone to get their share. Every Thursday and Friday – the traditional pay days – businesses, financial institutions and the gardaí across Ireland braced themselves for another wave of hold-ups by the terrorist and 'crime ordinary' gangs.

There were so many heists taking place that it became something of a joke. In contemporary TV comedy sketches a working-class newsreader character presented a robbery report in the form of a weather forecast. Gilligan later recalled how it was an exciting time to be a young gangster.

At weekends he and the rest of the criminal community would meet on the beach at Portmarnock, north Dublin, for horse trotting races, where they gambled and planned various jobs to recoup their losses. Gilligan was gaining a reputation for violence and was fond of handling firearms. Like his father, he also had a serious gambling problem. Sometimes he combined both vices. In September 1976 he was arrested and charged with an attempted robbery of a bookmaker's shop on Capel Street in Dublin's north inner city.

The following year Gilligan and his young family moved to a local authority house in Corduff Estate, in Blanchardstown, west Dublin – one of many such new estates to be built during the decade as the urban sprawl continued. But he wasn't going to be around to settle in. In July 1977 he received his first custodial sentence, eighteen months, after being convicted of receiving a van load of stolen goods from a shop in Ballyfermot. The following September he got another three months for larceny and a year for the attempted robbery at the bookmaker's.

A young garda called Tony Sourke had arrested Gilligan on the charge of receiving stolen goods. When Sourke took the thief into the local station to be charged with the offence, the diminutive would-be gang boss warned him: 'I'll blow your fucking head off for this.'

John Gilligan was making a name for himself.

CHAPTER TWO

FACTORY JOHN

Gilligan adapted to life in Mountjoy Prison once he got over the initial shock of his eighteen-month sentence. His first sojourn behind bars was made bearable in the company of friends from around Dublin who could teach him new tricks. He was also busy planning his future career and how to beat the system.

In November 1977 Martin Cahill, who was already seen as a major player on the gangland scene, arrived. He had been jailed for four years on a charge of receiving a stolen car and two motorbikes which were intended for use in a robbery. His brother Eddie joined them on the same rap.

The following month Gilligan's old friend John Traynor was also granted a long stay in Mountjoy after he was convicted of possession of a firearm with intent to endanger life. Years later the Coach recalled the incident with typical bravado:

> Most of my convictions were for stupid things I did when I was drunk. I was in a pub in Newcastle, outside Dublin and had a .22 pistol which I had bought for £100. I got in a row with a cop who was there. I hit him with the gun and swung it around threatening the people in the bar. It was more of a joke than anything else.

On 14 December 1977 Traynor's 'joke' turned sour when he was sentenced to five years for possession of a firearm, assault, burglary and larceny charges. A few days later he was given another five-year stretch, to run concurrently with the others, for assault causing harm.

Cahill and Traynor were well-seasoned villains compared to Gilligan. They instructed the relative novice on how to play what Cahill referred to as the 'game' – his war of wits against the police and the law. Gilligan admired how the psychotic Cahill had no scruples about using intimidation and violence against his enemies, and it didn't matter who they were. The two criminals had a lot in common. His older mentors taught Gilligan that there were many loopholes in the law which could be exploited using a clever lawyer to fight every step of the prosecutorial process. Trials could also be scuppered by scaring off potential witnesses or simply shooting them.

Gilligan was anything but a slow learner when it came to his criminal enterprise. His record of sixteen convictions, mostly for relatively short jail terms, over a thirty-year period of intense criminal activity demonstrates how he used both legal and criminal means to thwart the law. During the same period he was charged over thirty times with larceny, burglary and robbery. Over half of the cases collapsed when victims and witnesses suddenly developed amnesia.

When he was released from prison in 1978, after serving less than a year of his combined three sentences, Gilligan had decided to focus on a particular area of expertise which had nothing to do with pulling bank heists. He would later declare: 'I wasn't into armed robberies because that involved firearms and I could get shot.'

The criminal entrepreneur saw an opening in the market for stolen goods. Working in B&I he'd realized that the container ships were veritable floating Aladdin's caves, with every conceivable type of resaleable consumer product rolling off their ramps into Dublin. Security was lax and he had solid, corrupt contacts in the shipping business.

Gilligan saw a comfortable niche for himself in the burgeoning Irish crime industry. He would have no problem selling a container load of goods in the working-class estates across west Dublin. The punters would appreciate a bargain and he would turn a tidy profit in a short time.

After his release he established a team of local criminals around him and went to work. Shortly afterwards, one night in November 1978, Gilligan hijacked a truckload of frozen bacon as it left a storage depot at Grand Canal Harbour off James Street in central Dublin. Gilligan produced a .45 pistol and dragged the driver from his cab. He chained the terrified man by the neck to a lamp post and left him there in freezing temperatures.

A few days later Detective Garda Tony Sourke, the young policeman who had arrested him four years earlier, got information that Gilligan was behind the robbery. His informant led him to where Gilligan had hidden part of the haul, behind a ditch in a field near Ballyfermot. The rest of the haul was hidden in a shed. Gilligan had been paying the husband and wife for the use of the shed for several months to hide various truckloads of goods that contained everything from frozen bacon to sheets of galvanized metal, and even nuts and bolts.

The couple were arrested and taken in for questioning. The wife was the first to crack. She described John Gilligan, as 'a small, little man who wears a big Crombie overcoat' who had paid them for the use of the shed. Gilligan was arrested and the woman identified him in a line-up in Kevin Street garda station. On 17 November 1978 Gilligan was charged with the crime and released on bail.

Three months later Gilligan was again arrested. This time he was charged with taking part in an armed robbery at the Allied Irish Bank branch on the Naas Road in Bluebell, west Dublin. Cash to the value of €39,000 had been taken in the heist by a team of three armed men.

When Gilligan was questioned he swore on his children's lives that he hadn't been involved. His wife, Geraldine, then arrived at the station in tears, pleading her husband's innocence. She told detectives that Gilligan had been with her at the time of the robbery.

He was subsequently not convicted on either the hijacking or armed robbery charges. In the hijacking case the woman who'd identified him withdrew her statement after Gilligan threatened to harm her and her husband if she testified. In the armed robbery case forensic evidence was not strong enough to sustain the charge and the State bowed out. Before that, however, Gilligan had the audacity to offer a policeman in Ballyfermot a substantial bribe, equivalent to almost €20,000, for the name of the person who had informed on him and his cronies in the AIB robbery. The officer declined the offer.

The detectives were particularly interested in the .45 pistol that Gilligan carried with him on his various jobs. Sometime later they got another tip that he and his team were planning a major heist on Bluebell Avenue near Ballyfermot. Gilligan had arranged the theft of a getaway truck and was to be the driver. As usual a night watchman was to be tied up, the truck loaded, and the cargo taken to a safe warehouse Gilligan had rented in the country.

While a team of detectives from Kevin Street garda station was keeping the area under surveillance, they spotted another group of men hiding in the shadows some distance away. They turned out to be gardaí from Ballyfermot who had received the same information. The informant had been double jobbing. Both teams were after the prize – John Gilligan, his team, the stolen goods and his .45 pistol.

On the second night of the operation the Kevin Street team was about to abandon the job when they spotted the stolen truck pull up outside a flat in Bluebell, not far from the factory. Gilligan was behind the wheel with two members of his mob. They got out and went into the flat. At this stage the backup team for the arrest had moved off.

Detective Gardaí Tony Sourke and Gary Kavanagh decided to move in anyway and arrest the trio in the flat. When they burst in, Gilligan and his two pals were relaxing on a couch. They were arrested and searched, but the woman who lived there was left behind. Outside the detectives found that the truck was empty.

Unfortunately for the police, the thieves had been on their way to do the job. There was no sign of the gun. They later discovered that Gilligan had wanted to open fire when the detectives first banged on the apartment door. He quickly changed his mind and handed the weapon to the woman, who shoved it down her trousers.

Gilligan learned valuable lessons from the close calls and thereafter meticulously planned his future 'strokes'. He sorted out an impressive network of fences to receive and sell on the stolen goods and sourced hiding places for his loot around Ireland. He made a point of acquainting himself with truckers in a Ballyfermot pub frequented by drivers. They would tip him off about the various cargoes coming in and he would pay them for the privilege of hijacking their loads.

The young criminals soon branched out and began hitting large warehouses and factories in the sprawling industrial estates across Dublin. The Robin Hood Estate in Tallaght, south Dublin, was one of his favourite targets. By now he had earned such a reputation for violence that other criminals would not encroach on certain industrial estates because they were known to be 'Gilligan's turf'.

He became expert at short-circuiting alarm systems. Another modus operandi involved lighting a large fire at the exterior wall of a factory or warehouse. The heat from the fire would weaken the wall by drying out the mortar and blocks. The gang would return the next night and easily knock a hole in the wall separating them from the loot.

Gilligan's robberies during the 1980s were so frequent that alarm and security companies had to develop more sophisticated systems to prevent the heists. But just in case the security system was too elaborate for him, Gilligan had a few security men on the payroll to ensure that things went smoothly.

He planned every aspect of a robbery with painstaking precision and supervised his crew like a military commander. Gilligan knew the layout of every industrial estate he targeted: entry points, escape routes and what each warehouse had inside its doors. He carried out surveillance on each premises and knew the response times of both security staff and the police.

On robberies Gilligan used scanners to pick up garda radio traffic and his teams communicated with two-way radios. Lookouts would be positioned on the approach roads while the other gang members went about cleaning the place out. He became known in the underworld as Factory John. He later bragged:

> It was great fun and I got a buzz out of it. Sometimes we got stuff and other times nothing. We were chased by the cops now and again and we had plenty of near misses. There were a lot of times when we were in and out of a place and no one knew a thing for ages afterwards. The strokes [crimes] were a win-win situation for everyone. The owners of the truck or the factory got the insurance money...and me and the lads got a few bob. It was the perfect crime and doing no harm to anyone.

Gilligan's favourite time of year was winter. The long, dark nights provided excellent cover for a thief. As the evenings grew shorter each year the police in stations covering the big industrial estates braced themselves for a string of burglaries. In November 1981 members of the crime task force attached to Ballyfermot garda station had a lucky break when they spotted Gilligan and two of his pals driving his van near Greenhills Industrial Estate in Walkinstown, south-west Dublin. They stopped the van and found almost €20,000 worth of chocolates which had been stolen from a warehouse. Factory John was stocking up for the Christmas market.

The three crooks were arrested, taken to Ballyfermot and charged with burglary. Gilligan's van was impounded, and the men were charged and released on station bail pending a hearing in the lower District Court. But Factory John was not giving up the chocolates that easily. The following night an eagle-eyed officer spotted the three hoods in the process of trying to steal the van from the police station yard. The audacious thieves were arrested and charged for a second time.

The following March Gilligan was given a twelve-month prison sentence and banned from driving for fifteen years for using his van to commit a crime and then trying to steal it back from the police. Two months earlier he had been given another twelve-month sentence for burglary.

But Gilligan didn't mind. The two sentences would run concurrently and he would be out in a few months. He was beginning to play the system. In the course of 1981 Factory John was arrested and charged a total of nine times for larceny and burglary offences. He was convicted of only two crimes.

It wasn't cunning or luck alone that kept Factory John in business. He utilized his favourite 'get out of jail free' card – terror and intimidation. Gilligan left his gang members in no doubt of the deadly fate that lay in store for anyone who talked to the police about him.

Standing at just five feet five inches tall Gilligan demonstrated the classic traits of the condition known as 'small man' syndrome or Napoleon complex. It occurs where the individual holds a deep-rooted sense of inadequacy about their height and overcompensates with aggressive behaviour. Gilligan did a lot of overcompensating. He would threaten anyone who annoyed him or didn't give him what he wanted – and it didn't matter who they were. Gardaí, revenue officials and lawyers were just as eligible for his wrath as an errant gang member.

The aura around Gilligan crackled with menace and volatility. It was a defence mechanism to persuade those that he was meeting for the first time – criminal and law-abiding alike – that size didn't matter and he could do as much damage as a man twice his height. In street terms he exuded an air of 'don't fuck with me or else'. Striking out and dispensing pain were second nature.

According to some of those who worked with Gilligan, he would conduct his own 'court-martial' to see if there was an informant in the gang. Once when a member of his gang was arrested for the offence of buggery Gilligan saw him as a potential weak link. In that unenlightened time homosexuality was still a criminal offence and homophobia was embedded in the culture. The police used the law to put pressure on various gangsters who were known to be closet gays. In testosterone-charged gangland, calling a hard man a 'queer' was as bad as calling him a tout or informer. The gang member they nicknamed 'Jeremy Thorpe', after the British politician who had been at the centre of a gay scandal, was exiled from Gilligan's inner sanctum. At one stage members of the gang feared he was going to be murdered.

Gilligan was never afraid of the police. When they sat outside his house monitoring his various underworld visitors or searched the place, Factory John would confront them, hurling abuse and threats. His confident aggression was based on the fact that he never brought stolen goods home. After a search he would complain that he was being unfairly victimized by the cops. Often when he was arrested he threatened to murder officers and burn down their homes.

The gardaí wanted the violent armed robber off the streets. In the early 1980s a factory involved in making Atari computer games was burgled in Tallaght. The night before the burglary Gilligan and his crew had set a large fire causing the mortar in the rear wall to crumble. The next night the gang used sledgehammers and a truck to break a hole in it to get into the premises and bypass the security system.

The method was Factory John's signature and he became the top suspect. A few weeks later the police got a tip-off that Geraldine Gilligan was selling the Atari games to unsuspecting workmates in a factory in Blanchardstown, west Dublin. Detectives from Tallaght identified a woman who had bought one of the games. She made a statement and Geraldine was charged with receiving stolen goods.

Gilligan took over the handling of his wife's case instructing her lawyers to seek depositions. This is a form of pretrial hearing during which the various witnesses for the prosecution relate the testimony that they intend giving in the actual trial. It was a tactic Gilligan used many times to delay trials. It also gave him an opportunity to convince people that appearing in the witness box would be bad for their health.

On the Friday before the depositions hearing John Gilligan arrived at the home of the woman who had made the statement against his wife. He pushed his way inside and threatened to have her fourteen-year-old son shot if she gave evidence. The woman was deeply disturbed and withdrew her statement the following Monday.

Similarly a nineteen-year-old youth who had bought one of the games pulled out of the case after Gilligan threatened him on the morning of the hearing. The police informed the court of the intimidation but no action could be taken because the victims would not testify.

The case eventually foundered and Geraldine was off the hook. Gilligan openly scoffed at the detectives when his wife walked free. In the meantime Geraldine was fired from her job but her husband made it pay. She successfully sued the company for unfair dismissal and received compensation to the value of €35,000. Then Geraldine went on disability benefit for the stress which she claimed had been caused by the regular police raids on her home. She never worked again.

By the mid-1980s John Gilligan and the Factory Gang were among the top three organized crime gangs on garda intelligence files. Gilligan ranked next to Martin Cahill, the General. The third was the northside-based robbery gang led by a clever young villain called Gerry Hutch, the 'Monk'.

Intelligence reports describing Gilligan as the most prolific large-scale burglar in Ireland were circulated to detectives in every police division in the State. Gilligan and his associates were being spotted by garda units throughout the country and at one stage it was estimated that he was responsible for one major 'job' every week. At any one time Factory John was plotting up to a dozen robberies.

A detective who took a particular interest in Gilligan and would remain his nemesis for over twenty years was Felix McKenna. In 1978 McKenna, originally from County Monaghan, was appointed a detective garda and sent to the Tallaght garda M District. This was the area where Gilligan was committing most of his crimes and he treated the industrial estates as his exclusive turf.

As an investigator McKenna earned a formidable reputation for his abilities and tenacity in pursuing serious crime. He spent practically all of his career involved in the investigation of organized crime and would be one of the founding officers, and later chief, of the Criminal Assets Bureau (CAB).

Shortly after he arrived in the M District, McKenna had his first encounter with Gilligan when he caught him in possession of a stolen lorry and charged him with larceny. The case was dropped when the owner of the truck refused to give evidence after Gilligan threatened him.

On St Patrick's Day 1981, McKenna and his colleagues thought that they had at last nabbed Factory John. Gilligan and his team stole a truckload of colour TVs from an electrical engineering warehouse in the Cookstown Industrial Estate, Tallaght. At the time the haul was worth over €580,000. Gilligan broke in and disabled the alarm. He reversed a full-length transport lorry, stolen especially for the job, into the factory. After Gilligan and another criminal figure from

Ballyfermot loaded it up, they drove the truck to Sligo. It had been arranged that the TVs would be sold to a local businessman who specialized in the sale of smuggled goods – and was a fence for stolen merchandise.

Within a few weeks of the heist McKenna and his colleagues, Detective Sergeant John McLoughlin and Detective Garda Noel Whyte, received intelligence about who had carried out the crime and the name of the fence. By the time the three detectives arrived in Sligo most of the TVs had already taken pride of place in dozens of living rooms.

The unsuspecting customers thought they were getting a bargain smuggled from the North. McKenna and McLoughlin raided the fence's house and recovered thirty sets. The list of customers included some of the most respected people in the town. Over the following days word filtered out that detectives from Dublin were tracing stolen TVs. For weeks local people were handing in their cherished sets to the local garda station or hiding them in attics. In at least one case, a TV was broken up and dumped.

The Dublin detectives recovered seventy per cent of the haul and charged four people with receiving stolen goods. The fence identified Gilligan as the man who had offered him the TVs and who had actually delivered them. In the end, despite the opportunity of making a deal with the State, the fence opted to take the rap. He had come to the decision after Gilligan and one of his cronies visited him in Sligo, produced a gun and threatened to blow his head off.

Like Gilligan's other erstwhile 'clients', the fence was terrified. The risk of a stretch in prison was better than a spell in intensive care or worse, the grave, he told the frustrated investigators.

It was business as usual for the factory thieves. Demand was booming and the money was flowing in.

Factory John was beginning to believe that he was invincible.

CHAPTER THREE

HEISTS

The same year that Gilligan formed his Factory Gang, 1978, also saw the appointment of Dr James Donovan as the head of the State's forensic science laboratory at Garda HQ, Phoenix Park. The committed scientist spearheaded the advancement and modernization of forensic science so that, by the early 1980s, it had become a crucial component of every major criminal investigation in the country.

John Gilligan was well aware that Donovan's expert forensic evidence had proved pivotal in securing several high-profile convictions. These included the conviction of the IRA's top bomb-maker, Thomas McMahon, for the blast in 1979 which killed Lord Louis Mountbatten, his fourteen-year-old grandson, Nicholas, Lady Doreen Brabourne and fifteen-year-old Paul Maxwell. Dr Donovan's evidence had also helped to convict IRA and INLA members of the murder of three gardaí in 1980.

The scientist was also a crucial witness in several trials involving the 'crime ordinary' gangs, like Gilligan's mob. What the forensic scientist found under the lens of his microscope was often more hazardous to a gangster or a terrorist than the business end of a cop's .38 revolver. Gilligan and the other mobs had a new enemy and, inevitably, Dr Donovan began to draw unwanted attention.

On the morning of 6 January 1982 Dr Donovan was driving to his workplace in Garda Headquarters when a bomb ripped his car apart. Miraculously the scientist survived the murder attempt. However, Dr Donovan suffered horrific leg injuries which would blight the rest of his life. The motive for the attack was obvious from the outset – some organization or individual didn't want the forensic expert testifying in court.

Even in a country that had become inured to the use of extreme terrorist violence over the previous dozen years the attack was greeted with shock. This was the first time that a civilian employee of the State had been deliberately singled out and targeted.

At first the finger of suspicion landed on the IRA and the INLA. But even for them this seemed like a step too far. Although they did not express any sympathy for what had happened, the two terror gangs issued curt statements of denial, the Provos declaring: 'The IRA has more to lose by carrying out such an act because of the anti-republican hysteria it would arouse.' The INLA comment was even shorter: 'It serves no useful purpose.'

It wasn't long before gardaí discovered that the bombing was the work of Gilligan's old friend, Martin Cahill. Organized crime had set a deadly new precedent. The attack on Dr Donovan still stands out as one of the single worst acts of terrorism committed by organized crime gangs over the past fifty years.

The motive for the murder attempt was to stop the forensic expert presenting vital technical evidence at an armed robbery trial of the General and his close friend, Christy Dutton. From Ballyfermot, Dutton was also an associate of Gilligan. The General and Dutton had held up an amusement arcade and left vital forensic clues on the getaway motorbike they used.

The courageous scientist later recovered enough from his injuries to deliver his evidence in court. Despite the horrific methods they had used to scupper the case, in the end the pair was acquitted on a legal technicality.

The Donovan attack was to have repercussions for Factory John. As part of the huge follow-up investigation involving the Central Detective Unit (CDU), Special Branch and local detective units in the M District, every piece of information received at the incident room in Tallaght station was processed in detail.

One caller reported seeing a suspicious white van and a car in the Belgard area of west Dublin, close to Dr Donovan's home, a few nights before the bomb attack.

Detectives John McLoughlin and Felix McKenna were tasked with tracing the two vehicles which became a major lead. They discovered that the van belonged to a security man who patrolled the Cookstown Industrial Estate in Tallaght. He was a highly respected, trusted individual who had been appointed a peace commissioner with the power to sign garda search warrants and other sensitive police documents.

The detectives then uncovered something sinister. On the night that the white van had been spotted, the security man was meeting Factory John. Given his well-known association with the General, Gilligan now became a prime suspect for having planted the bomb device.

Over a number of weeks, however, the investigation team established that Gilligan had not been involved in the plot. Cahill had been assisted by the INLA and the Dunne brothers.

Due to a lack of evidence neither Cahill nor any of his associates were ever charged with the bombing. It sent a dangerous message to a criminal like Gilligan with a propensity for extreme violence – telling him that he could cross the line and get away with it.

The ongoing enquiry into Gilligan's relationship with the security man had produced a valuable lead in the investigation of the factory robberies. It emerged that the pillar of society had been working for Factory John as an inside man. It was estimated that in the year before the attack on Dr Donovan, Gilligan had robbed goods worth the equivalent of over €4 million today from the Cookstown Industrial Estate, at the rate of one job every month. Factory John's success rate was now making sense. If an alarm was raised the security man would head off the local police who had come to investigate, assuring them that everything was fine. He knew the gardaí and was trusted by them. When he was arrested and questioned the security man confessed to his involvement and detailed his dealings with Gilligan.

There was enough evidence on which to bring a criminal case against Factory John, but it was a non-starter. Once again the principal witness was too afraid to testify. The security man preferred to plead guilty to complicity in the crimes rather than incur Gilligan's, by now, infamous wrath.

One of the incidents in which the security man had helped Gilligan was a burglary from the RTV Rentals warehouse on the estate. The gang again punched a hole in the fire-damaged warehouse wall, bypassing a state-of-the-art alarm system. This time Gilligan drove off in a stolen truck with video recorders worth the equivalent of €2 million. McKenna got information that Gilligan had transported the luxury goods to the Midlands, stashing them with a farmer near Mullingar who was helping to sell them.

The investigation team raided the farm and uncovered half of the stolen machines. Most of the video recorders were eventually recovered and the farmer later agreed to make a statement outlining Gilligan's involvement in the crime.

A file was prepared for the Director of Public Prosecutions (DPP), the State's chief prosecutor, and a decision made to charge John Joseph Gilligan with burglary and receiving stolen goods. True to his modus operandi the increasingly confident gang boss used every legal device to stall the criminal case and play for time.

On the morning that the case was finally due to proceed, the Mullingar farmer arrived in court shaking and ashen-faced. 'I met John Gilligan last night and he stuck a shotgun in my ear and told me if I give evidence I am a fucking dead man,' he told the police. The farmer was adamant that he would not testify. He would take the rap himself.

The DPP was forced to enter a *nolle prosequi* and drop the charges. Not content with beating the system for yet another time, Gilligan jeered at the detectives as he strutted from the courtroom – knowing there was nothing anyone could do about it.

As his confidence grew, so did the size and frequency of the robberies. Just keeping track of the number of large-scale burglaries being reported throughout the country was a task in itself. Whenever Gilligan was in custody, the police, the factory owners and freight operators were given a reprieve as the number of robberies dropped dramatically. On his release, urgent criminal intelligence bulletins, including a photograph, description and list of associates, were sent to every police station in the country with the warning: 'Gilligan has returned to active service organizing burglaries on a grand scale.'

The Factory Gang was stealing anything that could be sold on the black market and even began taking orders. The astonishing 'shopping list' included agricultural medicine, hardware goods, double-glazed windows, pharmaceuticals, clothes, footwear, lingerie, chocolates, household foodstuffs, alcohol, cigarettes, computer games, TVs, video recorders and music systems.

The gang hit warehouses, factories and large stores, and hijacked freight vehicles throughout the length and breadth of Ireland. Gilligan's fleet of trucks was purloined from transport companies. The size of truck being taken depended on what the gang intended stealing. Gilligan began travelling independently of the loot while it was in transit, scouting ahead of the stolen goods and watching for police checkpoints.

He used walkie-talkies to co-ordinate the various burglaries. If the truck carrying the loot ran into the police, Gilligan and other gang members would move in to distract them. He and his gang were always armed. Guns were a helpful persuader if a security man got notions of being heroic. Officers were warned to approach the Factory Gang with caution, preferably with armed backup.

In Dublin the experienced officers involved in the investigation of serious crime were finding it impossible to get the resources to place around-the-clock surveillance on the organized crime gangs. Garda management had switched resources away from such specialist areas of investigation with the result that the crime gangs had virtually free rein. An internal report in the early eighties, colloquially known as the 'Three Wise Men's Report', inexplicably directed an organizational shift away from specialist crime squads, with the exception of anti-terrorist units. The theory was that every officer in the force should be able to do any job required.

Garda management had adopted an ostrich approach to the escalating crime problem by refusing to accept that organized crime even existed. Use of the term was more or less banned from police discourse. The sections dealing with collating criminal intelligence worked on a nine-to-five basis and never at weekends.

Gilligan was taking full advantage of the inadequacies in the system. Inaction, inefficiency and ignorance in the operation of the criminal justice system were creating a monster.

While the police continued to stagnate, Gilligan began doing business with Tommy Coyle, the country's biggest fence on either side of the border. Coyle had extensive underworld contacts in Britain and mainland Europe as well. Operating from his home in Drogheda, County Louth, Coyle was a remarkable character. He was the middleman for every illegal group, both paramilitary and criminal, on both sides of the border. Loyalist and republican terrorists were among his clients. A policeman once commented that the list of Coyle's contacts read like a who's who of 'every outlaw on the island'. He was the essential cog that kept the wheels of organized crime and terrorism turning.

A lot of gangland observers wondered why Coyle was never murdered by one of the many disparate groups he did business with (he died from cancer in October 2000). The truth was that, in addition to his complicated working arrangements, Coyle developed a relationship with the police and acted for several years as a double and treble agent.

It was also suspected in garda and criminal circles that Coyle moonlighted as an agent for Britain's counter-intelligence and security agency, MI5, which was active on both sides of the border. His death from natural causes bore testament to the fact that his usefulness outweighed any damage done through his complex set of relationships.

In 1985 Coyle took delivery of a consignment of TVs worth an estimated €1.2 million from Gilligan and Michael 'Jo Jo' Kavanagh. They had been liberated from Sony's main warehouse in the Cookstown Industrial Estate, Tallaght. Kavanagh, from Crumlin in Dublin, was an armed robber and one of the General's top lieutenants but frequently worked with Gilligan.

This was part of a now regular arrangement between the Factory Gang and Coyle, who had an impressive network of safe warehouses and distributors for every type of merchandise. Gilligan stole the goods and dropped them off to Coyle. In turn Coyle had them distributed within days. On this occasion the police were onto the scam and arrested Coyle.

After a long interview the fence agreed to show Detective Inspector Mick Canavan, an experienced officer in the Serious Crime Squad, where most of the TVs were hidden in a shed near Slane, County Meath. In the following weeks the police 'recovered' a number of other hauls of stolen merchandise around Counties Meath and Louth. Coyle gave no evidence or statement to link Gilligan or Kavanagh to the crime. He was subsequently charged but got off on a legal technicality.

Gilligan and Coyle were rumoured to have fallen out over the seizures but nevertheless continued to deal with each other. In

November 1985, for example, Coyle helped dispose of €388,000 worth of cigarettes stolen in a hold-up from a warehouse in Clondalkin, west Dublin. The truck robbed for the heist was later found across the border in Newry, County Down.

In some respects, despite his greedy and violent disposition, Gilligan could, on rare occasions, be pragmatic. Part of a stolen consignment could be recovered by the police as long as no one was charged and it caused no long-term damage to the operation. It was an acceptable occupational hazard.

Gilligan was also suspected of informing on some of his partners in crime or competitors but it was an issue no one would broach with him. Investigators who tried to break him during the heady days of the Factory Gang recall how he would steadfastly refuse to give the names of any of his fences. They were his bread and butter and their anonymity was non-negotiable.

Factory John continued to supply his fences with more stolen goods to sell on. At 6 a.m., on 2 January 1986, Gilligan and a gang of armed and masked men burst into the Nilfisk warehouse in Tallaght. The foreman and a security worker were tied up at gunpoint. Gilligan's men reversed a stolen tractor unit and forty-foot container inside and began loading it with a consignment of 850 brand-new vacuum cleaners worth over €410,000. They emptied the warehouse and disappeared in less than an hour. If there had been prizes given out for the country's most efficient cargo loaders, Gilligan and his gang would have won all the trophies.

Felix McKenna, who had been promoted to Detective Sergeant and assigned to the Serious Crime Squad at the Central Detective Unit (CDU), was brought back for the investigation because of his experience of dealing with Gilligan. He was under the command of Detective Superintendent Ned Ryan, known as the 'Buffalo', the tenacious legendary chief of the Serious Crime Squad – and the General's sworn enemy. Indeed, emboldened by the Dr Donovan bombing, Cahill had ordered a murder contract on Ryan. For a time the tough old-world cop was placed under armed protection by his colleagues until Cahill was convinced to change his mind.

McKenna had an impressive network of informants throughout the underworld. Within three days of the Nilfisk heist he got the tip-off that Gilligan had stashed the vacuum cleaners in a warehouse in the Weatherwell Industrial Estate in Clondalkin, only 5 kilometres away. This time Detective Superintendent Ryan ensured that McKenna got the go-ahead to mount a long-term surveillance operation, if necessary.

Detectives from Clondalkin, Tallaght and the CDU were involved. During a discreet search of the warehouse McKenna and his men discovered most of the stolen vacuum cleaners. In addition to the Nilfisk loot they found the stolen tractor unit and forty-foot trailer used in the robbery, a stolen Leyland truck and a stolen Ford Sierra car. The team withdrew and waited for their target to appear.

Eight days later the squad's patience finally paid off when a van drove into the estate and stopped outside the warehouse. John Gilligan got out of the passenger seat. He carefully scanned the area, checking for anything unusual, and then opened the warehouse doors.

He directed the van inside. It was being driven by a young member of his gang, twenty-two-year-old David Weafer from Finglas, north-west Dublin. Gilligan scanned the area again before closing the doors. McKenna waited for ten minutes to allow Factory John to get comfortable before giving the order to swoop.

The eight armed detectives burst through the doors with weapons drawn, screaming at the two men to get down on the floor. Such was the ferocity of the invasion that Gilligan, who was in the process of loading the Nilfisks into the van, soiled himself with the shock. One of the arresting officers recalled almost throwing up as he took Gilligan in for questioning under section 30 of the Offences Against the State Act. On 11 January 1986 Gilligan was charged with the aggravated burglary in the Nilfisk warehouse, Tallaght, and placed in custody.

Two days later another of Gilligan's jobs went ahead as planned without him. This time an armed gang struck at Connolly Haulage in the Bluebell Industrial Estate near Ballyfermot and drove off with a truck full of cattle drench, for the control of parasites in animals, worth over €270,000.

During the robbery the truck driver was locked into the back of a refrigerated lorry and almost died of hypothermia. Two of Gilligan's associates, George 'the Penguin' Mitchell and Gerard Hopkins, were caught with the cattle drench and subsequently sentenced to five years each in prison.

When Gilligan was released on bail a few weeks later he went back to work. On 6 April he took a truckload of video recorders from another warehouse in the same Bluebell Industrial Estate. They were never recovered.

As a result of the ongoing investigation into the Sony televisions heist the police discovered that the gang was also using a lock-up shed in Finglas. A team placed the lock-up under surveillance for a number of days. Finally a criminal associate of Gilligan's turned up.

Just before the detectives moved in, Gilligan arrived in his car with the wife and sister-in-law of another major criminal. The officers swooped and the group was arrested. Inside the shed the detectives found clothes stolen from a factory in County Kildare, crates of cooking oil taken from a warehouse at the Dublin docks and pharmaceuticals worth €355,000 from the Glaxo factory in Rathfarnham, south Dublin.

Gilligan was charged with the Glaxo burglary on 9 August 1986 and with receiving the other stolen goods found in the shed. Factory John opted for trial by jury while one of his associates made a statement admitting his involvement with Factory John and pleaded guilty. He was then subpoenaed as a witness against Gilligan. When it came to the case being heard, however, the State's only witness had disappeared and Gilligan walked free yet again.

A month after he was charged with the Glaxo burglary Gilligan was caught by gardaí in Limerick with two associates robbing mailbags at the city's train station. On 14 September the three criminals were arrested, charged, and then given bail.

Gilligan and his compatriots were using a BMW car registered to Christy Kinahan who a few days earlier had been busted with heroin worth around €300,000. The drugs seizure was one of the biggest recorded by gardaí at the time. Gilligan's use of his car exemplified the network of connections between the mobsters.

Meanwhile the mounting charges against him were not putting Factory John off his stride. A few weeks later, on 3 October, he took part in an armed robbery at a post office in Portlaoise with members of the General's gang. On the job was Martin Cahill's brother, John, Martin Foley, christened 'the Viper' by the General who suspected Foley was a police informer, and Eamon Daly, one of the General's closest lieutenants. The four got away with cash, cheques and registered letters worth an estimated €250,000.

In December, much to Gilligan's amusement, the Limerick mailbags case was dropped in the District Court on a legal technicality. On the same day he was arrested and taken to Portlaoise garda station for questioning about the post office robbery. There was insufficient evidence to charge him or any of his other accomplices with the crime.

For every seizure being made by the police there were several hauls they never managed to recover. In one case Gilligan and his team robbed two forty-foot container loads of the latest Adidas sportswear. The robbery took place in Cork on a Saturday night. By Wednesday the residents of Crumlin and Ballyfermot were proudly wearing the very latest Adidas gear, including some designs which hadn't yet made it into the shops.

In another job Gilligan, with the help of Martin 'the Viper' Foley, robbed a truckload of Aran jumpers from a factory in Falcarragh, north-west Donegal. Somehow Gilligan headed back to Dublin with the load and forgot to take Foley with him. The truck was later recovered in Dublin and taken to Crumlin garda station for examination. Gilligan then stole it back from the station yard and it was never seen again.

On 17 April 1987, Good Friday, the police pressure on Gilligan continued when he was nabbed red-handed. This time he and two associates were in the process of loading a truck with €197,000 worth of sweets at Rose Confectionery in the Robin Hood Industrial Estate in Tallaght. A security man had spotted them and called the police who quickly surrounded the premises.

When a member of the gang spotted the squad cars Gilligan remained calm. He joked that one of the gang should put him into a sweet jar and close the lid. But the fun stopped when he was charged with burglary and being found in the premises.

This time there would be no witnesses to silence. Prison was looking inevitable for Factory John.

CHAPTER FOUR

———

A GODFATHER OF CRIME

Geraldine Gilligan enjoyed being the wife of a notorious gangster. She was the driving force behind her husband's criminal activities, acting as his secretary and adviser. Between 1982 and 1984 John had been banned from driving for a total of forty years as a result of various convictions and mostly relied on his wife to be his chauffeur. Geraldine drove him to meetings with other gang members to plan jobs and to carry out surveillance on prospective targets for his expropriations.

But Geraldine harboured ambitions that went beyond helping with her husband's career and rearing children. While he was achieving his goal to become an untouchable godfather she craved respectability and wanted a legitimate business of her own.

From childhood she had a passion for horses and dreamt of one day owning a world-class equestrian centre, which she intended buying with the proceeds of her husband's crimes. By the mid-eighties Geraldine already owned eight horses stabled in Kilcock, County Kildare, and Tracey was taking riding lessons. Like her husband, she was a keen networker who ingratiated herself into the wealthy horsey set, attending riding schools and events around the country. However, her ultimate aim was to buy land so that she could build a riding school and stables.

In September 1987 the Gilligans bought a derelict farmhouse on five acres in a secluded area called Mucklon, near Enfield, County Kildare. Geraldine spotted the place for sale one day as she was driving through the village. She immediately recognized its potential and paid the equivalent of €17,000 in cash for the property. The couple began reconstructing the house and erecting stables for horses at the back. Geraldine's plans for their new home, Jessbrook, named after her favourite horse, Jess, put huge pressure on her husband. Factory John switched his attentions to robbing hardware outlets and warehouses to steal the materials he needed for the work.

Gilligan shared his wife's pretensions to respectability and began describing himself as a horse breeder and trainer. The couple also joined the Meath Hunt. As far as his new acquaintances were aware Gilligan was an inner-city Dubliner who had done well in business – a self-made man. Very few people knew the truth about the small man who talked a big game. But that was about to change.

From December 1987 and throughout the first six months of 1988 garda management launched a major offensive against organized crime in Dublin – in the full glare of media attention. It was long overdue. In 1987 alone there were almost 600 armed robberies throughout the country, with 500 of them in Dublin. Only 100 incidents had been solved. The number one target of the unprecedented police operation was the General and his gang.

Cahill had embarrassed the authorities so much that they were finally forced into all-out action. He had robbed millions of pounds in cash and jewels and was the first Irish gang boss to gain international notoriety when he stole the priceless Beit paintings in 1986 from Russborough House, County Wicklow. The robbery is still regarded as one of the world's biggest art heists of all time. Now it was the police's turn to fight back.

In criminal psychology Cahill could be classified as an anarchist, suffering from acute paranoia, with multiple personalities. Gilligan shared many of the same behavioural traits but without the different personalities. What you saw was what you got with Factory John. Cahill's development as a sociopath can be traced to the two years he spent as an inmate in a notorious reformatory school. With the full support of the law, the Irish industrial and reformatory school system was a dumping ground for the orphaned, the deprived and the wrongdoers. They were veritable gulags, asylums of appalling misery and suffering, run by sadistic religious orders.

Youngsters deemed 'troubled' or beyond parental control also qualified for forced admission to both institutions. Rape, gross sexual and psychological abuse, torture and starvation were constant features of life in this inhumane system. Cahill wasn't lying when he later recalled bitterly: 'If anyone corrupted me it was those mad monks down in the bog.'

Gilligan had been fortunate to escape the reform school's clutches, although it could be argued his father filled in for the mad monks. The former inmates were released with a deep-seated hatred for the rest of society. Although poorly educated they had learned one important lesson from their captors – that violence was the most effective tool in life. They would spend a lifetime getting even.

Unlike any other criminal, the General waged a personal war against the State and especially the gardaí, for whom he harboured a pathological hatred that grew more irrational over time. While other villains, including Gilligan, did everything to avoid the police, Cahill spared no effort trying to humiliate them.

The General equipped his extensive arsenal of firearms by robbing the garda depot where confiscated weapons were stored, and, out of spite, he stole the country's most sensitive crime files from the office of the Director of Public Prosecutions. Cahill had also blown up the State's top forensic scientist and plotted to murder the officer in charge of investigating his activities. He had become the undisputed Public Enemy Number One.

The Tango Squad was a novel approach introduced to take on the criminals. Young, enthusiastic officers from around the city were recruited for an overt surveillance operation to harass the hoodlums round the clock. The investigation turned Cahill into a household name as he paraded around in balaclavas and Mickey Mouse shorts to hide his face from the cameras. The team brought about impressive results, eventually forcing the gang members to make mistakes. Most of them ended up serving long sentences for armed robbery and possession of firearms, with the exception of Tango One – Cahill.

By the time the Tango Squad was sent into action in late 1987 the criminal intelligence assessment of gangland placed Gilligan's Factory Gang in the top three operating in the country. It wasn't long before the re-energized specialist police squads turned their full-time attention to him.

The intense pressure being exerted on gangland was unearthing valuable intelligence. Unfortunately for Factory John, Felix McKenna was appointed as one of the Tango Squad's team leaders. He received a tip-off that Gilligan was planning to hit a hardware store in Enniscorthy, County Wexford, and later stash the stolen goods in a yard at Ballymount, west Dublin.

Gilligan was still concentrating on robbing hardware stores around the country in order to equip Jessbrook. On 26 January 1988 Gilligan and gang members Christy Delaney, from Finglas, Robert O'Connell and James 'Fast 40' Kelly, both from Tallaght, hit Bolgers Hardware & Builders Providers in the town and took off with €36,000 worth of materials. In the previous weeks another large hardware store had been hit in Athlone.

The next evening Detective Sergeant McKenna and his Tango team raided the yard they had been tipped off about in Ballymount and found a lorry with half of the stolen hardware goods inside. The rest had already been moved.

The owner of the property, Maurice Griffin, admitted to McKenna that Gilligan had left the loot there for safekeeping and would be returning later to pick up the rest of it. Nine officers concealed themselves in strategic positions around the yard and waited for Factory John. At 11 a.m. two men drove in and began transferring the stolen gear to a van. As the two villains, Delaney and Kelly, chatted away, detectives were listening in from under the truck.

McKenna decided not to arrest the two thieves in situ. He ordered his men to allow the pair to leave the yard and arranged for them to be intercepted a few kilometres away. The Tango Squad then resumed their surveillance in the hope that Gilligan would walk into the trap.

Luckily for the police, mobile phones were not yet widely in use. When Kelly was taken in he tried to phone Gilligan on his land line to warn him off, but there was no reply. At 5 p.m. another van drove into the yard. This time it was being driven by gang member Robert O'Connell and Gilligan was in the passenger seat. The pair loaded up the rest of the stolen material in canvas bags and threw them into the back of the van.

McKenna again waited until they had driven down the road before he had them arrested. Gilligan, already on bail for the Nilfisk robbery and the Rose Confectionery burglary, was charged with receiving stolen goods but was released on bail yet again. He told the arresting officers that he had only been 'getting a lift' from O'Connell. Gilligan used every delaying tactic possible and the case did not come to court for another two years. In the meantime the arrests didn't deter the villains.

Three nights later Gilligan, Kelly and O'Connell were again arrested. This time uniformed officers caught them stealing wood from Chadwicks builders' suppliers in Sandyford, south Dublin. They were charged with burglary and given bail.

Gilligan assessed the four cases facing him – the Nilfisk job, the Rose Confectionary robbery and now the Bolgers Enniscorthy and

Chadwicks hardware heists. He took the strategic decision to plead guilty to both the Rose Confectionary and Chadwicks offences in the hope of getting shorter sentences which would run concurrently. It was another way of playing the system.

On 13 May 1988 he duly pleaded guilty and was given eighteen months for the burglary at the Rose Confectionary warehouse in Tallaght. But at the hearing in the Circuit Criminal Court Gilligan got more than he had bargained for. Detective Inspector John McLoughlin used the opportunity to expose John Gilligan to the public. He told Mr Justice Frank Roe that the mobster was 'one of Ireland's biggest criminals in organized crime'. McLoughlin commented:

> I have known John Gilligan for fifteen years and he is the leader
> of a gang which has robbed warehouses all over the country. His
> only source of income is from crime.

In mitigation, a woman with whom Gilligan stabled three horses said that he was a 'kind, generous and considerate person who placed his ponies at the disposal of disadvantaged children'.

Gilligan didn't mind the prison sentence but he was furious that the hearing had given the media a first opportunity to reveal his true identity to the rest of the world. The high-profile investigation of the General had generated huge public and media interest in organized crime in Ireland. Gilligan's trial was news and the following day a newspaper ran the story under the heading 'Crime godfather jailed' – thus blowing his cover among the horsey set Geraldine and he had so carefully cultivated.

Two months later Gilligan pleaded guilty to the Chadwicks job and was jailed for another four months. He spent eighteen months in prison in total.

When he was released from prison in December 1989 a criminal intelligence bulletin was circulated to all garda districts. The document warned:

Subject John Gilligan has recently been released from prison having served eighteen months for burglary and larceny. Information suggests that this man has returned to active services organizing burglaries at stores and warehouses, hijacking of freight vehicles and larcenies on a grand scale.

Having regained his freedom Gilligan was still facing charges for the more serious Nilfisk and Bolgers robberies, which he had decided to fight tooth and nail. As a result of his previous convictions and the size of the haul of stolen goods recovered, this time, if convicted, he was facing a much longer prison stretch.

David Weafer had pleaded guilty to the Nilfisk charge already and had been jailed for two years. Gilligan believed that Weafer had secretly done a deal with the police and was informing on the gang. He decided to send his former acolyte a message in prison. One day while he was showering Weafer suffered extensive injuries when his face was slashed with a knife by one of Gilligan's henchmen. The twenty-two-year-old was rushed to hospital. The attack was also intended as a warning for any other would-be snouts in the camp. And the intimidation was not confined to errant gang members.

Before the trial anonymous calls were made to Nilfisk's headquarters in Dublin threatening that the place would be burned down if employees gave evidence against Gilligan. The matter was reported to the police and Factory John's bail was revoked. He was placed in custody for almost two months. After pre-trial hearings he was returned to the Dublin Circuit Criminal Court on a charge of receiving the Nilfisk vacuum cleaners.

The trial lasted for two weeks. In the witness box Gilligan put on his best performance. He directly addressed the jury and claimed that he had been offered a lift in the van by Weafer. He protested that he had been helping a mate move a few things when the police burst in. He was an innocent man.

Gilligan's lawyers then made an application to the court on a point of law. Quoting English legal precedent, they pointed out that an individual cannot receive that which they stole in the first place. They pressed the case that there was substantive evidence that Gilligan had in fact actually stolen the vacuum cleaners but that he had only been returned for trial on the receiving charge. On those grounds, they argued, the case against their client should be dismissed.

Factory John's penchant for gambling paid off. He was acquitted and walked free. As was his wont Gilligan could not stop himself giving the Tango Squad the two fingers as he marched triumphantly from the court. He had played the legal system and won – again.

The case caused consternation in the offices of the Director of Public Prosecutions. An edict was sent to all District Court judges informing them that when a defendant was returned for trial, he should be returned on all the charges outlined by the police. It would not be the first time that Gilligan forced changes in the criminal justice system.

Despite the latest victory Factory John was still facing the charges for burglary and receiving in the Enniscorthy case. Every time he appeared in court Gilligan and his pals created a sense of fear and intimidation. He would stare out gardaí and witnesses. He even used Geraldine in a failed bid to blackmail an individual on the prosecution side. Felix McKenna and his colleagues were determined that their nemesis would not thwart the system this time.

McKenna furnished an extensive report on John Gilligan's history for the Director of Public Prosecutions. He itemized the number of times Factory John had used intimidation and fear to get off various charges and stated that he was suspected of threatening jurors. The experienced detective urged the DPP to issue a certificate returning Gilligan for trial to the non-jury Special Criminal Court as had been done for most of the Cahill gang.

At a pre-trial hearing for Gilligan, James Kelly, Robbie O'Connell and Christy Delaney, Gilligan's lawyers argued that he should not be returned for trial because of insufficient evidence. The District Court judge, having read the book of evidence, said there was a case to answer. He was about to return Gilligan for trial by jury at the Circuit Criminal Court when a barrister for the State suddenly stood up. She handed the judge the DPP's certificate directing that Gilligan be sent forward to the non-jury Special Criminal Court.

Gilligan was stunned and turned pale with shock and then anger. This was a game changer. He instructed his lawyers to fight the decision on the grounds that he was entitled to trial by a jury of his peers. In the meantime his three co-accused were sent for trial to the Circuit Criminal Court. O'Connell got three years while Kelly and Delaney's sentences were suspended.

While awaiting trial, and doing everything possible to stop it, Gilligan became involved in efforts to sell the Beit art collection. Cahill had given Tommy Coyle the job of offloading the priceless paintings. But even Coyle, with his impressive connections, was experiencing difficulty finding a buyer. Each attempt to sell the art had failed because of worldwide sting operations and traps set by police forces. Cahill's gang began to believe that the paintings had brought a jinx on them. Everyone who dealt with the stolen treasures experienced bad luck – as Gilligan soon found out.

Coyle was approached by a representative of the Portadown-based UVF, a group that was responsible for some of the worst sectarian atrocities against Catholics in Northern Ireland. The loyalists were interested in buying the paintings to raise cash for a number of arms deals they had in the pipeline with a South African gunrunner.

The fence arranged a number of meetings between the UVF representative and the General. For Cahill, now desperate for cash, politics meant nothing. Five years earlier he had been prepared to go to war with the IRA when they demanded a share of one of his robberies. In his eyes terrorists were cowardly criminals hiding behind the veil of a political cause. The loyalists' blood money was as good to him as the Provos'.

Coyle recruited Gilligan as a go-between in the complex negotiations which took place over the period of a year. Cahill, who was suspicious to the point of extreme paranoia, trusted Gilligan. He knew, at least, that Factory John would not have a cop on his shoulder. For his part Gilligan was hopeful of a massive payday if the Beit deal went through. The secret negotiations were still ongoing when Factory John's trial came up for hearing in the Special Criminal Court.

During the day-long trial Maurice Griffin, the owner of the Ballymount yard, was called to give evidence for the prosecution. He contradicted his earlier statements to the police and claimed that the stolen goods had been brought to his yard before the Enniscorthy robbery. He said he had been visited by a Mr Gilligan but that he wasn't the man in the dock.

Felix McKenna told the court that Gilligan was the leader of the gang and heavily involved in serious crime.

On 7 November 1990 the court cleared Gilligan of the burglary charge but convicted him for receiving stolen goods. He was jailed for four years.

Mr Justice Robert Barr, in handing down the sentence, said that he accepted Gilligan was the gang leader. 'He has been involved in serious crime for many years and it appears probable that he has never had lawful employment,' the judge said.

Leave to appeal was denied and Gilligan was sent to serve his sentence in Portlaoise maximum-security prison on E Wing. Other members of organized crime gangs and many of his old associates were already incarcerated there as a result of the garda counter-offensive.

This time it was the police who were triumphant as Gilligan, white with rage, was led away in handcuffs.

It was a significant victory for McKenna and the Serious Crime Squad that they had finally busted the country's most prolific thief. With Gilligan inside the Factory Gang had been smashed.

CHAPTER FIVE

———

A DEADLY ALLIANCE

The decision to send Gilligan to serve his sentence in Portlaoise Prison, the State's highest security prison unit, was an acknowledgment of Factory John's growing reputation and status in gangland. Until the late 1980s the heavily fortified prison complex, on the edge of Portlaoise town in County Laois, had been exclusively used to house subversives, members of the IRA and other republican groups.

This changed in 1988 when the fortified complex was deemed the most suitable facility to accommodate the increasing number of dangerous 'crime ordinary' villains being jailed as a result of the garda offensives against the crime gangs. Since it was first used to hold terrorists in 1973 there had been several elaborate escape bids, all of which had failed. As a result Portlaoise was transformed into one of the most impregnable prisons in Europe.

Today it is still used to house terrorists and some of the most dangerous criminals in gangland. When Gilligan arrived, the ratio of prison officers to prisoners was the highest in the country and they were backed up by a large number of gardaí. An air exclusion zone operated around the complex and a detachment of 120 troops, armed with rifles and anti-aircraft machine guns, patrolled the perimeter walls and rooftops, while others maintained constant surveillance from watchtowers. The complex bristled with state-of-the-art CCTV cameras and sensors, both above and below ground, and lines of tank-traps stood guard around the prison's entire boundary.

The new category of high-risk, violent prisoners sent there in the 1990s was a reflection of the changes that were taking place in gangland. On the E1 wing the inmates were segregated from their republican neighbours, who didn't see themselves as gangsters and didn't want to fraternize with them. In less than two years, the wing became home to a fearsome collection of Ireland's most dangerous drug dealers, armed robbers and killers.

Behind its escape-proof defences the prison quickly became organized crime's premier training academy as its inmates mapped out the future direction of gangland. Criminal concepts were debated, new trends explored and experiences shared. Contacts were made and new gangs formed for the eventual return to freedom.

The most popular subject on the curriculum was learning from the mistakes that had won the 'students' their state-sponsored 'scholarships' in the first place – and how to avoid them in the future. Gilligan was one of the academy's star pupils. This was where he formed the nucleus of his future drug gang.

The retired former head of the Drugs Squad, Chief Superintendent John McGroarty, recalled how the new gangs developed.

> Gangs normally come from blood relationships, from localized areas in the neighbourhood and particularly prison. You invariably find that they've served time in prison together and that is where strong bonds of friendship are forged. The criminals assure each other that when they get out they'll have a bigger and better plan. A gangster will have some information or an idea which he will develop and bring other individuals into the mix. Between them they will hatch a wonderful plan to do highly profitable crime and next time they won't get caught. That's what so many of them

like to think. And that is how the John Gilligan gang got started,
on E1 in Portlaoise.

While escape from his new home was not an option, Gilligan
mounted legal challenges against his conviction and the severity of
his four-year sentence. They all failed. When he recovered from the
shock of being beaten at last by the police, he fell into a depression
and was homesick for his wife and children. Friends recall how he
was worried that Geraldine might not be there for him when he
got out. The feared crime boss wrote romantic letters expressing his
undying love for her and how much he wanted to be home. He was
also concerned about the sensitive bit of business she was taking care
of on his behalf.

Geraldine, who remained loyal to her childhood sweetheart, was
the only person he could entrust with the complicated negotiations
to sell the Beit paintings. Her plans for Jessbrook were put on hold
as the supply of money dried up when John was imprisoned. Instead,
she focused on closing the deal with the UVF.

A few weeks after Gilligan was jailed Detective Inspector Tony
Hickey of the Serious Crime Squad attached to the Central Detective
Unit, received intelligence about Geraldine's involvement in the
proposed art deal. The squad's surveillance team was dispatched
to monitor her activities and her phone was secretly bugged. In
January 1991 the undercover team watched as a representative of
the Portadown terrorists visited Geraldine at the family home in
Blanchardstown, west Dublin. The UVF man actually asked one of
the undercover surveillance officers, who was posing as a pedestrian,
for directions to Gilligan's house.

Over the following weeks the undercover teams monitored a number
of meetings between Geraldine and two loyalist representatives. The
meetings took place in pubs on the outskirts of Dublin, including
a bar in Blanchardstown and another near Dublin Airport. At one

stage, while in the company of the Northern pair, Geraldine tried unsuccessfully to cash a bank draft valued at the equivalent of €66,000 in the Ulster Bank at Walkinstown Cross, west Dublin. She tried a number of other institutions, but these also refused to cash it. The draft was believed to be part of a down payment for one of the paintings.

As part of the negotiations Martin Cahill had agreed to hand over the least valuable piece in the collection, *Woman Reading a Letter* by Gabriël Metsu, so the loyalist middlemen could show it to a prospective buyer, as proof that they had the collection. But the jinx of the Beit paintings struck again when the conspiracy with the UVF went disastrously wrong for the General – and the Gilligans lost out on a big payday.

Two of the loyalists travelled to Istanbul to do a deal with a Turkish businessman. He claimed to represent a sheikh who was interested in buying the collection. On 24 February 1991 the terrorists gave the Metsu to the businessman as proof of their bona fides. But before they could be lured further into the trap the Northern terrorists were tipped off and advised to get out of Turkey. As they headed to the airport they were arrested by the 'businessman' and his associates, who were all undercover police. It was later suspected that the operation had been compromised by British intelligence.

The seizure of the stolen Beit painting, and the connection with the most notorious sectarian terror group in Northern Ireland, made big news back in Ireland. It was the last type of publicity that the General wanted. It also gave his old enemies in the Provos a new reason to watch him. After the fiasco, there was no further contact between the Gilligans and the UVF.

In Portlaoise John Gilligan overcame the loss of the Beit money by reassuring himself that the involvement of his wife in the conspiracy was not known. He eventually settled down to do his time, building contacts and plotting his next move on the outside. He got over his loneliness in the company of many old friends as E1 was a home from home for the top tier of Dublin's underworld, including most of the General's gang. Cahill's brothers, John and Eddie, his brothers-in-law, Eugene Scanlan, Albert Crowley and John Foy, and his lieutenants, Eamon Daly and Harry Melia, were all serving long stretches for armed robbery and drugs offences.

Another gang member, Seamus 'Shavo' Hogan, who had been sentenced to seven years in Portlaoise for possession of firearms, had been segregated after three other inmates tried to slice off his ears. Hogan had been accused of informing to the Tango Squad and the injuries were intended to make his ears resemble those of a rat, branding him as an informer.

Larry and Christy 'Bronco' Dunne, the two most senior members of the crime family, also called E1 their home. Larry was doing fourteen years for running the family's heroin empire and Bronco, the head of the clan, had been given eleven years for kidnapping and robbery.

Former INLA members Fergal Toal and Dessie O'Hare, the notorious 'Border Fox', also shared the wing. They got forty years each for the brutal kidnapping of Dublin dentist John O'Grady in 1987. O'Hare was also suspected of carrying out several cold-blooded, sectarian murders in Northern Ireland. They were shunned by the other republican prisoners who didn't want them on their wings.

Unlike anywhere else in the prison system Portlaoise offered plenty of educational and training programmes to occupy the denizens of E1 and their subversive neighbours. Several of the inmates took art classes and even put together an impressive exhibition that went on tour around the country. It included works by Eddie Cahill and Larry Dunne. Gilligan, however, had no interest in messing about with paint brushes.

His art was networking, making contacts and winning the respect of his fellow inmates, a lot of whom he had associated with in the past. Gilligan already had a formidable reputation and was known as a criminal not to be messed with. As one former inmate recalled:

For a small fellow Gilligan had a tougher reputation than some of the biggest fellas in E1. He was known for having mad bottle and he was a violent bastard who wasn't afraid to 'do' anyone who fucked around with him. Gilligan was a big mouth and always demanding to be the centre of attention, but he was still well liked. He was always slagging the other lads and having the craic and trying to help out. But he was making connections, nurturing fellas who could help him on the outside. Gilligan was a great grafter.

As Factory John continued his Machiavellian manoeuvring, he struck up a friendship with a sinister individual called Patrick 'Dutchy' Holland, a career armed robber and a professional hit man.

Holland was a bald, unattractive man with a large boxer's deformed nose and a tall build. To the ordinary observer there was nothing overtly threatening about him. He stood out from the rest of the underworld rabble as a most unlikely criminal.

In 1989, at the age of fifty, Holland was convicted of possession of explosives. He had been in the process of selling them to the IRA a year earlier when Detective Inspector Tony Hickey's squad arrested him and his accomplices in a Dublin flat. The former boxer was eighteen months into a ten-year sentence when Gilligan arrived on E1.

Holland, who was the oldest lag in the prison, came across as a gentle, soft-spoken man heading for retirement. A non-drinker and non-smoker, he projected himself as a deeply religious man. Holland never missed Sunday Mass and had a keen belief in an afterlife. He rarely used bad language and was courteous and friendly to everyone. But those who knew him well described a very strange and complex character, a man of many contradictions with a dark, dangerous side.

Unlike most other criminals, it is hard to find a reason why someone like Patrick Holland became a professional criminal. Gardaí who pursued him during his criminal career suggest that he was just born to be bad.

Born on 12 March 1939, he grew up at St Laurence's Road in Chapelizod, west Dublin, which at the time was still the countryside. He came from a respectable, middle-class background where there were no criminal influences. Holland later described having had an idyllic, privileged childhood, and he was very close to his parents and siblings. He was a dedicated athlete and played professional soccer for a time. There was no hint of deviancy through his teenage years and early twenties, and he was never in trouble with the law. Dutchy was a perplexing character.

In his late teens the future hit man went to America with a friend and joined the United States Marine Corps. He spent a few years with the American army before returning home to Ireland in the early 1960s.

Holland's first scrape with the law took place in 1965 when he was convicted for receiving stolen fur coats. He was twenty-six. He later claimed that he had been set up and that this first conviction put him on the road to a life of crime.

During the 1970s Holland became known to the police as the 'lone raider' responsible for a string of armed robberies in Dublin. In each incident the robber arrived heavily armed and disguised as a plump man. In fact it was not unusual for Holland to dress up as a woman for a 'job' and he always wore wigs. Thus in his early career he became known in criminal circles as 'the Wig'.

Eventually the Serious Crime Squad unmasked the mystery lone raider and he was charged with three hold-ups. He was also caught and charged with a robbery he had carried out with Michael and John Cunningham. On 7 February 1977 a warrant was issued for his arrest when he failed to appear for a remand hearing in the Dublin District Court. Holland had fled to America with his wife. He lived in Chicago for several years and was eventually captured when he returned to Ireland in 1981 and carried out another series of robberies.

Detectives arrested Holland as he was about to leave the country again in the summer of 1981. When officers searched a safe house he was using they discovered a large cache of firearms, including an Ingram machine gun, a .357 Magnum revolver, smoke grenades and ammunition. He subsequently received a seven-year sentence for the robberies.

After his release in 1986 Holland joined another gang led by the General's older brother, John Cahill. Cahill and two other members of the gang were arrested in a shoot-out with police a year later but Holland escaped. That was when he began dabbling in the sale of explosives to the Provos which in turn had earned him another rent-free stay in Portlaoise, this time for ten years.

When Holland was being questioned following his arrest with the explosives he made a startling admission to detectives. During an informal chat the detectives asked him what he had been doing while on the run in the US. In a matter-of-fact tone Holland claimed that he had worked as a contract killer for the Mafia in Boston and Chicago and carried out 'two or three' murders. He also claimed that he was wanted by the FBI. The police investigated the dramatic claims but found no evidence to back them up.

But those who knew him best reckoned that Dutchy was telling the truth. One of the people who believed Holland's version was John Gilligan. He recognized that an assassin like Dutchy, possessing his skills and personal discipline, would be an invaluable asset in the future.

It was the start of a deadly alliance.

CHAPTER SIX

———

THE MASTER PLAN

In Portlaoise John Gilligan lost no time in organizing the next phase of his criminal career: one which would make him wealthy and would not involve doing any more time inside. Within months he had recruited two young hoods who would become his loyal lieutenants in the years ahead. Brian Meehan and Paul 'Hippo' Ward, both from Crumlin in south-west Dublin, were well established as hardened criminals by their late teens. Flash, brash and violent, the two friends personified gangland's new brat pack of violent young thugs.

Meehan and Ward, both of whom were serving sentences for armed robbery, were elevated in the underworld hierarchy when they were transferred to E1 in Portlaoise Prison from Mountjoy Prison in the summer of 1990. When Gilligan arrived, he took the pair under his wing and started to groom them for better things. They would each play a major role in his future plans.

Factory John already knew Meehan, whom he had used as a driver on a number of jobs. He had long admired the cocky kid's 'bottle' and how he handled himself, especially the ease with which he could resort to violence when required. Meehan was to become his favourite lieutenant and he treated him like a son.

Over the next few years on E1 the trio developed a strong bond. Meehan and Ward looked up to Gilligan as a patriarchal figure and an accomplished role model, who would one day make them rich beyond their wildest dreams. They were steadfastly loyal to their new godfather. Gilligan implemented a Mafia-style hierarchy where Meehan would become the underboss and Ward operate as a capo.

———————

Born in Crumlin on 7 April 1965 Brian Meehan had a formidable reputation as an up-and-coming thug long before he took up residence on E1. Meenor, as he was known to friends, cut his teeth as a joyrider in his early teens, robbing high performance cars and jousting with the pursuing police squad cars during chases across Dublin.

Meenor had accumulated a string of convictions for car theft and larceny by the age of sixteen. He had been disqualified from driving before he even qualified for a driver's licence. His potential was first spotted by Michael 'Jo Jo' Kavanagh who became his mentor. Meenor had a fascination for guns and loved the buzz involved in a hold-up.

Despite being in his teens, Meehan impressed his elders in the way he handled the adrenalin rush during a robbery, maintaining his focus and control. He wasn't afraid of using a gun if the need arose and had no problem shooting at cops. Meehan began stealing getaway cars and driving them in heists for Kavanagh and the General. He also took part in freelance jobs with Factory John and his associates. The young hood was in big demand.

Meehan's name began appearing in garda criminal intelligence bulletins linking him to a growing number of serious crimes, including incidents where gardaí were threatened at gunpoint and shot at. By the time he was nineteen, Meenor was being regularly sighted in the company of Martin Cahill, Jo Jo Kavanagh, John Gilligan and other gangland celebrities of the day.

Meehan had been spotted driving Gilligan and Kavanagh on occasion and officers had also noted Gilligan calling to his home in Crumlin. Being treated with respect by such exalted criminals gave the dangerous youngster immense credibility among his peers – and a special place on the cops' most wanted list. It was obvious that Meehan was a rising star.

Garda intelligence reports warned that the leader of the gangland brat pack was 'dangerous' and 'particularly disposed to using violence on garda members'. On at least three occasions he had threatened gardaí at gunpoint. In one incident, on 19 February 1987, Meehan almost added the term cop killer to his CV when he shot and injured an unarmed garda following a payroll robbery. In the same incident he pointed his gun at the head of another officer who was trying to arrest him but the weapon misfired.

'Stay back, you bastard, or I will kill you!' the twenty-one-year-old hood warned, before he and his accomplices made their escape. The incident elevated him to the top league of dangerous villains but there was insufficient evidence to charge him. At the time DNA profiling did not exist.

On another occasion, one night in 1987, Meehan was stopped at a garda checkpoint in Clontarf, north Dublin while driving a high-powered, stolen jeep. His passenger was P. J. Loughran, a former IRA member and the leader of a highly efficient armed robbery outfit that became known as the Athy Gang. When the unarmed garda asked Meehan his name and address, instead of wasting time bluffing an answer, Meehan pulled a pistol and pointed it at the cop, telling him to 'Fuck off'. Then he drove away.

In December 1987 Meehan finally ran out of road following a daring armed hold-up with Jo Jo Kavanagh at the Allied Irish Bank on Grafton Street in central Dublin. The duo was arrested a few days after the heist but there was only sufficient evidence with which to charge Meehan and Kavanagh was released. The man in charge of the investigation was Detective Inspector Tony Hickey, who had also caught Holland. The detective would play a significant role in the future careers of both Meehan and Gilligan.

When Meehan's trial came to hearing a year later he was determined not to go down without a fight by taking a page out of Gilligan's play book. On the fifth day of the trial the judge was informed that two female jurors had reported to gardaí that they had been followed home from the precincts of the court. The judge immediately ordered an investigation and the jury was discharged.

Later one of the jurors positively identified a close associate of both Meehan and Kavanagh as the man who had tried to intimidate her. But the criminals had done their job. The jurors were too frightened to give statements and refused to co-operate with the investigating police. No one was ever charged with the attempt to nobble the jury.

Meehan was remanded in custody and a second trial date was set for April 1989. This time the young blagger pleaded guilty and was jailed for six years.

Sent to Mountjoy Prison, Meehan began a campaign of protest over conditions in the Victorian, medium-security prison. Seven months later he was joined by his friend and neighbour, Paul 'Hippo' Ward, who was the same age as Meehan and also had a reputation for violence.

Hippo had also been a joyrider and took part in robberies with his pal. He later lived with Meehan's sister, Vanessa. But Ward did not have the same personal discipline as his pal and became a heroin addict in his teens. He carried out several violent robberies while strung out and terrorized his old neighbours in Crumlin.

Police who dealt with Hippo and locals who knew him later described him as a 'two-bit violent robber' who was not afraid to inflict pain or shoot anyone. In November 1989 Ward was sentenced to four years for the armed robbery of a bookmaker's shop in Crumlin Village. He narrowly missed killing a detective as he and another accomplice made their escape before they were cornered near Crumlin Shopping Centre.

In the summer of 1990 the simmering tensions in Mountjoy boiled over with Meehan and Ward among the ringleaders of a full-scale riot. After wrecking a whole wing of the prison, they, along with dozens of other inmates, staged a rooftop protest and the stand-off continued for a number of days. When order was eventually restored, the prison authorities were determined that Meehan and Ward would not cause any further disturbances. The troublemakers were transferred to Portlaoise.

———————

The old video of a soccer match is a remarkable piece of gangland memorabilia. Recorded in Portlaoise Prison, on Saturday 23 May 1992, it provides a rare insight into how John Gilligan ingratiated himself with the rest of the prison population and placed himself at the centre of attention. The match was between the criminals on E1 and a team from the IRA.

In arranging the game Gilligan, the main organizer, had successfully broken down a cultural barrier between the criminals and the republicans. As political prisoners, the terrorists usually refused to associate with the gangsters or allow them onto their wings. They looked down on the gangsters as nothing more than undisciplined riff-raff. Yet Gilligan found room for compromise by devising a mini soccer tournament in each other's exercise yards. The games were classed home and away.

Gilligan organized a video camera to record the event and he granted himself the job of commentator for the seven-a-side matches. The 'home' game was played in the exercise yard beside E1 in splendid sunshine under the gaze of the armed soldiers patrolling the rooftops overhead. The video showed criminals and paramilitaries jostle, dribble and shoot at goal in a good-humoured atmosphere.

Gilligan's commentary, in his nasally Ballyfermot brogue, was monotonous. He showered praise on his team, which featured Brian Meehan, Paul Ward, Harry Melia, Eugene Scanlan, Martin Farrell, Fergal Toal and another young Mountjoy rioter, Warren Dumbrell. Gilligan was particularly glowing in his praise for the footwork of Toal, Ward and Meehan.

He jokingly cajoled the referee, former Dublin pimp John Cullen who was doing life for the murder of three women, and he gave nicknames to the Provos because he didn't know their real names. The video recorded one, almost comical, irony. Three years earlier the Provos had tried to murder the criminal team's star striker, Harry Melia, because of his drug dealing activities in Tallaght. Now Melia was exacting some revenge by scoring most of the goals for the criminals to beat the paramilitaries by an impressive sixteen goals to five.

Gilligan cracked jokes on camera about the players. At one stage a republican supporter reminded the criminal side that there were at least ten minutes more to play in the match. The criminals disagreed and said that the match had only a few minutes to run to the full-time whistle.

Gilligan turned it into a joke, reminding the Provo: 'When we're winning, there isn't another ten minutes to go. We're criminals for fuck sake...we have to rob ye!'

After the match the amateur sports reporter pointed out other major criminals who had come out into the sunshine to watch the two most unlikely soccer teams in Ireland. Adopting the role of a celebrity-spotting TV presenter, he pointed to Larry and Christy Dunne and described what they were wearing. Larry was the team coach. Gilligan ordered the victorious E1 crew to line up to be filmed and praised each individual player as they stood in front of the camera. He then prompted the cameraman to pan across to the republican team. Smiling, he walked over to commiserate on their loss but commended their efforts.

In the film Gilligan looks like a caricature of himself, dressed in blue shorts and a striped sweatshirt with white socks and runners. He literally had to look up to most of the prisoners. As Dessie O'Hare, who had missed the match, appeared in the yard Gilligan's commentary became excited:

> The Border Fox has come into the yard. He missed the match because he was on a visit. It's himself, the Border Fox! Would you come over here, Dessie, and say a few words to us, or I'll blow the whistle on ya!

The baby-faced psychopath smiled but didn't reply.

The fun continued as the criminal team and its supporters gathered for a group photograph with Gilligan snuggled up next to Dessie O'Hare. It all looks like a jolly day out for the lads.

The video continued in a recreation room where the criminals and terrorists celebrated the match with soft drinks, tea and cakes. The paramilitaries have distinctive, strong country and Northern Ireland accents. The criminals have heavy, loud Dublin brogues. Gilligan continued chattering into the camera's microphone and calling out to the two teams and their supporters.

After almost two hours of video footage, it was obvious that he was working hard at being popular. There was no doubt that the rest of E1 saw him as the main man.

Four years later the tape would provide the police investigating Veronica Guerin's murder with valuable corroboration of the close relationships between Gilligan, his co-conspirators and many of his gangland clients.

By the time Gilligan decided to chance his arm as a soccer commentator he and his acolytes had already decided on a change of direction – he was swapping factory robberies for the drugs trade. In the history of crime in Ireland the early 1990s saw a major paradigm shift which ushered in a new era for organized crime and law enforcement. It began on E1 with Factory John.

Gilligan and most of the other E1 residents had realized the hard way that armed robberies and factory heists were becoming too risky. The police were better organized and armed to take on the gangs. The fact that E1 had been filled with forty serious criminals in the space of a few years was due to the successes of the reinvigorated Serious Crime Squad which had absorbed the Tango unit. The squad had established a world-class surveillance team and were using state-of-the-art technology to track and eavesdrop on their targets.

Some of the inmates even had the bullet wounds to show after encountering the deadly new weapon the cops had deployed against them – the Emergency Response Unit (ERU). In 1990 the specially trained weapons and tactics squad first appeared on Irish streets with devastating consequences. The elite squad was based on similar police SWAT-style teams in America, Germany and Britain. Members had additional training with the Irish Army's Special Forces unit, the Army Ranger Wing. The ERU's thirty-two members were equipped with the latest in specialist firearms which were not available to the rest of the force: the Smith and Wesson Model 59 semi-automatic pistol, Heckler and Koch assault rifle and the Winchester pump-action shotgun.

The police were determined to turn the tables on the blaggers. In the first six months of 1990 the ERU's impact was measured by the number of dead and wounded robbers who had decided to shoot it out, rather than put their hands up. Three raiders were shot dead, Meehan's accomplice, P. J. Loughran, had been crippled and four others were seriously injured. As a result of his injuries Loughran never stood trial. The other survivors of the shoot-outs were all long-stay residents on E1 along with Gilligan.

In Dublin, where the majority of armed hold-ups took place, the ERU was being augmented by a quick reaction anti-robbery squad called the Cobra Unit. Pairs of heavily armed officers, wearing bullet-proof vests and driving high performance cars, cruised every division in the city. Armed robbery had become a decidedly hazardous undertaking even for the most professional crews.

Detective Inspector Tony Hickey was in the thick of the action. Running the Serious Crime Squad he witnessed how the counter-offensive against the gangs had forced a significant shift in gangland activity. He would later comment:

> We had plenty of evidence at the time that criminals exclusively involved in armed robberies looked around and said this is a dangerous business. The gardaí had shown the criminal fraternity that they had the ability to take them on and quite a lot of them decided that there was an easier way to make money with less risk, and that was drug trafficking.

While lounging around his cell, Gilligan would listen intently as Meehan and Ward told him about the huge profits being made in the burgeoning market for recreational drugs that was evolving outside the prison walls. As Ireland began to prosper economically it produced a hedonistic generation of young consumers with a fondness for hashish and the new drug ecstasy, which had arrived on the rave scene.

Meenor's best friend, Peter Mitchell, was already running a very lucrative business selling both drugs. He also dealt in cocaine, which was no longer regarded as the exclusive drug of choice for the social elite. The new generation of educated high-earning young people was increasingly partial to a line of the Colombian marching powder to celebrate the weekend. In less than a decade cocaine abuse had grown exponentially with one in five adults in the Irish Republic regularly using the drug. On a per capita basis, Ireland had one of the highest rates of consumption in Europe. It led to a dramatic escalation in violence as a new phenomenon, the gangland feud, became the norm.

Known as 'Fat Head' or 'Fatso', with a reputation as a loud-mouthed, violent bully, Peter Mitchell was born in 1969. From Summerhill in the north inner city, Mitchell first met Meehan while they were both in Mountjoy and the pair became best friends. Fatso had also taken part in the infamous riot but wasn't sent to Portlaoise because he'd been due for release.

When Mitchell got out he began dabbling in the drug trade, but steered away from heroin because it was considered too troublesome. Junkies were also difficult to deal with and the trade was loathed in the working-class communities. Instead his customer base consisted of mostly ordinary law-abiding citizens with plenty of money to spend.

In a short space of time Mitchell was a significant supplier in an area that stretched from Summerhill out as far as the working-class suburb of Coolock in north Dublin. During visits to Meehan in Portlaoise, he would brag about the huge money he was making. One lucrative drug deal could yield more hard cash than a whole fleet of Factory John's stolen trucks. And there was a lot less risk and aggravation involved. This was clearly a whole new world of opportunity – there for the taking.

Gilligan and his protégés resolved to become drug traffickers. Factory John was determined to set himself up as a wholesaler and take the lion's share of the cake. Dessie O'Hare and Fergal Toal taught him how to organize a gang based on a similar cell structure as that operated by the IRA and INLA. Gilligan planned to design an efficient importation and distribution system that guaranteed that he could maintain a safe distance from the merchandise – and out of the reaches of the police. He already had a wide network of potential customers from among his fellow lags who were also planning on a change of career when their sentences were served.

Gilligan also learned from the downfall of the Dunnes, the country's first big drug syndicate, dismissing them as 'Muppets' who had made the fatal blunder of getting high on their own supply. It wasn't a mistake Gilligan planned to make.

In November 1992 Gilligan's sojourn on E1 came to an abrupt end thanks to his legendary short fuse and lack of self-control. At this stage he was classified as a difficult prisoner who repeatedly made unreasonable demands of the warders. On this occasion he had asked for a copy of his prison file which he knew he was not entitled to get. A chief officer informed Gilligan on E1 that he would not be getting the file. As the officer turned to leave, the diminutive godfather attacked him from behind in a flurry of punches, leaving his victim bruised and stunned. Gilligan claimed that he 'lost the rag'. As a result he was transferred to Cork Prison and spent two months in solitary confinement without privileges.

The hours and days spent in a drab cell on his own were interminable and Gilligan's macho facade crumbled. He fell into a depression and became obsessed with losing his wife Geraldine. He stopped washing or changing his clothes and became dishevelled. The experience copper-fastened his resolve to never do prison time again.

In February 1993 he was convicted of the assault on the prison officer and given an additional six months to serve at the end of his existing sentence. Eventually, after pleading his case to the High Court, he was returned to Portlaoise for the remainder of his time.

On 9 September 1993 John Gilligan was granted temporary release and went home to his family. Until his final release date, two months later, he was required to sign on each week at Portlaoise Prison.

Three days after Gilligan's release, Brian Meehan was also granted temporary release. His full release date was set for April 1994. Paul Ward had been released six months earlier.

As John Gilligan walked out of the prison gates for the last time, he swore that he would never serve another jail sentence. He was instilled with one ambition in life – to become so big that no competitor, cop or judge could ever touch him again.

CHAPTER SEVEN

GETTING STARTED

Gilligan wasted no time dwelling on the welcome sound of the prison gates slamming shut behind him. He was an ambitious man in a hurry. He had his team of young Turks in place so the next step was to find a partner he could trust. It had to be someone with a proven criminal track record who would help him to organize the business, raise the seed capital and have the connections to launder the proceeds at the other end. To Gilligan there was one obvious choice – John Traynor. His timing could not have been better.

The Coach had already arrived at the conclusion that drugs were the future and was also seeking out a partner he could trust. Traynor had different requirements for his prospective collaborator. He wanted someone who had plenty of clout in the underworld and would be the de facto public face of the organization. Traynor was risk-averse, preferring to work in the background.

Gilligan was pushing an open door and Traynor enthusiastically agreed to the partnership. From their first encounter in B&I ferries over twenty years earlier the pair had been natural criminal accomplices. In temperament and intellect they were, however, poles apart. That was also reflected in their physical appearances. Traynor was a big, strong man, over six feet tall, who was, ironically, frequently mistaken for a policeman. Being an inveterate opportunist he often posed as one. The pragmatic Big John was happy for the pugnacious Little John to be the overall boss while he would pull the strings from the shadows and enjoy the proceeds.

In a conversation with this writer in 1995 Traynor described Gilligan in glowing terms although he was careful to distance himself from the drug trade:

> He is the best grafter I have ever met. In criminal terms he is a great businessman. He can turn money into more money, no problem, and is prepared to be hands-on, if necessary. But he is very dangerous if you fuck with him.

Like his future partner, Traynor's conversion to narcotics began while he was serving a lengthy prison sentence in the UK. He had been convicted in London's Old Bailey and sentenced to seven years for his part in the 1990 theft of Bank of England bearer bonds worth the equivalent of tens of millions of euro today.

Traynor had fled to London in 1987 as the Serious Crime Squad in Dublin prepared to charge him with receiving the equivalent of €130,000 worth of stolen goods which had been robbed by his former shipmate.

Before his sudden departure, the Coach had more than proved his credentials. He enjoyed celebrity status in the Irish underworld as an accomplished fraudster responsible for a string of sophisticated scams targeting banks and the Irish revenue commissioners. He was also regarded by other villains as a man of 'respect' thanks to his role as Martin Cahill's adviser – the Mafia equivalent of his *consiglieri*. Traynor initiated and helped plan several of the General's most spectacular crimes including the theft of gold, gems and diamonds valued at €3.5 million which, in 1983, was the largest heist in the history of the State. He also played a pivotal role with Cahill in organizing the theft of the priceless Beit paintings.

While Traynor was anxious not to end up in prison for receiving stolen goods, he had an even more pressing reason for his sudden departure in March 1987. In a fit of paranoia Cahill decided that his *consiglieri* had been ripping him off and wanted him shot.

However, time proved to be a healer for the oddball underworld couple. While Traynor was away the hard core of the General's mob had been locked up. Cahill had come to realize that his pal had not short-changed him after all.

In November 1992 the Coach qualified for temporary home leave from Highpoint Prison in Suffolk, England, where he had been transferred as a low-risk, model prisoner. When he returned to Dublin after a five-year absence Cahill welcomed him back with open arms.

As part of a shady deal, the gardaí then agreed to drop the outstanding charges for receiving stolen goods against Traynor after Cahill – in an uncharacteristic act of co-operation – returned a highly sensitive garda investigation file. It was part of a batch the General had stolen in his audacious burglary at the offices of the DPP in 1987. The deal gave Traynor a clean slate to make a new start in Dublin. He had been due to return to Highpoint Prison on 23 November but did not arrive.

Traynor had learned valuable lessons from his time inside. Serving his sentence in a range of English prisons, the charismatic chancer made invaluable international underworld contacts. In Wormwood Scrubs and Wandsworth prisons he befriended major players from England, the Netherlands, Belgium, Turkey, Spain and Morocco. Organized crime in the UK and much of the rest of Europe had already made the transition from robberies to drugs. Most of his fellow inmates were involved in drug-related criminal activity, either supplying large consignments of every kind of drug, from heroin to cocaine, or laundering the profits.

Traynor listened and learned a lot about the inner, complex workings of the business. The profits they discussed had the greedy Coach drooling. When he returned to Ireland, he began conducting his own market research, socializing with the city's new generation of drug dealers. Traynor was more intelligent than most other criminals and carefully worked out his strategy before making a move. The clever crook studied the dynamics of the drug business and the methods used to launder the profits. With this goal in mind he opened a second-hand car dealership in Rathmines, south Dublin, and began importing Japanese cars. In the years before the gardaí were given the powers to pursue the proceeds of crime, it was relatively easy to wash money through a used car lot. Ironically, the alliance between Gilligan and Traynor would be the catalyst for the creation of the Criminal Assets Bureau.

In criminal circles Traynor was a snob. He considered himself a cut above the rest of the underworld riff-raff whom he looked down on. When speaking to this writer about some of the bigger gangsters, he instinctively curled his upper lip and described them in a sneering tone as 'dirty, filthy cunts'. The manipulative con man also acted as a police informant, passing information on those he didn't like or considered to be competitors. But the duplicitous mobster's keen sense of self-preservation meant that he was remarkably coy when it came to passing information about Gilligan. Nor did he ever use disparaging terminology about his bombastic partner. The Coach knew when to keep his thoughts to himself. He was all too aware of Gilligan's lethal potential.

Gilligan and Traynor made the perfect team. Each had something the other needed in order to make the operation efficient and profitable.

Since his return to Dublin, Traynor had closely examined the trade in heroin and cannabis. Both drugs were in ever increasing demand with the guarantee of prodigious profits. Gilligan and Traynor were reluctant to dabble in heroin or 'smack'. Their reticence had nothing to do with moral qualms about the devastation heroin was causing on the streets of the capital. While very profitable, they felt it was a business that attracted too much political, media and police attention. The dealers were hated in the working-class communities where ordinary decent criminals were traditionally tolerated. Across the city whole communities were taking to the streets in protest against the drug scourge. Operations to break the heroin-dealing gangs were prioritized by the police. The courts were also imposing much harsher sentences on heroin dealers than their hash-dealing counterparts. It was the type of aggravation that Gilligan and Traynor wanted to avoid.

Their market research and analysis convinced the crooked pair that cannabis should be their primary business. They would also supply ecstasy and cocaine as the market demanded.

Former Assistant Commissioner John O'Mahoney spent most of his earlier career in the Serious Crime Squad and was a team leader in the Tango Squad. He was also a senior member of the squad who investigated the Guerin murder. He witnessed first-hand the evolution of organized crime and Gilligan's move into drugs and recalls:

> When John Gilligan came out of prison he identified a niche in the market [with John Traynor] and decided that cannabis resin was to be his business. He decided that for a number of reasons: one was that he felt that by operating in the area of cannabis that he would not be as big a target for law enforcement as if he was dealing in heroin. He also saw that there were more people

in this country using cannabis and the people who were using it had more money to spend. This was also the beginning of the Celtic Tiger era.

The most pressing requirement for gangland's latest narcotics entrepreneurs was hard cash. Buying drugs was an expensive business. They needed capital to get a seat at the table. Two months before Gilligan's release, Traynor and Cahill had started plotting the kidnapping of the family of Jim Lacey, the chief executive of the National Irish Bank (NIB). The plan was that Gilligan and Traynor would get a cut of the action from Cahill and use it as seed capital for their new venture.

The plan went into action on the night of 1 November 1993, but Factory John did not play a prominent role in the operation. Brian Meehan was recruited instead. The banker's terrified wife and children were taken hostage while Lacey was beaten by Meehan and held at gunpoint overnight.

The following morning Lacey was told by Jo Jo Kavanagh that his family had been kidnapped and that he had to get the money from NIB to pay their ransom.

Lacey and Kavanagh drove in a van to the bank's main cash-holding centre at College Green in Dublin city centre. The banker was instructed to load it full of cash from the vaults. But Kavanagh was outsmarted by Lacey who handed over cash to the value of €480,000. The vault was holding over €14.4 million at the time.

The disappointing result further convinced Gilligan and Traynor that the days of kidnapping and armed robbery were well and truly over. The Coach's share of the proceeds wasn't enough to start their drug dealing venture.

The General had come to the same conclusion that drugs were the way forward. The Lacey kidnap was to be the last major crime he carried out. Steered by his manipulative *consiglieri* Cahill had also intended investing the proceeds from the kidnapping in the drug venture. Cahill didn't want to be a drug dealer but was interested in becoming a silent investor who could sit back and collect a handsome profit without being directly involved. He agreed to loan Gilligan and Traynor the bulk of the money they needed to get started, handing over £100,000 (€206,000) worth of seed capital. Cahill at the time claimed that he had been ripped off for a similar amount of cash after investing in a hash deal organized by another former associate, Niall Mulvihill. Gilligan and Traynor convinced Cahill that he was guaranteed an attractive fivefold return on his investment, worth over €1 million.

The rest of the start-up capital came from Traynor's paltry share of the kidnap proceeds. Gilligan added to the pot by organizing two armed robberies in December 1993 and January 1994 when they robbed a security van in Tallaght and a Dunnes Stores supermarket in Kilnamanagh, south Dublin.

With the combined proceeds, the gang was ready for business.

———

Now that they had the money secured, the next priority for Gilligan and Traynor was to find a reliable drug supplier with whom they could do business. Shortly after his release, through Traynor, Gilligan met two English drug dealers with a view to setting up a supply route into Ireland. But the deal never got off the ground as they were under surveillance. Gilligan was secretly videotaped by undercover Scotland Yard detectives at the meet in a hotel in Brighton. He smelled a rat and didn't say anything incriminating. The two drug dealers were subsequently caught and charged, and the partners had to look for a new source.

Factory John recruited an old friend from Ballyfermot, Denis 'Dinny' Meredith, to assist in the new venture. Meredith was also closely associated with John Traynor. Dinny, who had grown up with Gilligan, was a member of the Factory Gang, driving the container trucks used in their many robberies. He had worked for a number of the transport companies which had coincidentally fallen victim to Gilligan's hijackings.

Through his job Meredith had criminal connections and a network of dodgy contacts in the transport industry around Europe. He had already been successfully involved in smuggling tobacco and alcohol from the Continent, as well as small quantities of drugs. Gilligan trusted Dinny and appointed him the gang's first bagman.

Traynor used more of his old UK prison connections to seek out potential contacts in Amsterdam. The Dutch capital had become the operational hub of Europe's illicit drug trade where every producer in the world came to sell their wares. The 'Dam', as Gilligan and his cronies called it, was to drug traffickers what Wall Street was to stock market dealers.

Traynor travelled to Amsterdam where he was introduced to a representative of one of the country's biggest international drug traffickers. Simon Ata Hussain Khan Rahman was a major league criminal who made gangsters like Gilligan, Traynor and Cahill look like pickpockets. Rahman's criminal tentacles stretched out to South America, Europe, the former Soviet Bloc countries, the Middle East and North Africa.

Born in January 1942 in Surinam, South America, a former Dutch colony, Rahman had moved to live in The Hague. From there he ran a criminal empire which, apart from narcotics, dealt in smuggling, fraud, firearms and money laundering. His convictions included burglary, road traffic offences and 'vandalism'. In 1989 he was arrested by Dutch police under 'opium laws'.

He had also been charged with drug trafficking in Britain but was acquitted in court and promptly returned to The Hague. In 1994 Dutch police intelligence estimated that Rahman was worth up to €100 million in today's value. He nurtured a veneer of genteel respectability and was chairman of Jamaat Al Imaan, a Muslim cultural association.

Rahman's front was that of a legitimate millionaire businessman who specialized in the import and export of goods, from foodstuffs to furniture. He had a superior, aloof presence and he privately sneered at the likes of Gilligan and his mob as uncouth ruffians. Rahman sourced his cannabis in Nigeria and Morocco. He had well-established supply routes organized throughout Europe for the import and export of his legal and illegal wares. He would export container loads of rice and nuts, for example, to The Gambia. When the containers returned to the Netherlands, they would carry imports of foodstuffs and furniture to conceal shipments of thousands of kilos of hashish. His operation supplied gangs in the UK and all over the Continent.

He was the quintessential businessman. If the customer had the cash, he would supply whatever they required. Rahman had a large network of people working for him and he stayed a safe distance from the physical operation of the business. He would live to regret the day that he sat down to deal with a vulgar Irish gangster called John Gilligan.

Two weeks after the Lacey kidnap, in the middle of November 1993, Gilligan and Dinny Meredith flew to Amsterdam to follow up on Traynor's initial approach. Rahman had agreed to meet them to hear their proposition. They also met with one of Rahman's closest associates, Johnny Wildhagen, a Dutch national from The Hague.

Forty-year-old Wildhagen was a violent cocaine addict who worked as an enforcer for Rahman. He organized the consignments of drugs and guns for export. He also oversaw the movement of cash, and dealt out brutal justice to anyone who failed to pay his boss.

Rahman took an instant dislike to Gilligan during their first meeting and later referred to him disparagingly as loud-mouthed and vulgar, calling him 'De Klein' ('the little one'). He didn't trust

Factory John, but business was business and Rahman wasn't looking to make new friends.

He laid out the terms of their business arrangement. Each consignment would have to be paid for in cash, upfront. The prices of the first shipments were equivalent in today's value to €2,600 per kilo of hashish, but it would be cheaper depending on the quantities being ordered, reducing to an average of €2,400 per kilo. Rahman also explained that, as trust and goodwill developed between the two sides, the payment for shipments could be broken into three parts: a portion would be paid in advance, another upon delivery and the final part after the drugs were sold. No new shipment would be sent to Ireland until the last one had been fully paid off.

Gilligan and Dinny stayed overnight, returning to Dublin the following day. The negotiations and talks continued. Flight records would later show that Meehan was sent to the Netherlands on 22 November and returned the same day. A week later, on 29 November, Traynor and Gilligan travelled to Amsterdam where they finalized a deal purchasing 170 kilos from Rahman.

Rahman and Wildhagen were impressed by Traynor, describing him as 'Big John, the real boss of Gilligan'. Using his charm and the persuasive skills of an accomplished con artist, Traynor convinced Rahman that if he reduced the price of the initial shipment from €2,600 to around €2,000 per kilo, it would mean more cash for Rahman in the long run. It would be a sort of introductory offer.

Acting on Traynor's advice, Gilligan had prepared for his new profession as a drug trafficker. He joined the Aer Lingus Gold Circle Club before his first flights to Amsterdam. Using the business class frequent flier card, Gilligan could book a seat on an aircraft minutes before it was scheduled to take off. Catching a plane without warning enabled him to shed unwanted police surveillance.

The morning after their meeting with Rahman, Gilligan and Traynor arrived back in Dublin on one-way tickets they had purchased in Schiphol Airport. The previous day in Dublin they had paid for two pre-booked open return tickets on Gilligan's Aer Lingus card. The return tickets could be used at any time over the following twelve months. When the flight arrived in Dublin, Gilligan was the first passenger to go through Customs, while Traynor ensured he was last off.

Gardaí attached to the immigration unit were not so easily fooled. The pair had been spotted flying out the previous day. The purchase of tickets that were never used was a scam intended to mislead the police about their movements. A report about the trips was immediately circulated to all garda units with an interest in Gilligan and Traynor. Little did anyone know that this trip marked the beginning of the biggest drug trafficking operation in the history of the State.

In the meantime Traynor put knowledge he had acquired from his cell mates in the UK prison system into action and drafted the gang's business model. He advised Gilligan that they should vary the size of the drug shipments. Each large consignment should be followed by a smaller one, in case the route was discovered and the drugs seized. It would also give them breathing space to collect their money.

Traynor also introduced the concept of operating what is known in bookie circles as a 'tank'. Gilligan agreed that the gang would use the initial investment money as the 'tank' and split the profits. This would give them an operational cash base and a kind of insurance to lessen the financial blow if the drugs were intercepted.

On 5 December the first portion of the consignment of drugs arrived in Dublin Port on a transport truck arranged with Dinny's assistance. The 150 kilos of hash were packed into six boxes, specially sealed, labelled as leather jackets and addressed to an engineering works in Chapelizod, west Dublin. The truck delivered the boxes to the transport company's main warehouse.

The following morning the boxes were picked up by a courier and sent to another address in Chapelizod. Gilligan and Traynor had the truck followed to ensure that it was not under surveillance. When it stopped at traffic lights, Brian Meehan knocked on the window and told the driver he had been sent to collect the boxes for the engineering works. He signed for them using the fictitious name 'Frank O'Brady'. The deal went off without a hitch.

Later that same day Gilligan and Dinny again flew to Amsterdam with money for Rahman and returned the following afternoon.

On 12 December the second part of the deal, 20 kilos, arrived on a transport truck from the same company. This time it was packed in one box, labelled 'compressor parts'.

In the early days of the operation Gilligan and Traynor distributed the hash through Peter Mitchell, Brian Meehan and Paul Ward. They, in turn, had set up a network of dealers who bought the drugs from them.

Over the following months the operation expanded rapidly as the gang began filling a huge demand in the market. They were soon the biggest wholesale supplier to dealers throughout Dublin and later to gangs across the country.

The proceeds of the sales were collected for Gilligan and Traynor who then sent cash to Rahman for the next order. Following the first successful arrivals in Dublin, each subsequent shipment was preceded by one or more trips to Amsterdam, most of them by Gilligan, to place another order. Traynor made sure he stayed in the background.

Gilligan flew to Amsterdam on 14 December and on 4 January 1994 another 50 kilos arrived in two boxes of 'oil coolers'. He flew to the Netherlands again on 7 January 1994 for meetings with Rahman and his representatives, carrying bags of cash. As Rahman only wanted payment in Dutch guilders, he suggested that the most efficient method of changing the cash was to use one of the many Bureaux de Change in the city. When the euro was introduced it made life easier for drug traffickers.

During the Guerin murder investigation detectives drew up a comprehensive set of records including flights, money exchanges and shipping details. When cross-referenced they gave an insight into the scale of the drug trafficking operation.

The records showed that Gilligan changed £31,950 (€65,594) into Dutch guilders on 7 January 1994. He then handed the money to one of Rahman's bagmen. The delivery of the additional 50 kilos followed this visit.

On 8 January Gilligan returned to the Bureau de Change in Amsterdam and this time changed £65,860 (€135,000) into Dutch guilders. Two days later another 55 kilos arrived in Dublin.

On 20 January 'the little one' handed Rahman £63,460 (€130,000) in guilders and three days later 75 kilos of hash arrived in Dublin Port. Just over a week later, on 28 January, Gilligan flew to Amsterdam and this time exchanged £117,865 (€240,000) which was followed, on 30 January, by a shipment of 100 kilos of hashish.

Less than four months after walking through the gates of Portlaoise Prison, John Gilligan was well on his way to achieving his ambitions to hit the big time.

Ten days later, however, the gardaí inadvertently scuppered another drug deal when armed officers burst into Gilligan's Blanchardstown home with an arrest warrant, rudely interrupting his plans to catch another flight to the Dam. He and his son Darren were arrested under the Offences Against the State Act and taken in for questioning about a shooting incident that had taken place in December 1993.

A doorman at French's nightclub in Mulhuddart, north-west Dublin, had been shot and injured a few hours after he barred Darren Gilligan from the club. Gilligan's eighteen-year-old son had been accused of selling drugs and thrown out. A file was sent to the Director of Public Prosecutions on the case but the injured man withdrew his complaint. Neither of the Gilligans was ever charged.

Gilligan did not have time to be annoyed about the arrest. He was too busy building a drugs empire. On 4 February Traynor flew to Amsterdam instead of Gilligan. This time a 45-kilo shipment was ordered, and it arrived six days later. On 11 February it was Gilligan's turn again, and his trip was followed by a shipment of 25 kilos. A few days later, on 14 February, Traynor returned to the Dam where he exchanged £30,000 (€61,000).

The following morning Gilligan checked onto the 7.25 a.m. flight to the Dutch capital. He was enjoying being a high-flying drug baron. Dressed in an expensive overcoat and carrying a briefcase, he relaxed in the comfort of the business-class cabin, rubbing shoulders with people whose companies and homes he would probably have robbed four years earlier. Drug dealing was an infinitely more civilised and lucrative way of making a dishonest living than breaking into factories on a frosty winter night.

Later that day Gilligan visited a Bureau de Change in central Amsterdam and changed £44,845 (€103,000) into Dutch guilders. The money was part payment for 100 kilos of hash. Gilligan then took the next flight home.

The previous day a container truck from a legitimate transport company had arrived in Hoofddorp, near Schiphol Airport in Amsterdam. The innocent driver had been instructed to pick up several pallets of computer parts for a company in Ireland. The truck was then dispatched to pick up five pallets of truck parts in Mechelen, near Antwerp, across the border in Belgium.

The trucker then had to make a further pickup from a warehouse near Antwerp Port. At the warehouse a pallet containing two boxes of 'oil coolers' was loaded. The driver was asked to hang on – there were other boxes for Chapelizod to be delivered to the same warehouse. As far as the driver was concerned this was a perfectly legitimate transaction and he had no reason to suspect that there was anything untoward occurring. About an hour and a half later the extra boxes, also labelled as oil coolers, were brought to the warehouse by Johnny Wildhagen.

The truck crossed on the ferry to Dover in the UK. The driver then headed for Liverpool to catch the ferry to the North Wall in Dublin. As the truck arrived off the ferry, on the morning of 17 February, members of the Customs National Drug Team decided to conduct a routine search.

They discovered that the 'oil coolers' were not what they purported to be and seized the truck and the 100 kilos of hashish. The driver was questioned but the officers were satisfied that he was unaware of his secret cargo. The customs officers called in the North Central Divisional Drug Squad based at Store Street garda station in central Dublin.

The squad and the customs officers removed most of the hashish and released the truck the next day, where it continued to its original destination, a warehouse at Bluebell Industrial Estate. Officers from Customs and the Drug Squad placed the warehouse under surveillance in the hope of nabbing the gang when they came to collect the 'oil coolers'.

On the following Monday morning at 10 a.m. Dinny Meredith arrived in a red van to pick up the 'oil coolers' from the warehouse. The officers later learned that the van was also under surveillance by Gilligan's mob. The cops secretly watched as Meredith drove to Chapelizod but failed to make a delivery. Meredith made another legitimate delivery and then returned the 'oil coolers' to the warehouse in Bluebell.

Gilligan and his old friend had smelled a rat and decided to pull back. Dinny was later interviewed about the incident and claimed that he tried to make a delivery but there was no one there to meet him. He admitted to having made seven other such deliveries of machine parts but denied that he had any knowledge of what was really in the boxes.

The loss of the consignment of hashish was a big blow but not fatal to the operation. There was still money in the 'tank' to buy further shipments. But when Meredith reported back, Gilligan and Traynor decided that they needed a new, safer route. The business was expanding at a dramatic pace and there were dealers to be supplied. If they couldn't keep up with demand, then their customers would go elsewhere.

Looking for a new port of entry, Meredith contacted John Dunne who he'd known for over four years. Dunne, who was thirty-eight years old and originally from Finglas, west Dublin, lived in Cork with his wife and three children. He worked as the operations manager with the Seabridge shipping company at Little Island in Cork Harbour.

Dinny had befriended Dunne through a relative living in Clondalkin. Dunne often arranged driving jobs for the trucker. Dinny told Traynor and Gilligan that Dunne was the type of guy who was open to earning some extra money without asking questions.

In his position at Seabridge Dunne would be perfectly placed to ensure that shipments from the Netherlands were collected and transported safely to Dublin. If Customs swooped, then Dunne could warn the gang off and no one would be caught. Shortly after the seizure in Dublin Port, Dunne was in Clondalkin spending the weekend with relatives. Meredith arranged to meet him for a drink in the Silver Granite pub in Palmerstown.

Gilligan was with Dinny when Dunne arrived. He introduced Gilligan by his first name only and the three had a few drinks together. Factory John was charming and chatty.

In late March Gilligan called Dunne at work and introduced himself as 'John, Dinny's mate'. Gilligan asked to meet Dunne, as he was down in Cork on business. Dunne agreed.

An hour later Gilligan rang him again. He told Dunne he was outside Seabridge and asked if he would come out for a chat. When

Dunne went out to the car, Gilligan was in the passenger seat and Traynor was behind the wheel. Dunne sat in the back seat. Gilligan and Traynor were friendly and made small talk before getting down to the purpose of their visit.

They wanted to know what services Seabridge had from the UK and the Continent, particularly from the Netherlands. Gilligan asked Dunne for the names and telephone numbers of reliable Dutch shipping agents he could use and asked Dunne if he would handle the Irish end. Dunne agreed and explained the system to Factory John. Gilligan would arrange to have his goods taken to the agent's depot in the Netherlands from where they would be shipped to Seabridge in Cork. Dunne would be expecting the arrival and take care of it from there.

Gilligan then discussed money and told Dunne that he would be paid £1,000 (€2,000) for every shipment he handled. Out of that Dunne would have to pay the shipping fee and the rest was profit. Dunne suspected that the whole business was 'shady' but, as Meredith had predicted, he wasn't going to ask awkward questions.

Dunne would later claim that he thought the boxes he handled for Gilligan were full of smuggled tobacco and admitted that he was motivated by greed. Gilligan and Traynor were delighted with the new arrangement. They were back in business.

In the meantime Gilligan's lieutenants were anxious to get a piece of the action and become full partners in the business. Ward, Mitchell and Meehan, along with two other associates, got their investment money at the point of a gun. On 28 April 1994 they hit the Jacob's biscuit factory on the Belgard Road in Tallaght. They held up security staff delivering wages and got away with €160,000 worth of cash.

With John Dunne safely recruited Gilligan had arranged the largest deal yet with Rahman. In observance of Traynor's business operating template, the first shipment was to contain 60 kilos and the second 175 kilos. Gilligan made three trips to Amsterdam in March to finalize the deal and collect money which had been sent to the Continent with truck drivers recruited by Dinny Meredith.

On 25 March Gilligan changed almost €185,000 worth of Belgian francs, sterling, punts and dollars into Dutch guilders at the Bureau de Change near Centraal Station in Amsterdam. He handed it over to Rahman's people and the following day returned to Dublin.

He called John Dunne in Cork, on 4 April, and told him that the first shipment would be delivered to the Dutch shipping company the following day. Three boxes, one large and two small, would be addressed to a bogus engineering works in County Cork. The cargo was described as being a type of chair. As usual the boxes had been packed and the false invoices prepared by Johnny Wildhagen.

But the inaugural run hit an unexpected hitch. The 60 kilos of hashish were mistakenly unloaded at Dublin Port on 11 April and then transported by road to Seabridge in Cork. Gilligan was furious. He rang Dunne several times to find out what time his precious cargo was due to arrive in Cork. An hour after the three cartons were offloaded, Brian Meehan and Paul Ward arrived to pick them up. Meehan introduced himself to Dunne as 'Joe' and the drugs were soon on their way back to Dublin for the second time that day.

A week or so later Gilligan rang Dunne again. Another load was coming through the Netherlands, and he told Dunne it would be due in Cork on 25 April. Gilligan said he had changed shipping agents. This time the shipment contained 175 kilos of hashish disguised as machine parts from a bogus Dutch company.

Dunne called Gilligan when the cargo arrived and was instructed to drive it to the car park of the Ambassador Hotel just outside Dublin. Dunne did as he was ordered. At the Ambassador 'Joe', aka Brian Meehan, was there to meet him and transferred the large boxes to another car. Half an hour later Gilligan arrived. He smiled and handed Dunne £1,000 in cash.

Gilligan had just established one of the most secure and lucrative illegal drug smuggling routes in gangland history. Between April 1994 and October 1996 over 20,000 kilos of hashish would arrive for the Gilligan gang by the same route. There were ninety-six individual shipments, none of which were detected.

Gilligan had worked out the perfect system.

CHAPTER EIGHT

THE SOLDIER AND THE GENERAL

Within a few weeks of the arrival of the first shipment using the new Cork route in April 1994 business was booming. By the early summer more than 1,000 kilos of cannabis resin had already been funnelled through Seabridge and transported to Dublin by John Dunne.

Gilligan was now buying the hashish from Rahman at a wholesale price of €2,400 per kilo. Factory John then sold the hash to Meehan, his underboss and confidant, for an average of €4,000 per kilo.

Meehan co-ordinated the gang's wholesale activities with Paul Ward and Peter Mitchell, selling it on to a network of clients for an average rate of between €4,600 and €5,000 per kilo. When each kilo of hashish had eventually passed through the drug dealing pyramid its street value had risen almost tenfold. It was making a lot of people rich and very happy in the process.

In the first four months of the new arrangement, records showed that, between them, Gilligan and Traynor had conservatively profited to the tune of €1.6 million. Meehan, Ward and Mitchell's take was equivalent to €600,000. Within a very short space of time the Gilligan gang had established the largest drug trafficking operation in the country.

The demand for Gilligan's hashish was growing so rapidly that the gang could barely keep up. They needed a discreet manager with good organizational abilities and a clean criminal record to handle the day-to-day running of the operation. They found the perfect candidate in Charlie Bowden, a former soldier.

Charles Joseph Bowden had a promising career in front of him when he joined the Irish Army in August 1983, two months before his twentieth birthday. Originally from Finglas, north Dublin, he was a keen athlete who stayed out of trouble with the law and wanted a life of adventure as a professional soldier.

Throughout his training and subsequent career, Private Bowden was considered a born soldier who loved military life and had the potential to rise through the ranks. After basic training he was posted to the 5th Infantry Battalion then based in Collins Barracks in central Dublin. In the same year he married a local girl from his neighbourhood. The couple would have three sons. The future looked bright for the young squaddie.

Tall, handsome and athletic, Bowden was one of the fittest soldiers in an entire brigade of over 2,500 troops. He won an Army Pentathlon competition and was the All-Army Karate champion three times. He was also an expert marksman and won the Eastern Brigade rifle championships.

In October 1984 Bowden began a six-month tour of duty with the Irish 56th UN battalion in south Lebanon. In the early 1980s several Irish troops were killed or injured trying to maintain peace in the war zone along the border between Lebanon and Israel. Bowden saw plenty of action as his unit regularly came under hostile fire. He was injured when his post was shelled by Israeli-backed forces and hospitalized for a short while but then returned to duty and completed the tour. Like the rest of his army record at that time, Bowden's overseas conduct and performance were deemed 'excellent'.

After his return to Ireland, his superior officers selected him for promotion. In late 1986 he passed a punishing four-month, noncommissioned officers (NCO) course with distinction and was promoted to the rank of corporal in April 1987.

Bowden's commanding officers were also considering him as a potential candidate for the army's elite Special Forces unit, the Army Ranger Wing. The new corporal was told that if he agreed to study part-time and completed his Leaving Certificate exams he could qualify to apply for a full commission as an officer. The sky was the limit. But then it all went catastrophically wrong.

Early in 1988 Bowden was selected to train a recruit platoon. One night he and another corporal, both of whom were drunk, stormed into a billet looking for a fight with their students. The drunken instructors used their prowess at martial arts to beat up eight of the recruits. Two of the recruits were hospitalized after the brutal incident.

The following day Bowden approached a recruit and warned him to tell the two injured soldiers to keep their mouths shut:

> Tell [soldier A] that he hit his head off a locker, if anyone asks, and tell [soldier B] that he just fell or something, and if anything gets out about this tell them they are going to be here for the next three years and I have a lot of friends in the battalion. Tell them that is not a threat.

The intimidation failed. A month later, following an investigation by the military police, an army court-martial convicted Bowden on seven charges of assault. He was busted back to the rank of private and given twenty-four days of detention.

When he returned to his unit Bowden had lost his taste for soldiering. Any chance of ever joining the Ranger Wing or becoming an officer had been wiped out by his self-destructive escapade. He knew he would spend the rest of his service as a private, with little prospect of even regaining his corporal stripes.

With his army career in ruins Bowden decided to leave the Defence Forces and was discharged on 8 August 1989. His conduct assessment on discharge rated him 'unsatisfactory'. Bowden's marriage was also on the rocks and he separated from his wife. After just six years his marriage and his army career had perished at the same time.

As his life imploded the ex-soldier was at rock bottom. Behind the facade of a womanizing tough guy, he was shattered inside. Bowden also found himself in dire financial straits. He had to support three small children and pay for a flat, his new home. He worked in a factory for a time and at night was a bouncer in a number of city-centre nightclubs. That was how he met Peter Mitchell and his life changed irrevocably for a second time.

Bowden and Mitchell became good friends and were members of the same kick-boxing club. At the same time Fatso had started dabbling in the drug trade, selling cannabis and ecstasy in the nightclubs where Bowden worked. Mitchell offered him a lucrative sideline if he wanted it. Desperate for cash, Bowden was seduced by the allure of easy money and began working as a drug dealer for Mitchell.

Fatso was drawn to Bowden's image as the tough ex-soldier and would have plenty of use for him. The former corporal was well organized and had extensive knowledge of firearms. It was also a major advantage that he was unknown to the police. Using his job as a doorman, Bowden distributed batches of ecstasy tablets to customers sent by his new boss.

As he got more involved, Mitchell paid Bowden £500 (€1000) each week in cash. Bowden also began distributing cannabis resin, between 5–10 kilos per week, for which Mitchell paid him £50 (€100) per kilo. The arrangement continued until around September 1993 when Bowden made an attempt to go straight again. He decided to go back to school to study book-keeping and domestic science for his Leaving Certificate exams.

But his return to the straight and narrow was short-lived. In 1994 Bowden again found himself in financial trouble and contacted

Mitchell. He proved to be the right man in the right place at the right time and Mitchell welcomed him back with open arms.

Mitchell introduced Bowden to Brian Meehan and Paul Ward so that they could assess his suitability as a potential operations manager. Meehan immediately approved of Bowden and agreed to take him on. As someone naturally drawn to violence Meehan was also impressed by the ex-soldier's hard man image.

Although it would be months before they met, Gilligan gave Bowden's appointment the seal of approval after receiving glowing reports from his underboss and lieutenants that he was 'rock solid'. Gilligan liked what he heard, especially that Bowden could operate below the police radar. He was the kind of unknown muscle, with a rare skill set, that gave the gang an additional edge. It also provided a further layer of management to buffer Gilligan and Traynor from the product.

Bowden began by delivering 80 kilos to a number of dealers and customers each week, for which he was paid £50 (€100) per kilo, or £4,000 (€8,000). Meehan and Mitchell would tell him how much and give him the customer's address for each consignment. Their clients were all regulars and included several of Gilligan's old criminal accomplices. Very soon Bowden became a vital cog in the workings of the gang's business.

By late summer 1994 huge amounts of cash were being collected, counted and then smuggled to the Netherlands and Belgium to buy further shipments of hash. Each month the quantities grew larger. It had become an industrial-scale operation.

Records showed that in the month of August 1994, Rahman shipped almost 900 kilos to Gilligan, generating a collective profit for the gang of €1.8 million. Meehan and Mitchell bought Bowden a car to deliver the drugs around the city. The fact that he had been banned for drunken driving was not an obstacle for the greedy ex-soldier. He registered the car in his brother's name and used his brother's licence.

At first Bowden kept the slabs of dope in his Ballymun flat, but that was proving too much of a risk. As the quantities continued to increase, he realized they needed a secure operational base. Bowden eventually rented a small lockup at Greenmount Industrial Estate, in Harold's Cross, south Dublin.

The ex-soldier's military training had given him impressive organizational and management skills. He created a smooth-running production line. He would take in the wooden crates containing the hashish delivered from Cork and then organize a list of customers, with the quantities they wanted, the price to be charged and a schedule of delivery times. Bowden also took care of credit control and collected money. He was in charge of quality control as well.

Bowden checked each shipment for sub-standard hash, described as 'diesel'. By now, such was the importance of the Gilligan gang to Simon Rahman, they had an arrangement whereby they returned inferior product in much the same way that legitimate companies did. If any 'diesel' was detected, Bowden would have new crates made up, repack the drugs and send them to John Dunne in Cork who in turn shipped them back to the Netherlands. Between 11 August 1995 and 5 September 1996, the gang returned over 800 kilos of sub-standard hash.

Bowden had become an invaluable asset to Gilligan's thriving drug trafficking operation. His efficiency, trustworthiness and discretion greatly impressed Gilligan, Traynor and Meehan. Within six months of starting his new career the ex-soldier was earning the equivalent of €12,000 per week. It was more money than he knew what to do with.

———

Around the same time that Charlie Bowden began working for the gang, Gilligan and Traynor had a problem. Their silent partner Martin Cahill had been hearing rumours of his pals' new-found prosperity and began putting pressure on Traynor for a return on his investment. He had been promised £500,000 (€1 million) and the General was calling in the debt.

By 1994 the once powerful General was a mobster in decline. Chronic diabetes, for which he refused treatment, had made him even more irrational, unpredictable and dangerous. He was seeing conspiracies where they didn't exist and embarked on vendettas against people he felt had crossed him. Cahill was busy accumulating enemies.

Perhaps as a result of Cahill's perceived weakness Gilligan and Traynor decided they would play for time in the hope that they might get away without paying anything. Traynor fobbed him off with excuses that the gang was not yet in profit. They reckoned that once Cahill learned of the money they were making, he would put the squeeze on them for a slice of the action. They knew that there were only two options for getting the paranoid General off their backs: either pay him what he was demanding, which wouldn't work, or kill him. But then an unexpected event occurred which would eventually let Gilligan and Traynor off the hook.

On Saturday 21 May 1994, a team of killers from the Ulster Volunteer Force (UVF) travelled to Dublin intent on murder. That night Sinn Féin was holding a fundraising function for the 'Prisoners of War Department' in the Widow Scallans pub on Pearse Street in the south inner city. It was a regular venue for republican functions and the event had been well advertised.

As negotiations to secure an historic IRA ceasefire were nearing the finish line in the fledgling peace process, the UVF had dramatically escalated sectarian violence in the North carrying out some of the worst atrocities in the history of the Troubles. That Saturday the terrorists were planning a massacre that would surpass their worst outrages.

At 10.50 p.m. two UVF members arrived at the door of the upstairs function room which was packed with over 300 people. One of them carried a handgun, the other a holdall containing an 18lb bomb. The plan was to leave it in the room and make their escape.

Fortunately for the people in the venue, the UVF operatives were confronted by IRA man Martin Doherty who was in charge of security at the event. He managed to raise the alarm and locked the door into the function room. In the ensuing scuffle Doherty was shot several times and died instantly. A second man was seriously injured when he was shot through the locked door.

Having failed to deliver the bomb the UVF men abandoned it and made their escape. Their getaway car was later found on the North Strand. Miraculously, the device failed to explode. Explosives experts said that if it had, the blast was powerful enough to kill everyone inside and knock down the actual building. The UVF later issued a statement claiming responsibility for the attack and warning that more would follow.

In the aftermath of the incident gangland was plunged into a state of fear. The Provos conducted an extensive investigation throughout the underworld to discover if gangsters had given the loyalist killers logistical assistance for the attack. Cahill became their focus of interest because he had dealt with the UVF in his attempts to offload the Beit paintings two years previously. Luckily for Gilligan the IRA had no knowledge of his role in the same plot.

There were also old scores to settle as well. In 1984 Cahill had gone to the brink of war with the Provos when they tried to extort money from him after the O'Connor's jewellery heist. The IRA dropped their demands and pulled back when a four-member active service unit was arrested by police for abducting Gilligan's old associate, Martin 'the Viper' Foley. Afterwards the terrorists sent a message to Cahill that the next time they crossed swords with him they would 'stiff him in the street'. The Provos, like any criminal organization, could not allow Cahill's temerity and lack of respect to go unpunished.

The subsequent police investigation established that neither Cahill nor any other Dublin criminal had been involved with the UVF operation. They discovered that the weapon used in the attack had been used in a string of other shootings in Northern Ireland and that the getaway car had been purchased a few days before at a used car auction in Belfast. But the Provos blamed their old nemesis regardless.

A number of republican figures even approached this writer at the time seeking information which pointed the finger at Martin Cahill. I had none to offer.

In the weeks that followed the Widow Scallans attack, the Provos invited criminals and drug dealers to attend further 'interviews'. In later years it emerged that the terrorists were merely using the conspiracy as an excuse to muscle in on the various drug rackets and to extract 'donations' from organized crime gangs. The patriots were preparing for peace and wanted to feather their own nests.

In the process most of the senior players in the Dublin Brigade of the IRA became completely corrupted and immersed in the drug trade. At the same time their propagandists in the Sinn Féin party claimed that they were doing what the cops couldn't – clearing up the crime scene.

Martin Cahill told the IRA to 'fuck off' when his presence was requested, but two individuals who were helpful to the Provos were John Gilligan and John Traynor. Ever the smooth-talking, convincing con man, Traynor is understood to have given the IRA the impression that Cahill *might* have been involved in helping the loyalists.

Gilligan, who was not so subtle, pointed the finger at the General. The treacherous pair had also spread rumours that the drug shipment seized at Dublin Port the previous December belonged to Cahill, to create the impression that he was becoming a powerful drug lord. Gilligan knew the IRA was anxious to find an excuse to whack their old enemy and wanted to assist in any way he could.

Factory John and the Coach had been considering murdering their silent partner, but the IRA offered a better solution. Treachery and greed are the principal characteristics of the drug business, turning friends into murderous foes. The Provos could save them the cost of hiring a killer to do the job for them. It was an odds-on wager for the two gamblers.

At this stage Traynor and Gilligan had also established a partnership with the INLA, which was heavily involved in organized crime. Gilligan had maintained the friendship he'd formed with Fergal Toal and Dessie 'the Border Fox' O'Hare on E1 wing in Portlaoise Prison. In fact his friendship with Toal was so strong that other inmates used to joke – well out of earshot – that they were lovers. After his release Gilligan often visited Toal and the other INLA prisoners in Portlaoise and regularly lodged sums of money to the prison account for them to buy snacks, cigarettes and clothes. Traynor, Gilligan and Paul Ward were also supplying drugs and guns to the INLA in Dublin.

It was established in subsequent investigations that over 4 kilos of high-quality cocaine had been smuggled through Seabridge in Cork for one of the INLA gang leaders, Declan 'Whacker' Duffy, who was based in Tallaght. At the same time Duffy had been fronting a supposed anti-drug vigilante group in the area.

There was also plenty of bad blood between the INLA and Martin Cahill. He had recently been involved in a number of confrontations with members of the gang and had burned an INLA member's flat.

Meanwhile the General continued to ratchet up the pressure for his share of the drug money. Traynor later claimed to this writer that Cahill was becoming increasingly prone to unreasonable temper tantrums.

Gilligan and Traynor had several meetings with Cahill over the following weeks. In the middle of August 1994 a garda surveillance team watched as Gilligan visited Cahill at the home of his sister-in-law and lover, Tina Lawless, in Rathmines, south Dublin. On both occasions Gilligan went to great lengths to avoid being spotted, arriving on foot after walking through a series of side streets.

The General's relationship with Gilligan was becoming particularly fraught. After one meeting, Cahill told a close friend that he had thrown Gilligan out of his home. 'He is a dirty bastard,' Cahill told the friend, although he did not divulge the nature of the row. Gilligan and Traynor would not have to fob the General off for much longer.

On the afternoon of 18 August 1994 a hit man stepped from the kerb at the corner of Oxford Road and Charleston Road, in the south Dublin suburb of Ranelagh. The assassin pumped five rounds into the General as he sat behind the wheel of his car at a stop sign. The man who had pioneered and dominated gangland died instantly. It was the highest-profile criminal assassination in the twenty-five-year history of organized crime in Ireland. But the seminal event soon descended into total farce.

Before the body had even grown cold, the INLA and the IRA swarmed like vultures to claim the kill. Ninety minutes after the shooting the INLA contacted a Dublin radio newsroom and claimed responsibility. But later that evening the same station was contacted by the IRA, using a recognized code word, claiming that they were responsible.

In their rush to claim the General's scalp the Provos took the extraordinary step of attacking the INLA's claim to the kill, describing it as mischievous and false. Such was their desperation to take credit that the Provos even provided information about the weapon and getaway bike used in the attack, facts which could only be known to the killers and investigating gardaí.

The farce deepened further when, 17 minutes later, the INLA phoned the same newsroom to repudiate its original claim. It was the terrorist equivalent of a *Father Ted* episode. This was followed up with two typed statements delivered to *The Irish Times*, purporting to be from the IRA, which again claimed responsibility.

Nearly three decades later there is still considerable scepticism among veteran cops and criminals about the IRA claims. There are grounds to speculate that the assassination was either carried out by Gilligan's gang or that the INLA did it at the behest of Gilligan and Traynor.

The timely execution saved the partners the equivalent of €1 million, not to mention a lot of aggravation from the increasingly volatile General. The drug kings had also given the Provos the propaganda coup they wanted. To add to the suspicion, two years later, Gilligan made an intriguing remark to a journalist, commenting: 'I know who murdered the General and it wasn't the IRA.'

In 1997 a woman who'd witnessed Cahill's murder came forward to the police when she saw a picture of Brian Meehan in the *Sunday World* newspaper. It was the first time his picture had appeared in public and the story, by this writer, named him as a suspect for the murder of Veronica Guerin. The woman was absolutely certain that Meehan was the man she'd seen near Oxford Road, just before the hit. It was impossible to substantiate the claim.

Another reason for the lingering doubt is that the modus operandi of the crime was chillingly similar to that later employed in the murder of Veronica Guerin, and the weapon used was the same type, a .357 Magnum revolver. Only a few people will ever know the truth.

But one irrefutable result was that, with Cahill out of the picture, Gilligan and Traynor were left with a free hand, and they went from strength to strength. Factory John had emerged as one of the most powerful godfathers in the country. He also had the INLA in his pocket and the Provos steered clear of him. Over time the INLA effectively morphed into a private army for Gilligan and Traynor.

In early 1995 the INLA provided protection to the Coach when members of the Cahill family and gang began putting pressure on him for payment of the General's €1 million. The INLA threatened to shoot one of Cahill's sons and a message was sent to other gang members in Portlaoise Prison that they had better back off.

Aside from these few diehard loyalists, the rest of the General's gang had no interest in seeking revenge. As they were released from prison Gilligan and Traynor gave them a start in the drugs trade, and they became loyal customers. In the meantime the business thrived.

On the day of Cahill's violent demise, Dinny Meredith exchanged £142,000 (€286,000) for Dutch guilders in Amsterdam. Ironically, it was a similar amount that Cahill had given the gang to do their first deal nine months earlier. On the day after the murder, 19 August, two consignments of 180 kilos and 205 kilos of hash were booked in for shipping to Cork. The boxes, addressed to one of the gang's bogus companies, were being sent as 'motor parts' from one of Rahman's companies.

Cahill's murder was not the only high-profile shooting in gangland that year. In 1994 there was a noticeable increase in the number of what became known as gangland murders. In October a former close associate of Gilligan and Traynor, Paddy Shanahan, was gunned down as he walked into a gym in Crumlin. Another of Gilligan's E1 wing friends, Dutchy Holland, was later arrested and questioned about the murder. The former US Marine had been released from prison a month earlier. He became an important player in Gilligan's operation, working as his personal assassin. Holland also ran his own cannabis distribution racket sourcing his supplies from Factory John.

At the time Gilligan circulated a rumour that his organization had carried out the murder because Shanahan was suspected of being an informant. However, the prime suspect behind the hit was an associate of armed robbery mastermind Gerry Hutch, the Monk, for whom Shanahan had fronted a number of construction projects in the city.

Garda intelligence sources at the time believed that Gilligan used the murder to scare off members of the General's old gang who, along with Shanahan, were in the process of reforming the old mob.

In 1995 two former members of Gilligan's old Factory Gang, David Weafer and Christy Delaney, were also shot dead in separate incidents in June and December. Both deaths were officially classified by gardaí as 'drug-related'.

Gilligan was losing a lot of old friends. But he was too busy making money, and hanging on to it, for sentimentality.

CHAPTER NINE

VICTORY OVER THE LAW

On 31 August 1994 a garda patrol car pulled over Brian Meehan and Peter Mitchell driving on Dorset Street in central Dublin. As two of gangland's most openly hostile hoods they were always worth searching, if for no other reason than it pissed them off.

In a search of the car the officers found a plastic bag full of money behind the front seat. The two underworld pals had just collected over £46,000 (€92,000) in cash and were in the process of delivering it to Gilligan. Meehan told gardaí that the cash belonged to him.

The pair were arrested under the Misuse of Drugs Act and taken to Fitzgibbon Street station for a drug search. Meehan had a change of heart and told the officers that the money belonged to a friend, but he refused to name his pal. The police held on to the money, gave Meehan a receipt and released him and Mitchell.

A short time later John Gilligan arrived at the station and informed gardaí that the money was his and that Meehan was a 'good friend who has been minding it for me'. He said he could prove ownership of the cash and arranged an appointment at the station the following day.

In a rare display of co-operating with the police, Meehan attended as well and made a statement in which he named his boss as the true owner of the cash. Gilligan also made a statement.

Gilligan claimed the money and produced photocopies of bookie's cheques that he said he had received from winning bets on horses over the previous few weeks. 'I am a gambler, a successful one,' he claimed in his statement. He also produced documents stating that he was a horse breeder registered with 'Weatherbys Ireland Ltd'.

Gardaí, however, knew who they were dealing with and decided to seize the money under the Police Property Act. Under the Act a court could only determine the ownership of the property or cash which had been seized by the gardaí. The person from whom the money was taken was not required to prove how they had come by it. The legislation was archaic and completely unsuited to the modern age. Yet it was the only legal mechanism available to the police to try to seize suspect money. Inevitably they almost always had to return it. The anomalous situation meant that a criminal, who for example had been cleared of a burglary in court, could legally seek the return of the stolen property by claiming ownership. The law had fallen ludicrously out of touch with the changing nature of organized crime.

Gilligan was furious that his precious cash flow had been interrupted and had no intention of giving up his money. He applied to the courts to have it returned.

Traynor also approached a detective in the Serious Crime Squad and asked if there was a chance that some kind of deal could be made to get the cash back. The Coach said that Gilligan was prepared to give the police a few 'good arrests' by tipping them off about a number of drug dealers. In fact the dealers on offer were Gilligan's customers whom he deemed dispensable. The proposed 'deal' fell through when the cop told Traynor that he would be happy to do a deal, but the drug dealer he wanted was called Gilligan!

The seizure highlighted the gang's main logistical problem – transporting the ever increasing amounts of cash from Ireland to the Netherlands to pay for the drug shipments. The smuggling route into Ireland appeared secure but moving large sums of cash was a constant headache. In the first months of the business Gilligan brought the cash with him in briefcases and bags. Apart from a few trips, Traynor had cleverly stepped back from that side of the operation.

Dinny Meredith also transported large amounts of cash. Throughout 1994 he changed £1.6 million (over €3.2 million) into Dutch guilders at the Bureau de Change in the Centraal Station in Amsterdam. Gilligan changed over £200,000 (€400,000) in the same place.

In addition Dinny had established a network of truckers travelling to the Continent to bring parcels stuffed with cash to be delivered in Belgium and the Netherlands. The drivers were paid £50 (€100) for each delivery and were told that the parcels contained cash to buy cigarettes and tobacco. They handed the money to Thomas Gorst, another key member of the Rahman organization. Gorst was well known to Interpol and several European police forces.

Born in Liverpool in 1940, Thomas Gorst moved to live in Antwerp, Belgium in 1970. He had been involved in international drug trafficking for years and organized Rahman's smuggling routes through Belgium. Gorst, who was known as 'Scouser', also organized warehouse storage and transport.

In April 1983 Gorst was convicted and jailed for four years by a court in Plymouth, England, for drug trafficking. His brother, Eric, was a major drug dealer in England and, via Thomas, bought his product from Simon Rahman.

Two years earlier a Tangiers court had sentenced Thomas Gorst to a year in prison after he was caught with 25 kilos of powdered hashish that he was preparing to smuggle to Spain. His second wife, Mariette, who had been arrested with him, was acquitted. Gorst and Mariette were also identified on Interpol files as running a brothel in Antwerp and were regularly observed in the company of known South American drug traffickers.

Johnny Wildhagen introduced Gilligan to Gorst and his wife

early in 1994 during one of his visits to the Netherlands. Gorst also met and socialised with Traynor. He would later tell police that he liked Traynor but detested 'Gillon' or Gilligan, whom he considered a loudmouth. Gorst had agreed, at the behest of Rahman, to help with the delivery and conversion of the drug money coming from Ireland.

Mariette Gorst was working in a sleazy lap-dancing bar near Antwerp. Gilligan loved the place. When he discovered how cheap sex could be bought in such clubs, he was known as an enthusiastic and regular customer on the overnight visits when Geraldine wasn't with him.

Scouser began collecting the parcels of cash from the truckers coming from Ireland and then organizing the transport of the money across the Dutch border. He took delivery of scores of parcels of money, containing sums with a value of between €10,000 and €160,000. The money would be delivered by a number of different drivers on alternate days.

Dinny instructed the drivers to call Gorst's Belgian telephone number when they arrived at Zeebrugge Port. The meetings with the bagman normally took place at a BP filling station on the main motorway outside Antwerp.

Between November 1994 and January 1995 Mariette Gorst changed over €200,000 in Irish and English currency into Belgian francs at a bureau de change in Antwerp. Belgian nationals obtained a better rate of exchange than foreigners. Her husband and Gilligan would watch while the transactions took place – but not all the cash being sent to Gorst actually reached its final destination.

On 11 December 1994 Dinny approached Dennis Larrissey, who was preparing to board the ferry at Dún Laoghaire. Dinny appeared beside the truck and tapped on the window. He threw in a parcel wrapped in Christmas paper and asked him to drop it off when he got to Belgium.

The forty-year-old trucker from County Meath had already made a number of such deliveries for Dinny and two other associates. He was led to believe that he was delivering wages and that there wasn't anything illegal about it.

When Larrissey arrived in Holyhead Port he was stopped by a customs officer for a routine search. She spotted the package sitting on the passenger seat of the cab and asked what was in it. Larrissey said that he didn't know, but that he had been asked to deliver it to the Continent. The officer opened the package and saw the money. Larrissey was detained while the cash was counted. It took the Customs staff five hours to complete the count, which amounted to £67,000 (€135,000) in used notes.

When Larrissey was released later that day he contacted Meredith and told him what happened. The trucker was informed that the money belonged to Gilligan and that he should call him immediately. When Larrissey rang Gilligan in Dublin and nervously informed him about the seizure of the money he received an unexpected non-aggressive response.

Gilligan reassured the driver that he had nothing to worry about and claimed that it was all a mistake. The money was being sent out to build a golf course on the Continent and there should have been 'documents' in the parcel explaining this. Gilligan reserved his fury for the people who had taken his money.

He rang Her Majesty's Customs at Holyhead and spoke to a senior officer, Dave Winkle. Gilligan was furious at the unwarranted interference by HM Customs in his illegal affairs. In a menacing tone he demanded the return of his money and claimed that he could produce documentation proving that it was for 'investment in property in Ireland'.

Winkle told him that the case had been passed to Roger Wilson of the Customs National Investigation Service based in Manchester. An experienced investigator, Wilson believed that the money was suspect and decided that it should be confiscated under drug trafficking legislation. When Gilligan was informed about Wilson's decision he flew into a rage and snarled:

> He's [Wilson has] backed me into a corner...it's not a problem for me to get someone to shoot him...I'm not goin' down that road. I just want me money back. But if someone messes with my family, I'll have them fucking shot.

The threat against Roger Wilson was taken seriously and he was subsequently placed in a special protection programme.

While Larrissey was driving on the Continent the following day, he received another call from Gilligan. He told the trucker to call HM Customs in Holyhead on his return journey and sign forms confirming that he had no claim to the money. In the meantime Gilligan instructed his legal team to fight the case at Holyhead Magistrates' Court.

A week later, on 22 December, Gilligan was fighting another legal battle for the return of his cash. This time he was in the Dublin District Court seeking the £46,000 (€92,000) in cash which the gardaí had seized from Brian Meehan in August.

During the hearing Gilligan gave evidence of how the money was the proceeds of his activities as a professional gambler. Counsel for the State wanted to know why he had entrusted such a large amount of money to a convicted armed robber. Meehan, Gilligan replied, was a trusted friend and he had no reservations about leaving the cash in his possession. The court had no choice but to grant an order returning the cash to Gilligan.

The following day Gilligan swaggered triumphantly into Fitzgibbon Street garda station to collect his drugs money. He smirked at the officers across the front desk as they handed over the cash. Gilligan's confidence and narcissism grew with each new victory over the law, each death threat that worked and each new shipment of hash successfully delivered.

The gaping deficiencies in the criminal justice system were conspiring to validate his arrogance and justify his attitude that the authorities were not so much a threat as a nuisance.

Flushed with success Gilligan continued his case against HM Customs. He subsequently attended the magistrates' Court in Holyhead on four occasions to apply for its return. Each time HM Customs sought adjournments, arguing that their case was not yet ready.

Gilligan's solicitor insisted that he and his client were prepared to go ahead on each occasion and accused Customs of deliberately delaying the proceedings. His persistence eventually paid off.

On 21 July 1995 the magistrates ordered that the £67,000 (€135,000) be returned to Gilligan. He left court a happy man. The law in the UK was just as impotent as it was in Ireland. The world was Gilligan's oyster.

On the same day that he was getting his dirty money back, Simon Rahman's couriers shipped 100 kilos of hashish to Gilligan's gang in Ireland.

It was back to business as usual, and no one was going to get in the way.

CHAPTER TEN

——

GREED

On 8 May 1995 Peter 'Fatso' Mitchell was in an interview room in Coolock garda station in north Dublin, mouthing off at the two Serious Crime Squad detectives across the table. He was complaining in his customary loud, hoarse tone, but Mitchell's diatribe was not, for once, about police harassment or the fact that they were detaining him for two days. The cocky underworld mouthpiece was giving out about drug dealers – more specifically, the ones he employed! Mitchell whined:

> Youse think that drugs is an easy business? Well, it's fuckin' not. I'm payin' fellas £1,000 (€2,000) a week to sell hash and a few Es for me and do you think I can get the bastards to work? You can't get the fuckers out of the pubs or their beds. It's just not fuckin' easy.

The cocky crook then complained about an RTÉ documentary which he claimed had referred to his drug dealing activities. 'They claimed that I was makin' £50,000 (€100,000) a week from drugs. Well, that's a fuckin' lie. I don't know where they got that figure,' Mitchell grumbled, as he leaned across the table to impart a confidence to his new friends. 'I'll tell ye I don't earn anything like that...I'd say that I'm only makin' about £30,000 (€60,000) a week and nothing more and that's the fuckin' truth, lads.'

Even by Mitchell's voluble tendencies, it was an extraordinary outburst. It illustrated the contempt Gilligan and his henchmen had for the law. They considered the gardaí powerless to touch them and, in any case, bragging about involvement in crime was not an offence.

Mitchell and Meehan had been arrested for questioning about a gun attack on the home of Garda Inspector Willie Stratford in nearby Raheny. Around 4 a.m. the day before a gunman had fired two shotgun blasts through Stratford's downstairs and upstairs windows. Miraculously, no one was injured in the attack. It was another reminder that the crime gangs were out of control.

Inspector Stratford's two sons, John and Kevin, were young, enthusiastic cops based in two north-central police stations. They were dedicated policemen with reputations for giving criminals a hard time, especially the likes of Meehan, Mitchell and their associates.

When the shooting took place at the home of Inspector Stratford, Mitchell and Meehan were the obvious suspects. The two young hoods were not intimidated by the police and were openly antagonistic towards them on the street.

A week before their arrest in May Meehan and Mitchell had threatened Garda John Stratford when he arrested them for possession of offensive weapons. It was believed they were on the way to inflict pain on an errant customer. The hoods told Stratford that they could get him or his family anytime and they knew the address of the family home.

Mitchell's astonishing boast at Coolock station was prompted when the detectives told him that they meant business over the Stratford shooting:

> If you had anything to do with this, Peter, we'll hound you until you and your friends are charged. You'll get big time for this – we'll see to it. The good life will be over.

His brief display of honesty was intended to show that he was simply too busy to be bothering with attacking the homes of gardaí. Gilligan's boys were subsequently cleared of involvement and another criminal was eventually given four years for the incident.

When Fatso boasted to the detectives about his income, it was probably the first time in his criminal career that he had even approached the truth when talking to the cops. In any case, they didn't believe him. The police had still not realised the kind of cash being generated by organized crime. While they knew that Gilligan was in the drugs business there didn't appear to be any will at garda senior management level to authorize a full-on targeted investigation to bust him. Even though his gang was operating on an industrial scale and was the biggest in the country, the police had no workable intelligence about Gilligan's operation.

Factory John had kept to the plan outlined in Portlaoise Prison and adopted a cell-type structure in the gang. Similar to the set-up used by the IRA, it prevented leakage of information to the police. It was a vindication of the gang's internal security measures that the drug distribution network and supply route continued to run smoothly. The criminals were also indirectly abetted by some in garda management who had adopted a head in the sand approach. This writer was contacted in 1995 by a senior garda detective after publishing a story which highlighted how criminals were becoming millionaires on the back of the burgeoning drug trade. The article did not name Gilligan at the time. The senior officer admonished me for a grossly exaggerated piece of journalism. 'There is no such thing as a criminal millionaire,' he opined.

By the end of the year Gilligan and his gang were making huge money. Four days before the arrests of Mitchell and Meehan in May a consignment of 250 kilos of hash had arrived at Seabridge in Cork. As the consignments got larger, the gang got greedier.

Retired Detective Chief Superintendent Tony Quilter, the former head of the Garda National Drug Unit (GNDU), would later describe the key to Gilligan's success:

> The Gilligan gang brought drug trafficking to another level in this country. They brought a highly organized, businesslike structure to their empire. They dealt directly with associates on the Continent. They bought in bulk, and they had a sophisticated and logistical distribution network. They ensured that people worked on a need-to-know basis and kept the actual running of the operation a closely guarded secret. This was why the gardaí received very little intelligence about them.

Garda investigations, based on shipping records obtained in the Netherlands and Ireland, would later show that during 1995 Gilligan imported an estimated 8,700 kilos of cannabis resin into Ireland. Based on an average profit of €1,600 per kilo, Gilligan's take was almost €14 million, out of which Traynor got his cut.

The rest of the gang, collectively, made over €5 million based on a profit margin of €600 per kilo. These figures are still considered conservative. From subsequent investigations in the Netherlands, Belgium and Ireland it was understood that there had been many other shipments. Gilligan was also running a secondary operation trafficking large consignments of ecstasy which was equally profitable.

In 1995 Bowden's hard work was rewarded when he was 'appointed' an equal partner in the business. Shay Ward, a brother of Paul 'Hippo' Ward, who had a long criminal record and a heroin habit, also joined the gang. Shay began working with Bowden controlling the day-to-day running of the business. They would collect the consignments from John Dunne at the Ambassador Hotel and move them on to their long list of clients. The customer list, which was later seized by the police, and confirmed by Bowden, gave a fascinating insight into the sheer scale of the distribution network.

As each consignment arrived, Ward and Bowden would divide it into the individual orders for distribution. They worked fast, distributing an entire shipment within a few days. Bowden eventually had to buy a van from Traynor in order to make all his deliveries.

At the peak of the operation the gang was distributing an average of 200 kilos per week. Dunne got fed up with the frequent jaunts to Dublin and began paying a Cork van driver to do the deliveries for him.

Drops were made to customers around Dublin at pre-arranged locations and at the same time each week. Without Bowden the system would not have worked so well. He later recalled how there was a very poor work ethic among the other members of the gang. Meehan and the rest would often disappear for days on drink and drug binges, leaving the work to him. However, they tended to be more conscientious and punctual when it came to the cash.

Each Friday the five gang members – the Ward brothers, Meehan, Mitchell and Bowden – met in Meehan's flat and counted the week's turnover. The money for Gilligan was the first to be counted and packed for delivery to him. The rest they divided among themselves. Each man was earning an average equivalent of €14,000 per week today. A slow week earned them a paltry €6,000. To put the sums in context the average weekly wage that year was equivalent to €700. Money was re-invested in large consignments of ecstasy and cocaine as a sideline.

Gilligan's henchmen splashed their endless supply of cash on expensive clothes, luxury cars, five-star exotic holidays, gifts, drugs, drink and women. Whatever they wanted, the young hoods could buy. Their main difficulty was where to put all the cash.

Two years later Charlie Bowden would tell the Special Criminal Court that he had personally accumulated a profit worth at least €400,000 in just over a year. He explained where the rest of his fortune had gone:

I spent a lot of money on cocaine. I bought designer clothes and went on foreign holidays. I would go out. I would live well. I would buy stuff for the kids.

He also revealed how handling the bundles of drug cash was a problem for the gang:

This was a constant refrain throughout the whole time when we were earning this type of money, where to put it. I used to stuff it in a laundry basket. When it was full, I got another one. We spoke about offshore accounts and how we would go about doing it. We were thinking about getting the money into bank accounts in the Isle of Man.

Bowden bought a comfortable semi-detached home and a hairdressing salon which was run by his girlfriend Julie Bacon. The mortgage repayments and the hairdressing salon, which never turned a profit, soaked up some of the mountain of cash. He spent as much as €2,800 a week on socializing and snorting cocaine. He bought BMWs for himself and Julie. He had a special safe sunk in the floor of a shed at his brother's house to store more of the cash and he hid a large carrier bag stuffed with more than £200,000 (€400,000) in a friend's flat.

The rest of the gang also ploughed cash into high-powered cars, houses, apartments and investment bonds. Bank accounts were set up in the names of family members and filled with money. Meehan, as Gilligan's managing director, was the wealthiest of the five henchmen. He bought a luxury apartment and a number of investment rental properties.

Times were also good for John Traynor. After the initial contacts and meetings with Rahman in the Netherlands, Traynor stood back from the day-to-day running of the drug business. Records showed that between 1994 and 1996 Traynor only visited the Netherlands seven times. Gilligan had more than forty trips recorded on his Aer Lingus account and several others which he paid for in cash. In Dublin, Traynor and Gilligan met regularly to discuss business and to sort out money, but Gilligan had assumed the role of the overall boss. Much to Traynor's annoyance he also controlled the purse strings. He drip-fed his partner a few hundred thousand at a time. Traynor once complained to an associate that 'the little bastard owes me £1.75 million' (€3.5 million).

Gilligan knew that the only way to ensure Traynor's loyalty was to owe him money and he needed the Coach to help launder the drug money. In the months following the General's death, Traynor had a visible change in fortune. He no longer had to hide his wealth from Cahill for fear that he would take it. The Coach partied every bit as hard as the younger members of the mob, splashing out on booze and drug orgies with his many girlfriends. He bought a racing car, a small yacht and investment properties.

Traynor invested in the expansion of his used car business, opening two more dealerships in Counties Laois and Kildare. The companies were one of the Coach's clever money laundering fronts. He imported hundreds of used cars from the UK and sold them on at a loss. The deficit represented a good return for cleaning his ill-gotten gains when compared to paying the standard rate of income tax.

––––––––

The fortunes being made by Traynor and the rest of the mob, however, were modest in comparison to the wealth being enjoyed by John Gilligan. When the millions began rolling in, 'the little one' got greedy and wanted more. He was determined to hang on to every dishonest cent of it.

On the ground, Meehan and his hoods ensured that the 'little man' got his money on the button. If a dealer didn't pay, then they threatened him, broke his legs or shot him. No one was allowed off the hook. If someone was permitted to take liberties and not pay up Gilligan would be furious and order that the dealer get a more severe going-over. Owing him a few hundred pounds was as intolerable as owing a million.

Geraldine Gilligan had also become intoxicated with the mountains of cash her beloved husband's success had brought. At last they could be 'somebodies'. After all, she had stood by him since she was a teenager, supported him in his criminal activities and had suffered hard times when he was in prison. She had even taken a huge personal risk in getting involved in the negotiations with the UVF on his behalf. Geraldine believed that she was entitled to enjoy everything that the drug money provided. She convinced John that they should use the money to build a world-class equestrian centre and own and breed their own racehorses.

Within weeks of his release from prison in September 1993 Gilligan set about expanding and developing the land they had purchased in County Kildare in 1987. Geraldine planned to call it the Jessbrook Equestrian Centre. The investment would be an effective instrument to launder the drug money.

Gilligan's inimitable method of conducting legitimate business soon had local tongues wagging and people in fear of their lives. In negotiating land deals, Gilligan made an offer that could not be refused. If it was rejected then threats and intimidation followed. As he grew more arrogant, on the back of his new-found success, 'the little one' refused to take no for an answer.

On 14 November 1994 John Gilligan purchased 30 acres of land valued at €100,000 near his existing holding. Another man had a piece of land that Factory John was determined to buy but the man repeatedly refused to sell. Gilligan beat him up on a village street and reportedly urinated on his face. He bought the land and no charges were ever preferred.

He also threatened another local at gunpoint in a row over a right of way through land he had purchased. Gilligan no longer made any secret of the fact that he would do what he liked and no one could stop him. His presence in Jessbrook shattered the peace of what had been a quiet pastoral backwater. The people of the area were terrified of the drug dealer from Dublin and at least one family moved out as a result.

The police on the ground had been the first to notice the sudden rise in the fortunes of Gilligan and his cohort of thugs. In fairness the gangsters made no effort to conceal it. Garda units throughout Dublin were sending reports up the line about the gang members' extravagant lifestyles and property acquisitions. But they were powerless to do anything about it in the absence of legislation to seize the proceeds of crime. Yet senior officers could have sanctioned an investigation into the source of the wealth by placing the gang under surveillance. When they finally took action, it was too late.

Over two years Gilligan paid £162,000 (€330,000) for 77 acres of land despite having no visible means of income. No mortgage or loans of any kind were ever sought. The land was paid for with shoe boxes and plastic bags full of used notes. In September 1994 Gilligan paid £73,000 (€147,000) for a new detached house in Lucan, County Dublin, as a present for his daughter Tracey's twentieth birthday.

Tracey was her father's favourite, and he always wanted the best for his little girl. She had been sent to an exclusive private school, but she left before completing her education and had a child. On paper, Tracey's only income was a Lone Parent's Allowance of £79.70 (€160) per week and she had been assessed by the Department of Social Welfare as having no means. But in May 1994, after a tip-off from the gardaí, inspectors from the department called her in for an interview to discuss the allowance claim. It was actually unlawful for government departments and the gardaí to share such information. In an ironic twist, in order to see some justice done the public servants had to break the law. In reality, in the prevailing atmosphere of intimidation, often nothing ever came of the interventions.

At her meeting Tracey Gilligan denied that she had any means. When the social welfare inspectors asked about a car she owned, she told them it was a present from her father. They pressed her for evidence of this and threatened to cut off her payments if she didn't provide it.

When Tracey told her father, he saw red and dealt with the problem in his usual way. The psychopath believed that no one had a right to interfere with his family. Gilligan twice telephoned the officer dealing with his daughter's case. On each call he was aggressive and made a number of veiled threats that harm would come to anyone who treated his family unjustly.

The welfare inspector later passed the file on to the head office without recommendation. A note in Tracey's social welfare file recorded how 'unspecified threats' had been made by John Gilligan, who was described as a 'very dangerous man'. A memo by department officials stated that they had 'decided to drop the subject about the car and to continue paying her Lone Parent's Allowance'.

Around the same time the Revenue Commissioners, also acting on information unofficially supplied by the gardaí, sent a tax demand to Gilligan at Jessbrook. The aspiring godfather was infuriated by the effrontery. He took the letter and wrote the words 'fuck off' on it before sending it back. No action was taken. The system was acknowledging that John Gilligan was untouchable.

The civil servants had ample reasons for accepting the gangster's chilling threats. In 1989 Martin Cahill had Brian Purcell, a social welfare inspector, abducted and shot in the legs. Purcell's 'crime' was that he had been assigned to investigate Cahill's unemployment assistance payments. Brian Purcell later became the Secretary General of the Department of Justice. Neither Cahill nor any member of his gang was ever charged with the appalling crime.

Gilligan's actions were another warning that the criminals didn't care who they threatened or intimidated. The lack of joined-up thinking by the State meant that public servants were scared to do their jobs and the gangs could undermine society with apparent impunity.

As Veronica Guerin observed around this time, 'the law favours the criminal more than anyone'. Gilligan would ultimately change all that.

A former member of the Serious Crime Squad recalls the growing sense of frustration among the police:

> After Cahill attacked the social welfare officer there was no way we could get anyone in the relevant government departments to cut these guys off the dole or serve tax assessments on them. The unions who represented them were opposed to pursuing criminals on the grounds of health and safety. No one could blame them because we had guns and they didn't. But we had no powers to look into bank accounts and whenever we seized cash from a criminal, his lawyer could walk into court and have it returned under a Police Property Application. Some people in our job began to seriously question why we couldn't go after the criminal's money but there didn't seem to be the will to do that. We often asked why the legislation could not be changed so that we, the gardaí, could do the job for the social welfare people. Young gardaí who have joined over the past twenty-five years cannot believe that the system was like that.

In the meantime Gilligan kept on splashing his cash. In 1995 he paid £78,000 (€156,000) for a house for his son Darren's twentieth birthday. At the same time Darren was receiving £64.50 (€127) per week in unemployment assistance, even though a Bank of Ireland account in his name in Blanchardstown contained sums to the value of €160,000. He was also dealing in large quantities of highly profitable ecstasy which he sourced through his dad. Gilligan even bought the family's rented corporation house at Corduff in Blanchardstown.

In the year between 1995 and 1996 Gilligan spent another £78,000 (€156,000) in cash buying new vehicles, including two jeeps for the equestrian centre. On 9 January 1996 he walked into a car showroom in west Dublin with his two children. One picked out a new car and the other a jeep, which John agreed to buy, in much the same way children pick up toys in a store.

When the salesman asked how they wanted to pay for the vehicles, Gilligan produced a plastic bag full of used notes. On the same day the adoring dad lodged £20,000 (€39,000) in cash in each of his children's bank accounts. Gilligan could well afford it. Over the following fortnight, two shipments containing 387 kilos of hashish arrived in Cork. Gilligan's estimated profit was worth over €600,000, more than compensating him for his paternal generosity.

In 1995 the Gilligans paid £60,000 (€120,000) for a promising racehorse called Rifawan. Gilligan paid cash for it which he carried in a shoe box. Rifawan was put in training at the stables of Arthur Moore at a cost of £24,000 (€47,000) between February 1995 and May 1996. Moore did not know the name of the real owner of the horse and, as far as he was concerned, he was training it for a perfectly legitimate client. Rifawan did well, coming second in two races. Following the murder of Veronica Guerin, the trainer discovered the horse's true owner and returned it. Rifawan was subsequently sent to an English trainer but broke his leg in a novices' chase at Ayr in Scotland.

Owning Rifawan had given the Gilligans a tantalizing glimpse of the respectability and glamorous lifestyle they craved, allowing them to enter the prestigious owners' enclosure at races in Ireland and England. Gilligan once bragged he had got within winking distance of the Queen Mother herself.

At the same time Geraldine Gilligan's dream of owning her own equestrian centre was taking shape. In April 1994 the Gilligans drew up plans for the complete renovation of Jessbrook and the construction of fourteen stables. A single-storey six-bedroom mansion was built, hidden from view at the end of a long driveway behind electronic gates, overlooked by surveillance cameras. The Gilligans liked their privacy.

Gilligan used the threat of violence and large wads of cash to get things done. The builder who took on the construction job found himself in a living nightmare at the hands of a monster. In one incident, when a bricklayer didn't turn up for work, Gilligan went looking for him with an iron bar. When Factory John couldn't find him, he rang the man's wife and told her that if he didn't hear from the brickie he would put her husband in the hospital by nightfall. He later spoke to the builder and threatened to put him in a wheelchair if the workmen didn't turn up.

On another occasion Gilligan called the builder, the architect and another contractor together for a meeting where he berated them that the work wasn't progressing fast enough. During the conversation Gilligan's mobile phone rang and he passed it to the builder. In a rough Dublin accent the caller told him that if he didn't do what Gilligan wanted, he would be waiting for the builder up the road and would 'get' his wife and family. The architect was given the same message. The two men, who were honest, hard-working people, had never experienced anything so bizarre or terrifying. They were afraid for their own safety and for their families.

One day Gilligan rang and asked the builder: 'How many times have I said that I will kill you?' The builder stuttered back: 'Loads' and Gilligan began ranting about a piece of work which he said had not been properly finished. In the end the builder completed the house and stables and left. It was a harrowing ordeal.

Gilligan then refused to pay the outstanding £36,000 (€72,000) owed for the work simply because he could. The builder would never dare go to the police or try to seek recourse through the courts. In any event he didn't have the money. The unpaid bill left the builder's small business practically bankrupt, and he was living in fear that the new squire of Jessbrook would kill him.

In May 1995 Geraldine Gilligan sought planning permission for a full-size indoor show jumping arena with stables and groom living quarters, a floodlit outdoor horse exercise arena and large car park. It would be one of the biggest centres in the country, modelled on Millstreet, County Cork, and capable of hosting major international events. Again Gilligan did business his way.

As part of the planning process Kildare County Council made several amendments and finally gave it the go-ahead in March 1996. But by then Gilligan had ploughed on regardless and Jessbrook had been built in blatant contravention of the guidelines laid down by the local authority. He more than doubled the capacity allowed for in the original planning notice, increasing it from 400 to 900 seats.

Gardaí who later dismantled Gilligan's empire suspected that he had intimidated officials at Kildare County Council. When detectives began investigating Gilligan's wealth in 1996 they discovered that parts of the planning files were missing. The fearsome godfather seemed to have succeeded in scaring off another arm of the State.

A subsequent financial investigation revealed that Gilligan spent over €3 million on Jessbrook in less than a year. Most of the money was paid over in cash from shoe boxes and plastic bags. The rest of the payments were from cheques drawn on Geraldine's bank account. Between 1994 and 1996, Geraldine, using her maiden name, Matilda Dunne, paid over the equivalent of €1.6 million through various bank accounts.

The Gilligans were proud of their masterpiece but agreed that it would be best to keep John as far away as legally possible from any claims on the property. To cover their tracks, they drew up a legal separation agreement in July 1995 in which he assigned ownership of Jessbrook to Geraldine.

They reckoned they had covered every angle.

CHAPTER ELEVEN

———

THE GAMBLER AND
THE MISTRESS

As gangland's new top dog Gilligan made little effort to hide his good fortune because there was nothing anyone could do about it. But the tedious interference by HM Customs and the gardaí confirmed for him the prudence of making the money look as legitimate as possible. He opted for the front he knew best, that of a professional gambler.

Like his father, John junior was a problem gambler. In the early days Gilligan thought nothing of wagering his entire earnings from a warehouse robbery on a bet. Once he wagered the equivalent of €20,000 on one greyhound race but the dog broke its toe leaving the trap and never even started the race. Now he was in the big league Gilligan used his previous gambling experiences and worked out a relatively crude, but effective, system for laundering his dirty money.

Gilligan and a network of his couriers laid bets on short odds in bookmakers' shops throughout greater Dublin. He would often bet money on all the horses running in a single race, betting to the value of €20,000 a time. When he won Gilligan insisted on being paid with bookmakers' cheques, which he then used as evidence that he earned a living as a professional gambler. It was these cheques he had used to successfully reclaim the money seized in Dublin in 1994.

Gilligan washed the majority of his dirty money through the bookies. The examples below, uncovered in the subsequent investigation of the mobster's financial affairs by the CAB, show how his system worked.

On 18 March 1995 Gilligan laid twelve bets. At the time £1,000 was the equivalent of €2,000 today. The first bet was for £5,000 and the horse lost. Gilligan also lost the following two races, bringing his losses so far that day to £16,390. But his luck changed when he had the winner in the fourth race with a bet of £4,000. It paid £8,400, thus reducing his losses to £12,000.

Gilligan also won the next flutter of £3,800 which paid £10,450 and he lost £3,300 in the sixth. In the next three races Gilligan wagered a total of £12,000. All three horses won, lowering his cumulative losses for the day to £1,220. On the next race, the tenth of the day, he lost another £2,000. He called the final two races right, which left him up £2,000 on the day's betting.

With taxes, he had bet a total of £53,900 (€107,800) in cash and won £55,900 (€111,800, received in bookmaker's cheques). In the process the money had effectively been laundered. Some bookies began to limit the amounts that Gilligan could wager. It was not unusual for him to saunter up to the counter and empty a plastic bag full of bundles of cash to place his bets.

Gilligan was barred by a number of bookmakers and others classified him as a 'monitored customer' where the staff would first have to seek approval from head office before accepting his bets. One bookmaker conducted detailed analysis of Gilligan's betting patterns, including the type of races he backed, the horses and jockeys, but could not identify a discernible methodology or scam.

In 1995 Gilligan recruited thirty-three-year-old Derek Baker as his personal driver and general gofer. Originally from Aylesbury in Tallaght, Baker had been in the same class in school as Gilligan's brother Thomas. In the late 1980s Factory John had invested money in a bookie shop Baker opened but it folded in less than a year.

Baker, who didn't have a criminal record, had also owned an industrial cleaning company but it too had gone out of business. When Gilligan offered him a job Baker was working in the dispatch department of *The Irish Times* which he then quit. He became Gilligan's full-time personal bagman. He was soon earning up to €2,000 a day.

Apart from being his driver, Baker collected money from Gilligan's associates, paid staff at Jessbrook and co-ordinated his betting operation. He also began travelling to the Netherlands to deliver cash to Simon Rahman. Over the period that he was working for Gilligan, Baker was estimated to have personally exchanged £1 million (€2 million) through a bureau de change in Amsterdam.

Following the murder of Veronica Guerin the former bookie gave police a detailed statement outlining his dealings with his temperamental boss:

> I often placed bets on his behalf and organized other people to do the same. He would give me the instructions as to the horse and the amount to bet. I would collect the winnings if any. The payment would be made by cash or cheque. He was betting £5,000 (€10,000) to £10,000 (€20,000) on a horse. He would invest £20,000 (€40,000) to £30,000 (€60,000) in a single day and other days he would gamble only £5,000 (€10,000). I felt that he was winning at the bookmakers but he never indicated to me whether he won or lost. I knew he was winning through the dealings I was having for him and I am also aware that Ladbrokes curtailed his betting because of his success. We always paid tax at 10 per cent on the bets.

Baker said he had played 'cat and mouse' with betting shops for over two years as he placed proxy bets for Gilligan with bookies in Dublin and Kildare. He also recalled how he collected briefcases full of money from Gilligan and delivered them to the Netherlands.

In an interview with this writer in 2007 Baker claimed that he never saw his boss doing business:

> John never let his right hand know what his left hand was doing and he was very secretive. When I was driving him around, he would tell me to stop the car and then he would make telephone calls on a coin phone so nobody could hear him. He was very mad. He could spot someone on the street who he hadn't seen in a while and get out and give them £300 (€600) and then he could turn the other way and beat someone up out of the blue.

Analysis by the CAB later discovered that between March 1994 and June 1996 Gilligan wagered a total equivalent to almost €10 million in today's money. Betting tax at ten per cent raised the overall total to almost €11 million. Gilligan's return was just under €9.5 million, showing a loss of €1.2 million or 11.3 per cent. Given the standard rate of income tax, then and now, it was extraordinary value for money and all perfectly legal.

As his business continued to flourish Gilligan found himself a mistress who was twenty-five years his junior. Carol Rooney, from Palmerstown, was an attractive eighteen-year-old who worked as an assistant in Ladbrokes chain of betting shops where her mother Bernadette was a senior manager. One day in 1995 John Gilligan swaggered through the door and Carol's life took a turn for the worse. The youngster was easily impressed as the gang boss piled eye-watering bundles of cash on the counter to bet on horses.

Rooney had heard plenty of talk among the staff about Gilligan, the dangerous gangster. But she found him witty and charming as he showered her with compliments. He made the innocent teenager feel special. To her, the diminutive mobster had an exotic aura.

When one day he asked her out to dinner she laughed off the ridiculous request from a man who, at forty-three, was older than her own father. 'He cannot be serious,' she commented to a friend.

But Gilligan continued grooming the impressionable girl who was younger than his own daughter and she eventually agreed to meet him for a drink. Within a few weeks she was sleeping with the man who would become Ireland's Public Enemy Number One. Gilligan showered his teenage conquest with expensive gifts. He gave her wads of cash to bet in European casinos and bought her a car and an expensive Raymond Weil watch. There was also a five-star holiday in the Bahamas. The teenager was mesmerized by the life of luxury that Gilligan provided.

Behind Geraldine's back, and without the knowledge of her parents, Gilligan brought his mistress to Belgium, the Netherlands and the UK, when he met Rahman and his representatives to discuss business. Unlike her friends, Carol was living the high life and flying business class. She was also finding herself in the company of some of Europe's top drug dealers and gunrunners.

In 2017 the *Irish Mirror* published a taped conversation between Gilligan and an unknown interviewer in which he described his ill-matched relationship with the former mistress:

> I asked Carol Rooney to go for a meal. I was enjoying her company. She was a very pretty girl. It wasn't boyfriend-girlfriend. I said, 'This is not a relationship.' She was a very, very pretty girl, a really beautiful girl. She had a personality second to none. And good-looking, very good-looking. Body second to none. Gorgeous-looking woman. I don't know how many years I was older than her – it must have been 25 or 26. I think I was 42 [he was 44] when I got locked up and she was 20 [she was 19]. If she went out with someone else, it didn't bother me for half a second.

Gilligan said having a teenage lover did not cause him problems with wife Geraldine:

> No, we were legally separated since 1995. But I wasn't going to rub her nose in it. When I came out of prison, she was giving out to me, not to do this, not to do that and it done my head in eventually. Geraldine wanted me to be holier than the Pope.

As the relationship with Rooney intensified Gilligan decided he needed a little love nest. He instructed Derek Baker to find a suitable house for the purpose. In the summer of 1995 he rented a three-bedroom semi-detached house at Oaklawn West in Leixlip, County Kildare.

Carol Rooney and another young woman, Baker's mistress, moved into the house. Gilligan spared no expense on decorating and furnishing the place. Each week the godfather gave her money to pay the bills. She had fallen out with her parents who had learned of the affair and disapproved. But their daughter, legally an adult, didn't have to listen to them.

Over the subsequent eighteen months or so Carol Rooney found herself trapped in a terrifying situation as she became privy to her lover's criminal activities – and discovered that a monster lurked behind the charismatic facade. But by then it was too late.

She would later tell gardaí that she realized that she had made a 'childish, immature mistake' and was too scared of Gilligan to make a run for it. She was in so deep that she was left with no choice but to continue to play the role of the quintessential gangster's moll.

Meanwhile Gilligan began using the house for more than just sex. It became the gang's safe house. Rooney would watch in astonishment as Gilligan and other members of the gang arrived with big bags of cash, dumping them in the middle of the sitting-room floor to count. She often saw them count up to £200,000 (€400,000) at a time.

Gilligan regularly brought bags of automatic weapons into the house as well and hid them under the stairs. 'He asked me to guess where the cash came from. I was afraid to ask questions. "Hash and guns," he said,' Rooney would eventually reveal.

But Factory John was not prepared to depend on romantic fealty for his lover's discretion. He told her that if she ever opened her mouth to anyone about his business he could have her and her family killed.

The gang had regular meetings with their boss at the safe house. In this secure setting they openly discussed their dealings with money, drugs, guns, shootings – and the plot to murder Veronica Guerin.

Meanwhile the business continued to prosper. Simon Rahman thought Gilligan's method of laundering cash was a reflection of the rest of his organization and his personality – vulgar and unsophisticated. Rahman described the gang, with the exception of Traynor, as a bunch of 'Neanderthals'.

From the start of their business arrangement Gilligan had tried hard to impress Rahman and his associates by projecting the image of a major league international drug trafficker, a godfather with considerable clout. The global drug dealer, however, was amused at 'the little one's' efforts to ingratiate himself with the Dutch gang, while deploring the stupidity and arrogance of Gilligan and his mob which attracted unwelcome attention. Rahman later commented to associates that he always reckoned that the gang's arrogance and indiscretions would someday lead to their downfall.

But business was business and Gilligan was spending a lot of money with him. Rahman wanted to ensure that he continued doing so. At the same time he maintained a safe distance from Gilligan so that he would not get caught himself. He wanted someone he could trust to keep an eye on Gilligan and take care of the financial transactions. He appointed Martin Baltus to be his liaison man with the Gilligan gang.

Born in September 1946 in The Hague, Baltus became a business associate of Rahman a year before Gilligan came on the scene. He was described as being Rahman's equivalent of John Traynor. Baltus specialized in fraud and was a general underworld wheeler dealer and money launderer. He set up a labyrinth of bogus shell companies through which Rahman organized various smuggling scams and funnelled dirty money.

In December 1994 Rahman introduced him to Gilligan as a potential investor in a holiday home development which Baltus was supposedly organizing in Zeeland. While Gilligan didn't invest in the project he later visited the development with Baltus. He used pictures of himself taken at the property, together with sales documents, to convince nosy customs officials that he was a legitimate investor. Gilligan reckoned it provided an extra layer of flimsy explanation if he was stopped with a large bag of drug money.

In his role as Gilligan's client relationship manager Baltus took control of his drug payments. On 3 January 1995 Baltus was dispatched to Schiphol Airport to collect Gilligan and drive him to a meeting with Rahman in the Victoria Hotel in Amsterdam. Gilligan handed over a sports carrier bag which Baltus took away to exchange at the Bureau de Change in nearby Centraal Station.

The bag contained £138,000 (€276, 000) in cash. Baltus used his Dutch driver's licence as evidence of identity for the transaction. He returned to the hotel and handed the bag of guilders to Rahman.

Between January 1995 and April 1996 Martin Baltus exchanged over €5.5 million delivered by Gilligan's bagmen. He was very conscientious in his work and would even iron out crumpled notes before he took them to the Bureau. On each of the twenty-nine recorded occasions that he made an exchange at Centraal Station, Rahman was always a short distance away to monitor the transactions. When Gilligan was in Ireland during the handover, Baltus would ring him to confirm the rate of exchange he had received on the day.

Baltus also attended meetings with Thomas Gorst, his wife Mariette, Rahman, and John and Geraldine Gilligan. On one occasion the Gilligans brought their little grandchild with them. The Gorsts regularly brought parcels of money, supplied by the gang, similar to the one seized at Holyhead Port and gave them to Baltus for changing.

Baltus also helped Johnny Wildhagen pack shipments of hashish into wooden and cardboard boxes at Rahman's offices in The Hague. The boxes were lined with polystyrene, the drugs placed inside and expanding foam pumped in around them. Baltus then drew up shipping documents using one of his bogus companies and delivered the goods for transportation to Cork.

On 16 June 1995 Baltus attended a meeting with Rahman, Wildhagen, Gilligan, Meredith and Havid, a major Moroccan drug trafficker. Havid had smuggled a shipment of hash into the Netherlands and the purpose of the meeting was to make a deal. The gangsters met in an upmarket restaurant for lunch. To the innocent observer it looked like a group of well-dressed businessmen discussing the markets over a bottle of Chablis. Rahman, acting as a broker for his client Gilligan, agreed to purchase 208 kilos of hash at £1,200 per kilo. He bought drugs from other traffickers further down the food chain whenever his own stocks were low. Another trafficker he regularly dealt with on Gilligan's behalf was a man referred to as the 'hash farmer'. This usually happened in times of peak demand. Following the meeting with Havid, Baltus packed the drugs in boxes and shipped them to Cork.

From their first dealings Rahman was also supplying the gang with weapons. In the rapidly changing underworld a godfather's strength was judged by the firepower he possessed – and if he had the people to use it.

Through Johnny Wildhagen, Rahman supplied Gilligan with an awesome array of weaponry including Agram 2000 machine pistols, Sten sub-machine guns, fitted with silencers, automatic pistols, revolvers and ammunition. The arms were packed by Baltus with consignments of drugs between March 1995 and January 1996.

Rahman would hide the weapons in the ceiling of one of his offices. On 9 March 1995 Rahman sent Baltus to meet a criminal referred to as 'Koos'. He handed Baltus a carrier bag, which Baltus placed in the boot of a Mercedes car belonging to Rahman. As he drove around the corner, he was stopped by armed police who were waiting for him.

Baltus was arrested when they found an Agram 2000 in the bag. The gun was intended for the Gilligan gang. Baltus was later released pending an investigation and his arrest did not compromise the operation. Rahman continued sending guns to Dublin.

Charlie Bowden, who had now become the gang's armourer, cleaned, oiled and wrapped the weapons in cloth before they were hidden away. One shipment in January 1996 included a gleaming new .357 Magnum Colt Python revolver, the most powerful handgun in the world.

The ex-soldier carefully cleaned the weapon. He wrapped it up and put it in a plastic Tupperware box before hiding it with the gang's other weapons in a grave in the Jewish cemetery at Oldcourt Road in Tallaght.

The next time it was unearthed from its burial chamber the weapon would be used with deadly effect and with far-reaching consequences for its owner – John Gilligan.

———

CHAPTER TWELVE

THE INQUISITIVE CRIME JOURNALIST

When John Gilligan was released from prison and starting his new career as a drug baron, Veronica Guerin was making her mark on the world of journalism. Although from totally different worlds and backgrounds, their lives were destined to collide with tragic consequences.

In November 1993 Guerin won universal admiration with a front-page scoop in the *Sunday Tribune*. It was an exclusive series of interviews with Bishop Eamon Casey. The one-time celebrity bishop had gone into hiding in 1992 when it was revealed that he had fathered a child from an affair with an American woman called Annie Murphy. The Catholic Church was seriously embarrassed by the controversy and, in order to cover its tracks, Casey was spirited away to work as a parish priest in a secluded community in Ecuador. There, they thought, no one would find the controversial bishop and the whole embarrassing situation could be forgotten. But then Guerin got on the case.

She spent almost a year pursuing the story and eventually discovered where Casey was hiding. She flew to Quito in Ecuador at her own expense to doorstep the shamed cleric. Guerin spent several hours discussing the story with him and eventually persuaded him to give his first interview about the affair. The Casey story put Veronica on the map of Dublin journalism and the *Sunday Tribune* had a surge in sales.

Veronica's tenacity and dogged determination were key characteristics which got her some of the best stories. She was a natural investigative reporter who loved the sheer buzz that comes from breaking the big story.

Born in Dublin in 1958, Veronica was the second youngest of three girls and two boys. The family lived in the Dublin suburb of Artane. Her father, Christopher, an ardent Fianna Fáil supporter, was an accountant. Her mother, Bernie, was from Donegal. The Guerin children had a happy childhood.

Her siblings would later recall how Veronica was strong-willed and full of life. She was a passionate sportswoman and a life-long, fanatical Manchester United fan. As a pupil in the Holy Faith Convent in Killester she played football and represented Ireland internationally. She also played several times for the Irish national basketball team.

Like the rest of her family, she was a staunch Fianna Fáil supporter and Charles Haughey, the controversial party leader at the time, was her hero. Together with her brother Jimmy, she joined Ógra Fianna Fáil, an organization for young party supporters, and canvassed for Haughey during elections. In 1982 Haughey rewarded her loyalty by appointing her to the board of the National Institute for Higher Education, now Dublin City University (DCU). The twenty-four-year-old was the youngest person ever to serve on the board.

When she married builder Graham Turley in September 1985, the nuptials were attended by Haughey and his family. Graham and Veronica spent part of their honeymoon on Inishvickillane, Haughey's island retreat off the Kerry coast. The couple had one child, a son, Cathal.

Before settling on journalism Guerin had studied to be an accountant and worked in public relations and other business ventures.

She joined the *Sunday Business Post* in 1990 and her first major story was an investigation into the Aer Lingus holidays company. She left the *Post* in 1993 to work freelance for the *Sunday Tribune*. Early in 1994 she moved to work at the *Sunday Independent*, where her career took off.

Veronica was fascinated by crime and began writing about the complex world of Ireland's gangland. During the summer of 1994 she approached John Traynor and nurtured him as a source. The smooth-talking con man, who was making a fortune as part of Gilligan's organization, was intrigued by the gutsy female reporter. Always the opportunist, Traynor saw an advantage in having a journalist on his side. He could dish the dirt on his enemies and keep himself out of print.

In the weeks following Martin Cahill's murder Veronica produced a series of sensational exclusives which had been provided by Traynor. One concerned the General's tangled love life with his wife and her sister. Guerin also penned a number of speculative stories about who had actually shot Martin Cahill, pointing the finger at Gerry Hutch, the Monk. The journalist was then tipped off that she was under threat from the enigmatic crime boss, which she also published on the front page.

But the truth was that while Hutch was seriously angered by being implicated in a crime that he had nothing to do with, he was not in the business of harassing journalists. He had no intention of attacking Veronica Guerin. As an Ordinary Decent Criminal he accepted reporters, viewing them as an occupational hazard, like the police.

Then things took a dramatic turn. On 7 October a shot was fired through the front room window of the reporter's home in north County Dublin. It was clearly a warning for the journalist to back off. This was the first time that a journalist in the Irish Republic had been targeted in such a way. The shooter was never identified.

It turned out that the man who was pulling all the strings in the unfolding drama was the arch manipulator, John Traynor. In his unofficial role as a police informant the Coach had told them that the Monk was considering retaliation, omitting to reveal that he was the source of the story. He also tipped off Veronica about the bogus threat which was how it ended up in the newspaper.

Traynor's phoney narrative implicating Hutch diverted the attentions of some of the General's remaining lieutenants who suspected he'd had something to do with Cahill's killing. And if it led to a gang war then so be it. Traynor survived as a double agent by creating confusion and chaos – it was what he did best.

The shooting at Veronica's home was deliberately timed by Traynor so that the finger of suspicion automatically landed on the Monk. But the investigation couldn't find enough evidence to arrest Hutch for questioning. The detectives on the ground also were convinced that Hutch wasn't responsible – it just wasn't his style.

The shooting served another purpose for its author. It was intended to convince Cahill's family that he wasn't the source of the salacious love triangle story and had taken action to warn the journalist off.

The warning did nothing to dampen Veronica's enthusiasm for the job. In January 1995 Gerry Hutch pulled off a spectacular €5.55 million robbery from the Brinks-Allied cash-holding centre in north Dublin. The heist, the biggest cash robbery in Irish criminal history, had been meticulously planned and executed with military precision.

Ironically, the robbery took place less than a mile from Veronica's home. The government and gardaí were embarrassed when the *Irish Independent* ran a story revealing that the police had been watching the Monk's gang in anticipation that a major robbery was being planned but had failed to stop it.

On the following Sunday, 29 January, Veronica added fuel to the fire when she exposed the fact that Hutch had availed of a tax amnesty for his robbed cash a few years earlier. Veronica was upsetting the organized crime bosses again and providing Traynor with another opportunity.

Shortly before 7 p.m. on the following evening Veronica heard a knock on her front door. Her husband and son were out and she was getting ready to go to a *Sunday Independent* staff party. When she answered the door a man wearing a motorcycle helmet and brandishing a gun pushed her back inside the house, knocking her to the floor.

He pointed the gun at Veronica's head and then lowered the weapon. He shot her in the thigh, narrowly missing a major artery. Veronica was hospitalized and underwent emergency surgery. Doctors said she was lucky to be alive. She made a full recovery and courageously vowed to continue her work despite the attack.

The incident was a chilling warning from the criminal underworld that they were becoming more reckless. The day after the shooting detectives found a reconditioned .45 revolver, a pair of shoes and a jacket in a field close to Veronica's home – the shooter had abandoned them when he got stuck in the mud making his escape. It was suspected that the weapon was from a consignment of seized firearms the General had stolen from a garda storage depot in the 1980s.

Security was beefed up around the Guerin home and armed gardaí were assigned to protect her. But Veronica asked that the protection be lifted because it interfered with her work, making it hard to meet sources.

As Traynor had hoped, the gardaí initially suspected the Monk of carrying out the near-fatal attack. Just twenty-four hours earlier she had published a story about his tax affairs which brought even more media scrutiny and had politicians demanding that revenue inspectors should subject him to a full investigation. But detectives eliminated Hutch from their enquiries. They had seen through the ruse. The finger of suspicion fell on the Coach.

Traynor was arrested and questioned about the incident but there was no evidence linking him with the crime. He had, as the police expected, a rock-solid alibi for the evening of the shooting. Detectives drew a blank as the usually reliable criminal informants had no information to give. No one knew who had been involved.

Over a year later, in March 1996, Veronica interviewed the Monk in the kitchen of her home. He had agreed to do the story because he claimed he had been wrongly accused of drug dealing and of being involved in her shooting. Hutch was also impressed by Veronica's courage. After she was released from hospital she had personally delivered letters to Hutch's home demanding to know if he had been responsible. She was still determined to get to the bottom of her own story.

Veronica subsequently published an article on 31 March based on the interview:

> The Monk was immediately identified by gardaí and the media as the man responsible for both crimes. He denies both and, although I am still convinced he was responsible for the Brinks-Allied raid, I know he was not connected to my own shooting.

Even though Veronica was aware of the suspicions that Traynor had organized the shooting she inexplicably remained in regular contact with him. Her reasons for this remain a mystery, although it cannot be ruled out that the con man convinced her of his innocence. He was more than capable of doing so.

In May 1995 Veronica warned this writer to be careful with Traynor, commenting: 'He is a dangerous, two-faced bastard. He would have no problem setting you up.' Her warning was to prove tragically prophetic.

During the summer of 1995, as his drug business continued to boom, Gilligan was being referred to in police and underworld circles as a new, big-league godfather. But he continued to run a secure hermetically sealed operation and there was no hard information or leads on where to start looking for evidence against him. Instead garda management was focused on the criminal organizations being run by George 'the Penguin' Mitchell and Gerry Hutch.

Veronica Guerin, however, had John Joseph Gilligan in her sights. A police contact had told her about Gilligan's unexplained new-found wealth. The cop was typically frustrated by the lack of resources and legislation to enable him to take on the new crime boss. Traynor also piqued her interest about Gilligan. He famously told Veronica: 'You think I'm big...he's fucking huge.'

In August 1995 Traynor told this writer that Veronica was 'chasing' a story about Gilligan. She had asked him to introduce her to the 'little man'. Traynor said he had advised against it. Around the same time, I had featured Gilligan in an investigation in the *Sunday World* about the new bosses of gangland. The article revealed that Gilligan was heavily involved in the hashish and ecstasy trade. It also gave specific details of how he had illegally imported a number of machine guns with the drug shipments.

Traynor had provided the information, which ultimately proved accurate. With the benefit of hindsight, it is hard to understand the Coach's motivation. For legal reasons Gilligan wasn't named in the story and his eyes were blacked out in the garda mugshot.

Traynor said Gilligan had 'gone ballistic' over the story and warned me not to write about him in the future, cautioning: 'He is a very dangerous man. He will come after you and your family.' Traynor said he didn't want to give me any more information on Gilligan but he was happy to share secrets about the activities of criminals he did not like. George 'the Penguin' Mitchell and Martin Foley, 'the Viper', were his two pet hates. 'Dirty filthy cunts,' he called them.

Veronica was not giving up on Gilligan. On 7 September she sent a letter to him at Jessbrook, requesting an interview. In the letter Guerin wrote that she wanted to talk to him about his sudden success and the source of his wealth. Gilligan didn't respond.

A week later, on Thursday 14 September, Guerin decided to call on Gilligan in person and put her questions to him directly. She left Dublin around 8 a.m. and drove to Mucklon, County Kildare.

Around the same time, Dinny Meredith was catching the early morning flight to Amsterdam clutching a briefcase with £156,100 (€307,000) of Gilligan's cash, which was due to be exchanged routinely by Baltus in Centraal Station.

Guerin followed the signs for Jessbrook Equestrian Centre, which Gilligan had erected without council permission. She arrived at 8.50 a.m. and drove up to the centre, which was already open. She was stunned by the size of the place.

Guerin asked a woman in reception if 'Mr Gilligan' was around. The woman told Veronica that she could get him at his private residence. She was directed to call to a different gate.

At the main gate to Gilligan's house Guerin pressed the intercom button and looked up at the security camera overhead, so she could be seen. The electronic gates opened and she waited to see if someone would come to meet her. When nothing happened, she drove up to the house. The little man's jeep was parked outside.

Veronica was impressed with the splendour of Gilligan's country mansion. Inside, he was watching her on the security monitors. He already knew that she was making enquiries about him. Gilligan had warned Traynor to get her off his back or he would deal with her himself. His blood was boiling at her temerity in turning up unannounced at his family home.

A short-tempered brutal bully at the best of times, that morning 'the little man' had a hangover. The previous night the family had held a boozy party to celebrate Darren's twentieth birthday. But it ended badly when Geraldine confronted Gilligan about his mistress, Carol Rooney, and a flaming row ensued. Gilligan beat up his wife as he had often done in the past.

Unsuspectingly Veronica got out of her car and knocked on the front door. Gilligan watched her on a camera which followed her every move. He shouted at his wife to answer the door but she refused. He had given her a black eye and she wasn't facing the world with that.

Still wearing his silk dressing gown, he stormed out to the door to see off this latest irritant in his life. He opened the door and snapped: 'Yeah?'

'Mr Gilligan?' she asked.

'That's right,' he fired back.

Veronica explained who she was and said she wanted to ask him some questions about the source of his wealth and the equestrian centre. Gilligan lost his temper and lunged at her. He grabbed the journalist, punching her about the head and face with his fists.

He screamed at her as he did so. 'If you write anything about me I'll fucking kill you, your husband, your fucking son, your family, everybody belonging to you, even your fucking neighbours!' Gilligan fulminated in a mist of spittle.

Later Veronica told gardaí that Gilligan seemed to be physically carrying her towards her car. He pushed her onto the bonnet, still pummelling her with his fists in the head and body. She was terrified and subsequently said that she thought Gilligan was going to kill her.

When he let her go, she slid onto the ground beside her car. Crying and trembling with fear, she struggled to get to her feet. 'Get the fuck out of here! Get off my fucking property!' Gilligan raged.

As she opened the door of her car, Gilligan grabbed her again and shoved her violently into the driver's seat. He continued spitting out threats that he would murder her and everyone belonging to her if she wrote anything about him. Veronica was fumbling with her car keys in the panic to get away from the demonic madman who was screaming obscenities.

Gilligan reached into the car and grabbed her again by the neck. 'Have you a fucking mic? Where's the fucking wire?' he demanded. Gilligan tore open Veronica's shirt and ripped her jacket. 'No, I have nothing,' she cried. 'I'll kill you and your whole fucking family if you write anything about me,' Gilligan continued as he slammed the car door shut. 'Now get the fuck out of here!'

Veronica drove away at speed as Gilligan loomed in her rear view, still fuming. She could barely focus on the road through tears of terror and pain and got lost on her way back to Enfield. Her upper body and head were aching from the brutal attack. When she gathered her thoughts, she phoned a number of garda friends.

One of them was Deputy Commissioner Pat Byrne. When Byrne answered his mobile phone he could only hear sobbing. Eventually Veronica composed herself enough to speak. 'He's...he's after beating me up...he threatened to kill me...he beat me black and blue,' she told the man who less than twelve months later would be waging war against John Gilligan.

Later she went to her doctor who diagnosed shock and extensive bruising. She was advised to rest. Veronica called to see her mother Bernie. In the hallway of her mother's home she collapsed on the stairs and sobbed.

Pat Byrne had already mobilized the police and ordered that Guerin be given full-time protection while the assault was being investigated. After the incident Gilligan got dressed and went to see Traynor. He was still in a blood-curdling rage and said that he was going to have 'that interfering bitch done once and for all'.

Traynor tried to pacify his foul-tempered partner. His sense of feral self-preservation told him that if Gilligan escalated the situation so publicly then he too would be caught up in the slipstream of unwanted police and media attention. Beating someone up and threatening them was not as effective as sending a gunman in the dark of night. Gilligan decided to lie low for a while and took refuge with Carol Rooney in Leixlip.

In subsequent statements to the police Rooney recalled how that day Gilligan was in such a rage that it scared her. It was the first time in the few months she had been with him that she saw the real John Gilligan. She told the cops that he was 'going mad that a woman was trying to intimidate him and his family'. She said Gilligan ranted:

> No one messes with my family or my business. Something's going to be done about her, she's not getting away with this. She's going to ruin Jessbrook.

Rooney said that from that day John Gilligan became obsessed with Veronica Guerin.

The following morning solicitors for the *Sunday Independent* contacted barrister Felix McEnroy requesting that he meet with Veronica to discuss the assault.

It was just before 1 p.m. when Veronica called to McEnroy's office. She was still shaken and had bruises and swelling around her face. As they were talking, Traynor called Veronica and spoke to her about the assault. He was being conciliatory, but Gilligan, who was standing beside him in the safe house, snatched the phone and repeated his previous threats. Veronica hung up.

About five minutes later Gilligan rang Veronica's mobile phone again. This time McEnroy listened to the call. Gilligan identified himself and, in an aggressive tone, told her that he and Geraldine were separated and that 'all the property is in her name'. Then his voice became clear, controlled and menacing:

> If you do one thing on me, or write about me, I am going to kidnap your son and ride him. I am going to shoot you. Do you understand what I am saying? I am going to kidnap your fucking son and ride him, and I am going to fucking shoot you. I will kill you.

McEnroy was shocked by the venom in Gilligan's voice. He immediately told Veronica to cut off the conversation and advised her to make a statement about the assault and the threats to the police. In the meantime it became clear that Gilligan's attack on the journalist was causing panic in his own ranks.

Later that evening Geraldine Gilligan called Veronica. She asked her if she was 'Miss Guerin' and then continued:

> This is Geraldine Gilligan. I was told that you are doing an article about my place. Me and my husband are separated, and I am glad that we are separated. Everything is in my name. I just want you to know that.

Geraldine was clearly worried that publicity about her husband would damage her equestrian business.

Veronica told her that she could not discuss the matter any further and hung up. But the mob wasn't giving up. Later Traynor called Veronica exhorting her not to have anything more to do with Gilligan:

> I have told you before that he is a very dangerous man. He means what he says. Let it sit and I'll calm him down if you leave him alone.

However, Veronica ignored Gilligan's henchman and that evening gave a statement about the incident to Detective Inspector Tom Gallagher from Coolock garda station. Her statement concluded:

> I am fearful for my life and for the safety of my family. I believe that the threats made to me by John Gilligan were meant to put me in fear in relation to my personal safety and that of the members of my family. I am bruised around my upper body and head. I have serious bruising and swelling in the area of my left eye and my injuries are painful.

The *Sunday Independent* decided to run a story about the assault. On Saturday 16 September, the journalist who was writing the story phoned Gilligan to obtain a quote about the incident. The nasty little godfather was only too happy to oblige. 'If anyone interferes with me or my fucking family, I'll fucking kill you. I'll find out who you are and I'll kill you, me old flower,' Gilligan fumed.

His attack on the journalist, who was a household name, attracted a lot of media attention which infuriated Gilligan who blamed everyone but himself. Another layer of anonymity had been blown as the media spotlight turned on him. His insouciance, combined with a lack of self-awareness or self-control, prevented Gilligan from being able to see how much trouble he was creating for himself. In his head he was untouchable and he would trample on anyone who got in his way.

The investigating detectives decided to question Gilligan about the incident but when they went looking for him he had gone to ground. He stayed at the Leixlip house until 25 September when he flew to Amsterdam with Carol Rooney. Dinny Meredith, who was booked on the early morning flight, offloaded himself at the last minute and Gilligan took his seat.

The mob boss stayed in the Netherlands for a number of weeks in the hope that the police at home would forget about the assault. He ordered Traynor to convince Guerin to drop her assault charges against him. Within a week of the incident this writer met with Traynor to discuss what had happened. He maintained:

> I told her [Veronica] not to fuck around with that man and do you see what happened? The man is mad. He feels like he is defending his family and if anyone crosses that line they will end up dead. When Veronica arrived on his doorstep at Jessbrook it drove him ballistic. She was intruding on his part of the world. No one ever goes near the place except if he is invited and I mean that.

He said he had conveyed this to Veronica but gave the impression that they had fallen out over Gilligan. I later spoke to Veronica about the attack. She said it had been more terrifying than when she was shot. She was happy about the way the police were handling the case, but she again warned me to be careful with Traynor.

A few months later Traynor claimed that the assault had been 'sorted'. He said that he had offered Veronica over £100,000 (€200,000) in cash on Gilligan's behalf to drop the charges. But the truth was that the courageous journalist had rejected the offer and was determined that Factory John would face justice for the brutal attack.

Gilligan blamed Traynor for his predicament – if he hadn't been shooting off his mouth to Guerin in the first place she would never have come looking for him. In the weeks that followed Traynor contacted his garda handler to see was there anything Gilligan could 'offer' to get himself out of the 'Guerin hassle'.

The detective advised Traynor to urge Gilligan to give himself up and face the music. The Coach replied that the little man was determined not to go back to prison. On 10 November 1995 Gilligan arranged to meet with Detective Inspector Tom Gallagher and Chief Superintendent Jim McHugh. He was arrested and brought to Santry garda station for questioning.

Gilligan denied that he had assaulted Veronica and told the detectives that he thought he must have frightened her because of the way she 'flew down the driveway'. 'I never assaulted a woman and never will,' Gilligan lied. He also denied that he had torn her clothes.

'On the advice of my solicitor,' he continued confidently, 'I have already been tried and convicted by the *Sunday Independent*. I have nothing to say.' He repeated the same mantra in response to most of the questions he was asked. Gilligan was anxious, however, to point out that he and Geraldine were 'separated'. 'It was a happy separation...she got everything.' He smiled.

A file on the case was prepared for the Director of Public Prosecutions. Gilligan was charged with two offences, unlawful assault and causing criminal damage to Veronica's clothing. If convicted in the District Court, Gilligan was facing at least a year in jail.

Such an enforced absence at this critical time would cause untold disruption to his burgeoning evil empire. He was determined not to go back behind bars. He had grown too big and powerful to be brought down by a woman.

On the morning Veronica drove to Gilligan's house, she also put herself in the sights of the rest of the dangerous mob. His forced leave of absence would have worrying consequences for the gang's all-important bottom line.

Tony Hickey, who would later lead the investigation into the murder of Veronica Guerin, said the motive was clear-cut:

> Gilligan had a history throughout his criminal career of intimidating witnesses and he threatened Veronica with dire consequences if she pressed charges against him. If he was out of the picture and in prison for twelve months then his international contacts would dry up. That was the reason for her murder. It was pure greed.

Each month, week and day that Gilligan was inactive in the 'business' would cost them all obscene amounts of money. He was the pivot for the entire operation. Without his presence the gang was in trouble. Gilligan's cocky lieutenants agreed with their boss that there was only one option open to them: the meddling journalist had to be silenced – permanently.

CHAPTER THIRTEEN

PARADISE LOST

'This is a lovely bleeding place for a wedding, wha'? It's fucking beautiful it is,' John Gilligan said in his thick Dublin brogue. It was March 1996 and the gang was living the high life on St Lucia.

The Gilligans had travelled to the Caribbean paradise island for the wedding of Brian Meehan's sister, Leslie, to an electrical engineer with no connection to gangland. Meehan's parents, Kevin and Frances, and his siblings, Brad and Vanessa, were also there. Peter Mitchell, Meenor, their two girlfriends, Fiona and Sonia Walsh, and Paul Ward, made up the party of fourteen. Meehan's sister Vanessa was living with Ward.

The group stayed at the Sandals luxury resort for a week, swilling champagne, snorting cocaine, eating fine food and lounging about the pool. The Gilligans had paid the equivalent of €14,000 in cash for the week and Brian Meehan had paid for his family's trip. It cost him almost €60,000.

The idyllic wedding was recorded on a home movie, with Brian Meehan as the best man, looking awkward and uncomfortable in his black tuxedo.

'He [Meehan] looks great. I dressed him meself. Doesn't he look great? I got him out of all those rave clothes,' Gilligan joked on camera.

Peter Mitchell's unmistakable voice causes some raised eyebrows from the staff as he shouts: 'I have to zoom in on the bouncer [Meehan]. You'll get a job at home as a bouncer. Ya dirty fuck, ya.'

The wedding party's vulgar, raucous behaviour was incongruous in such a beautiful setting. Behind the din, the camera showed an idyllic scene. As Meehan was filmed signing the wedding register, Mitchell guffaws: 'I hope that's not a fuckin' statement for the fuckin' police.'

Later the video shows Meehan, Ward and Mitchell jumping into the pool, laughing and shouting 'This one's for Veronica Guerin. Crime doesn't pay, eh?'

The crime reporter was never far from their drink- and drug-addled minds. Gilligan's young hoods joked with him about the impending assault charge, calling him 'John Gotti' after the infamous New York Italian-American Mafia boss. Nicknamed the Teflon Don when he was acquitted in three high-profile trials with the help of intimidation and jury tampering, Gotti was Gilligan's hero and role model.

A few years later in the Special Criminal Court Paul Ward described the scene:

> The woman's [Guerin's] name was brought up and they [Mitchell and Meehan] were laughing at Gilligan. He was convinced he would get off the charge. It was funny that they were slagging Gilligan and winding him up. They were slagging him about what happened. He was laughing back and saying he didn't think he would go to jail [for the assault].

Throughout the tapes Gilligan was constantly by Geraldine's side. They seemed to be the perfect loving couple and certainly did not behave as if they were separated or that he beat her.

In another video the wedding group are sitting round a hotel lounge drinking and singing songs. Gilligan sang part of 'The Wild Rover' before forgetting the lines. Then Brad Meehan, Brian's drug-addicted criminal brother, began to sing an old country song. The lyrics could have been written with Gilligan and his henchmen in mind: 'I've got everything a man could ever need.'

Gilligan clapped as the song ended, looking smug and confident in the bosom of his mob family, like a miniature Don Corleone.

But the 'Guerin problem' was a constant irritation. Since she had rejected his offer of compensation Gilligan had hatched a preposterous plan. He considered kidnapping Gavin O'Reilly, the son of Tony O'Reilly, the multi-millionaire proprietor of the Independent Group which owned the *Sunday Independent*. Gilligan discussed the plan with Traynor who, along with Meehan, had helped organize the Lacey kidnapping. He thought their lackeys in the INLA could be prevailed upon to help abduct Gavin O'Reilly and take him to a safe house. Gilligan wanted the executive to be threatened and terrorized, but not harmed. Before his release he would be instructed to convince Veronica to drop the charges or the O'Reilly family would be 'hit' again. He would be warned not to report the matter to the police.

Traynor had eventually convinced Gilligan that it was not a wise course of action. Then the double agent informed his contact in the Serious Crime Squad of the plot. Traynor wanted cover just in case Gilligan went ahead with it and he also wanted some credit points as a valuable informant. An armed surveillance squad was placed at a discreet distance around O'Reilly until the authorities were satisfied that the executive was not being watched and that the kidnapping plans had been abandoned, which Traynor, the puppet master, duly confirmed.

As they worked on their suntans in St Lucia the Guerin problem was the only downside. The gang's drugs empire was thriving. The distribution system organized by Charlie Bowden was working like a dream and their Dutch suppliers were efficient and giving value for money. They had a formidable arsenal of firearms. Gilligan and his gang were dangerous men to cross.

The trip provided a welcome break from the hassle of the drugs world for Brian Meehan, Mitchell and Ward. In February 1996 they had been involved in two incidents with underworld rivals in Dublin. The most dramatic was the attempted murder of Martin 'the Viper' Foley.

Forty-six-year-old Foley had become one of the gang's minor customers, buying a kilo or two of hash from Charlie Bowden most weeks. Traynor and Gilligan now hated their old associate. Foley and his best friend, Shavo Hogan, had been exerting pressure on Traynor for money they believed he and Cahill had received for some of the Beit paintings. Traynor, a born coward, began to fear a hit from Foley and Hogan. The Viper had a formidable reputation as an underworld hard man with thirty-seven convictions ranging from crimes of violence to road traffic offences. He was infamous as the criminal with nine lives, escaping from an attempted IRA abduction in 1984 and another assassination attempt in December 1995. Something had to be done

The Viper, an incorrigible gossip, had an extraordinary capacity for irritating people. As part of his campaign against Gilligan and his gang, he began spreading rumours that they were involved in heroin dealing. In January 1996 Brian Meehan had been called to a meeting with the IRA and questioned about the rumours. The Provos, who had taken money from the Gilligan gang before, said they could not turn a blind eye if they were selling smack. They told Meehan the information had come from Foley, who wasn't one of their favourite people. Meehan convinced the Provos that the gang was not involved in heroin. Later, at a gang meeting, he told Gilligan and the others what had happened. Gilligan and Meehan suggested they kill Foley, and everyone agreed.

On 29 January Meehan and Ward met Charlie Bowden by appointment at the car park of Bridget Burke's pub in Tallaght. The trio went to the Jewish cemetery on the nearby Oldcourt Road. Bowden and Meehan exhumed an Agram 2000 machine pistol and a .45 automatic handgun from a cache which had been interred two weeks earlier.

The Agram is a deadly, close-quarter street-fighting weapon manufactured in Croatia. Agram is the old name for the city now known as Zagreb. Its design was based on the mechanism of the German Heckler and Koch machine pistol, the MP5, which was, at the time, the preferred weapon of specialist police and army units throughout the world, and for professional assassins.

Meehan asked Bowden to show him how to use the weapon. The former corporal fitted the silencer to the Agram and put a plastic bag on a bush in a field at the back of the graveyard. Meehan fired the full magazine at the bag, hitting it only a few times. He also tried the handgun.

Happy that they were in working order, Bowden put the weapons in a black bag and brought them to the Greenmount lockup. On Thursday 1 February, Meehan was to meet Foley around 7 p.m. on the pretext of collecting drug money from him. In reality Meehan and Paul Ward intended ambushing the Viper.

At 6.55 p.m. Foley left his home on Cashel Avenue in Crumlin and reversed his car away from the house to turn onto Captain's Road. Meehan and Ward were waiting for him on the corner of Cashel Avenue in a stolen car. Foley, who was constantly on his guard, spotted them and paused for a moment. Ward, who was driving, pulled over on the road.

They jumped out and ran towards Foley's car. The two gangsters wearing balaclavas opened fire with the Agram and the pistol, peppering the car with bullets. Foley reversed up the road with the two shooters after him on foot. One of the bullets hit his finger. Foley abandoned the car and jumped across the side wall of a garden.

Meehan, still firing his machine pistol, ran after Foley. Ward had thrown the automatic pistol to Meehan as a backup weapon while he went back to the getaway car. Foley burst through the back door of a house and turned the lights off. 'Call the police! They're after me,' Foley yelled at the stunned occupants.

The family was terrified and ran to get out of the house. When they opened the front door, Meehan came racing towards them, wearing a balaclava and holding the automatic in both hands. 'Where's the fucker? Get out of the way!' he shouted.

They ran out into the street as Ward was reversing the getaway car towards them. The woman was screaming that someone was being murdered in her home. Ward shouted: 'Shut the fuck up! There's no one fuckin' goin' near youse!'

At the same time Foley raced upstairs as Meehan opened fire again, this time hitting his target once in the back. Other bullets went through a bathroom door. Foley jumped through a window, landing on an extension roof.

From there he jumped into the garden of the house next door. Meehan followed and fired more shots at Foley as he ran through several gardens in a desperate bid to escape. He burst through the back door of another house and bolted it. He ran through the house, locked the front door and phoned for the police and an ambulance.

Fortunately for the Viper, Meehan was a poor shot and had fired off the full magazine on the machine pistol. The .45 handgun had jammed so Meehan calmly walked out onto the street and into the car. Ward drove off and headed back to his house on Walkinstown Avenue.

Charlie Bowden, Mitchell and Shay Ward were waiting for them in Ward's house. They were listening to the police radio communications on a scanner. As soon as they heard reports of the gun attack, Shay Ward opened the garage at the back of the house. Meehan and Paul Ward arrived within seconds, high on adrenalin. Meehan was cursing about the weapon that had jammed. He said that he had hit Foley in the back and was wondering if he was dead.

But the Viper had survived yet again. Martin Foley would survive another two assassination bids in 2000 and 2008 in which he was shot and left for dead both times. His body is peppered with at least twenty-two bullet wounds, and he's lost the top of a finger and his spleen. No other gangster has survived so many murder bids. Foley rightly deserves the title of the mobster they couldn't kill.

Following the shooting Gilligan castigated his underboss for his poor shooting and advised him to get his eyes checked. In the months after the incident, the Viper discovered who had shot him and why. Amazingly, he and Meehan effectively kissed and made up. After that it was business as usual, and Meehan continued supplying Foley.

A week before the trip to St Lucia, Meehan and Mitchell had been arrested and questioned about another shooting incident, this time involving a drug dealer who worked for a notorious criminal, P. J. Judge, alias the Psycho, who controlled a large heroin-dealing racket and was one of the underworld's most feared killers.

On 28 February 1996 Meehan fired two shots outside a northside pub as a warning to Judge's dealer. He had begun selling drugs on Mitchell's turf and the encroachment rekindled an old dispute. Two years earlier the dealer had shot Fatso in the same pub, causing him minor injuries. Peace was restored on that first occasion when the dealer agreed to pay Mitchell substantial compensation. The incident was never reported to the police.

Following the second shooting, officers at Store Street station were tipped off that Judge and the dealer were planning to murder Meehan. The two criminals had obtained a high-powered motorbike and were carrying sawn-off shotguns, cruising the area looking for Meehan.

To avert a bloodbath, detectives raided the homes of the dealer, Judge, Meehan and Mitchell, searching for weapons. Nothing was found. The hoods were left under no illusion that the police had found out about their feud. They decided to postpone 'straightening out' the situation until they got back from St Lucia.

When Gilligan and his mob returned from the Caribbean, the violence continued. On 1 April Johnny Reddin, a drug dealer and underworld heavy, was sitting in the Blue Lion pub on Parnell Street in the city centre. The forty-two-year-old was then facing a charge of causing grievous bodily harm leading to the death of a teenager, Sean McNeill, in a north city nightclub. Reddin was also an associate of Paul Ward's and sold drugs for the Gilligan gang. As he sipped a pint at the counter, a man walked up to Reddin and produced a pistol. 'Here, Johnny, take it out of that,' he said, and then shot him once in the head. The gunman ran out the door and got away on a motorbike.

Gardaí later obtained intelligence which led them to believe that, with Gilligan's blessing, Dutchy Holland had carried out the Reddin hit because of the fatal assault. Underworld sources told officers that Paul Ward was 'very annoyed' about Reddin's murder. No one was ever charged with the offence.

The involvement of the Gilligan gang in a number of other murders only came to light after the mob was broken up. One of them concerned the 1995 execution in Cork of local crime boss Michael Crinnion. At the time Crinnion was involved in a feud with a rival drug trafficker, Michael Danser Ahern, who was a close business associate of Brian Meehan. It was claimed that Brian Meehan and another gang member did the hit as a favour to Ahern. It demonstrated how deeply the Mafia code of *omerta* (silence) ran in the Gilligan mob.

———

The gang members were growing ever more arrogant. Instead of keeping their heads down, they were openly flaunting their criminal success. On one occasion Gilligan and his young hoods were out on the town in an upmarket hotel on Dublin's southside. They regularly hired a suite and partied like rock stars, indulging in orgies of sex, drink and drugs with prostitutes hired for the event.

Gilligan and his pals were downstairs drinking at the bar being aggressive and flashing money about when a detective walked in for a drink. He had a bulge under his jacket and Meehan began abusing him for carrying his gun.

The policeman ignored the jibes and ordered a beer. As his glass stood on the counter, Gilligan took off his expensive gold Rolex watch and slid it in the direction of the cop.

The detective looked down at the watch and said nothing. Gilligan shouted at him: 'Here, take the fucking thing – that's worth more than you'll earn in a year.' His entourage cackled with laughter. The detective shoved the watch back up the counter and left.

The gang's contempt for the gardaí was unrelenting. A few days after the Reddin murder, Brian Meehan was arrested in the early hours of the morning by uniformed officers from the Bridewell garda station. He had been at Reddin's funeral and spent the day drinking and doing lines of coke. He was in a belligerent mood and up for a row when the cops stopped him on the street.

The officers took Meehan to the station for a drug search. On the way Meehan taunted a female officer, calling her a lesbian and telling her: 'You fancy my arse.' When her colleague told him to behave himself, Meehan threatened him. 'I will get you, your wife and family. You think you're a big man now, but you will not be so big the next time I meet you with a bally' [balaclava].

At the station Meehan was taken to a custody room for a strip search. In front of a male garda Meehan began handling his penis and asked the astonished officer: 'Do you like men with big cocks?' Meehan then began masturbating and turned around, grabbing his buttocks and exposing his anus. 'Maybe you fancy me arse instead,' he snarled and resumed masturbating.

'Do you want a repeat performance?' he asked before being told to put his clothes back on. Gardaí found over £600 (€1,200) in cash in Meehan's pockets, which they seized for forensic examination. Meehan told the officers to keep it, sneering:

Youse fuckers need it more than I do. Give it to the police benevolent fund. Youse are a bunch of fucking idiots working and paying tax. I earn more in a week than you earn in a month.

Then he turned his attention to the desk sergeant and called him a 'shite bucket'. He was charged with causing a breach of the peace and indecent behaviour. Meehan couldn't have cared less. However, he did care about the nickname he was subsequently given. He became known as Brian 'the Tosser' Meehan.

A few weeks later Meehan and Gilligan demonstrated just how confident they had become. They had been contacted by an underworld associate to help spring Thomas 'Bomber' Clarke from a prison van and were happy to oblige.

Bomber Clarke was a ruthless, violent criminal who specialized in armed robbery and was an old friend of Meehan and Ward's. He had also served time in Portlaoise Prison with Gilligan. At twenty-seven years of age he had notched up twenty-two convictions in Ireland. Clarke fled to England to avoid an armed robbery charge and lived in Leeds where he continued to rob banks. On 20 May 1994 Clarke was convicted at Leeds Crown Court on three counts of armed robbery and sentenced to nine years. In October 1995 he escaped from prison and returned to Ireland. That December he was tracked down and arrested in County Kerry. He was questioned about the murder of Christy Delaney, a former member of Gilligan's Factory Gang, but was never charged. Clarke was held in custody and subsequently convicted on the outstanding robbery charge and sentenced to five years' imprisonment. While in custody he was further charged with another building society heist and had to attend a number of remand hearings in the District Court in Dublin.

Gilligan and his gang had no problem doing Bomber a favour. After all, they were above the law and a daring escape would raise respect for them in criminal quarters. But the police received intelligence about the plot and the Emergency Response Unit shadowed the prison van ferrying Clarke between Portlaoise Prison and the District Court in Dublin. As a result, the operation was called off.

On 25 April 1996 Clarke was being transported for another remand hearing. Gilligan had given the go-ahead for Brian Meehan and other associates to spring Bomber on the way to court. Peter Mitchell was to provide a backup car for Clarke's getaway.

A garda driver and four prison officers accompanied Clarke in the prison van from Portlaoise. As it drove past the village of Rathcoole, on its way to Dublin, the three hoods followed the van in a stolen 5 series BMW. The van approached the junction of the Naas Road and Boot Road at Clondalkin, and the gang struck. This was the same location where Veronica Guerin would be shot two months later.

The BMW swerved into the van's path, blocking a possible escape. Two men jumped out of the car and ran to the prison van. One had bolt cutters and the other a handgun. While his partner broke the van window, the gunman ordered the prison officers to open Clarke's cuffs.

Bomber Clarke had been expecting the ambush and was poised to react. He climbed out through the broken window and jumped into the car which sped off. As a major manhunt began across the city, Clarke was brought to the safe house in Leixlip where his girlfriend was waiting to celebrate his liberty. The house was another example of how Gilligan had successfully insulated his organization. The entire gang had been around there for months but not a whisper had reached the ears of the police.

In her subsequent statements to gardaí Carol Rooney described how Gilligan arrived with Dutchy Holland shortly after Clarke. They dyed Clarke's hair and dressed him in a disguise while Gilligan organized for him to be smuggled out of the country in a container truck driven by one of the gang's many couriers.

In Amsterdam Johnny Wildhagen provided a safe house for Clarke, who came with a glowing reference from Gilligan. To impress his

Dutch partners he bragged about Clarke's violent CV and offered his services as a hit man to Rahman and Wildhagen.

Some time later Clarke was arrested by the Amsterdam police on suspicion of staking out houses for the purpose of carrying out 'burglaries'. But that was probably the last thing on Bomber's mind as he'd been caught near the home of one of Rahman's underworld rivals.

It also later emerged that in return for Gilligan's kindness, Clarke was to murder George 'the Penguin' Mitchell who was dividing his time between the Dam and Dublin. George Mitchell had become an important player in the international drugs market, although he was a lot more discreet than Gilligan and his 'Neanderthals'. If the Penguin was out of the way, the Gilligan gang could take over his substantial slice of the action, dramatically increasing the size of their own operation in Dublin. But Mitchell, who a year earlier had almost come to blows with Gerry Hutch, had a formidable group of hardened criminals around him, including a number of accomplished assassins.

In 1995 he had been involved in supporting one side of a deadly gangland feud between two south London crime families, the Brindles and the Daleys. In September of that year the Penguin's hit man, Mickey Boyle from Bray, County Wicklow, was shot and seriously injured by police seconds after he had shot Tony Brindle, outside his home in Rotherhithe, south-east London.

By the time Bomber Clarke was sprung from prison it's possible Gilligan saw an opportunity to take the Penguin out and have someone else blamed. In any event Mitchell was never touched.

Gangsters are capricious, unpredictable creatures at the best of times and Gilligan was no different. In a fit of temper the impulsive gangster might order the murder of a rival today and then drop the plot tomorrow. Outwardly Gilligan and Mitchell remained on friendly terms.

Exactly a year after his dramatic escape Bomber Clarke pleaded guilty to the additional armed robbery charge he had been facing before his escape. When that sentence was served he was then extradited to the UK to serve the remainder of his prison sentence in Leeds.

In the first four months of 1996, up to the time of Clarke's break out, the gang imported 3,247 kilos of hash. Gilligan and Traynor's cut was estimated to be worth €4.8 million, while the five gang members each made €254,000. Business was brisk for Gilligan and the money was flowing in so fast that the gangsters could barely cope.

Records from the Bureau de Change in Amsterdam showed that they had exchanged over £1 million (€1.9 million). But these figures did not take into account the revenue being earned from separate rackets Gilligan controlled, including smuggling guns, tobacco and drugs such as ecstasy and cocaine.

The gang had also become the single biggest supplier of cannabis and ecstasy to Northern Ireland. A young, Newry-based drug dealer, Brendan 'Speedy' Fegan, began buying up to 100 kilos per week from Meehan and the gang. Fegan was introduced to the mob by his boss Paddy Farrell, a veteran drug baron and associate of Gilligan and Tommy Coyle. Fegan supplied loyalist and republican paramilitary gangs with ecstasy, cocaine and hash.

As the Gilligan operation grew in scale and power, the gang needed to cover its tracks. They had so much money they could buy anything: guns, drugs, cars, houses and holidays. By the middle of 1996 they had also bought a hero cop.

John 'Buffalo' O'Neill was thirty-one years old when he met Paul 'Hippo' Ward and agreed to act as a secret agent for the Gilligan gang. Having a cop on the inside would be of immense use.

O'Neill, from Ballyfermot in Dublin, had known Paul Ward and Meehan growing up. Unlike them, however, he had opted for a life on the other side of the thin blue line and joined the gardaí in November 1985. The married father of three had spent his career so far as a uniformed officer attached to the Divisional Task Force based in Tallaght and Crumlin.

In 1990 he was awarded the Scott Medal for bravery, the highest accolade bestowed by An Garda Síochána. O'Neill, who was unarmed, had confronted and arrested an armed robber who pointed a shotgun at him. He was a model citizen.

O'Neill was the last person anyone would suspect of being corrupt. His superiors considered him to be a dedicated cop who, if anything, was seen as being over-enthusiastic and often physically excessive when confronting criminals. A keen GAA football player, he didn't drink, smoke or gamble. He was a dedicated family man. But the hero cop had a weakness – he was a spendthrift who was hopeless at handling his finances.

John O'Neill had always wanted to give his family everything that he hadn't had growing up in deprived circumstances. He bought a nice home for his family and lavishly furnished it. He extravagantly splashed out money, buying a four-wheel-drive jeep for himself and a new car for his wife's birthday. He bought his children expensive toys, including small motorbikes for his sons. But it was all done on a garda's basic wage.

The hapless hero soon found himself in debt to the tune of €200,000. Apart from a mortgage, he also had four Credit Union loans. When he paid his various loans each week from his garda pay he was left with about £10 (€20). Buffalo had worked as a part-time bouncer in a nightclub whose manager was a criminal associate of Hippo Ward, Mitchell and Meehan. O'Neill was desperate for cash and approached the manager to ask if he knew anyone who could loan him money. The manager was delighted to oblige and contacted Hippo Ward.

In December 1995 O'Neill collected £1,500 (€3,000) in cash from Ward in the car park of the Red Cow Inn on the western edge of

Dublin. Ward told his childhood friend that he might be wanted to help sort out the odd summons or warrant.

Shortly before Christmas, Ward gave O'Neill £1,000 (€2,000) in the car park of another pub. Rather than pay off some of his debts, O'Neill spent the cash on presents for Christmas. A month later Ward asked O'Neill to 'pull' (quash) two summonses for a criminal friend of his from Drimnagh, by taking them out of the list for hearing in court. O'Neill did what he was asked. In the meantime the former hero-turned-traitor was added to the payroll of other gangsters.

In May 1996 Ward paid him the equivalent of €3,900 for pulling two arrest warrants for an associate of the gang. O'Neill took the warrants from his station and showed them to Hippo, who paid him another €1,000. A short time later he pulled two arrest warrants for another gang associate from Ronanstown, south Dublin. O'Neill tore up the warrants in front of Ward, receiving the equivalent of €4,000. Ward also arranged for the Buffalo to 'find' 3 kilos of cannabis to make him look good with his bosses. The corrupt cop later had summonses for motoring offences pulled for Paul Ward, Vanessa Meehan and Brian Meehan.

O'Neill was in above his head and sinking fast in the gangland swamp. Ward and the other members of the gang liked to brag that they had now bought their very own policeman. Gilligan loved the idea but he steered clear of meeting O'Neill. A bent cop was an invaluable asset for a drugs gang.

Nothing could touch Gilligan and his gang.

———

CHAPTER FOURTEEN

UNWANTED ATTENTION

Clean-cut Russell John Patrick Warren did what he was told. He was not a career criminal and was easily manipulated. Warren had an industrial cleaning company which cleaned out newly built properties for construction firms in preparation for sale. One builder recalled: 'He was the most useless man I ever had on a site. He was a nice bloke but you always had to go over his work a second time.'

Warren, a friend of Gilligan's current bagman Derek Baker, was also a 'quick buck' merchant. He had no qualms about making money dishonestly, as long as he didn't have to dirty his hands with a serious crime. Warren had been making money from the smuggled cigarettes racket which was one of Gilligan's peripheral activities. He was an ideal bagman for the mob boss. Baker introduced his friend to Gilligan as his potential replacement. At the time Baker had set up an on-course bookie business and told Gilligan he was concentrating on that. The truth was that Baker was scared of his boss and how 'heavy' he had become. He could see how the money and power had turned the little man into a dangerous monster. Years later Baker told this writer:

> I got suspicious about the drugs when the volumes of money
> I was collecting went through the roof. All of a sudden it went

from 30 or 40 grand to £120,000 and £180,000. That's when I
got out. I was a fucking eejit to get involved with him [Gilligan].
It has ruined my life. I knew nothing about Veronica Guerin and
I had distanced myself from Gilligan.

Baker was doing his old friend Warren no favours. Warren was no
match for a bully like Gilligan and once inside the organization, he
was too terrified to contemplate leaving. The only way out was in a
body bag.

Dinny Meredith had also become concerned at the how big the
operation had become. He opted out of delivering and laundering
cash for Gilligan. He later disingenuously claimed that he had received
a visit from the IRA warning him about his relationship with Factory
John. He also claimed that he had fallen out with Gilligan. In any
event Gilligan now needed a new bagman who was reliable, did what
he was told and kept his mouth shut.

At first Baker asked Warren to count bags of cash which he claimed
were the proceeds of Gilligan's betting and cigarette smuggling
activities. After some time counting and sorting the cash, Baker asked
Warren to fly to the Netherlands to deliver the money to Gilligan.
He would be paid the equivalent of €1,000 per trip.

Warren's first flight to the Netherlands was on 11 January 1996. In
Schiphol Airport he handed over a package to Gilligan and Martin
Baltus and then caught the return flight to Dublin. Eventually
Warren also exchanged bags of cash at the Bureau de Change in
Centraal Station, which by then had been used to exchange at least
£7 million (€14 million) for the gang. In twenty-two trips over the
next seven months Warren personally exchanged another £2.2 million
(€4.3 million). Records showed that the new bagman exchanged a
further £1.7 million (€3.3 million) while in the company of two
gang members. Warren had quickly become an essential cog in the
gang's operation.

The previous year Gilligan's success had brought bad luck down on Simon Rahman's organization. Early in 1995 police in Antwerp, Belgium, had received an investigation report from their money-laundering unit concerning Thomas and Mariette Gorst. The report detailed five suspect transactions at the KB Securities bank in Antwerp by Mariette Gorst between November 1994 and January 1995. Large amounts of Irish currency had been exchanged for Belgian francs on behalf of Gilligan. The police began to investigate.

On 5 October 1995 Thomas Gorst and his wife Mariette were arrested at their home in Berchem by officers from the Belgian Federal Police under Belgian money laundering laws. During questioning about the transactions, Mariette Gorst said that she had changed the money for a professional Irish gambler called 'John Gillon':

> I select a bureau de change. I wait outside the door and somebody approaches me to give me money to change. Sometimes it's a woman, other times it's a man. I presume that Gillon gave that person a description of me. The money is in a bag. Without knowing how much I am taking inside I go into the bureau de change and change the money into Belgian francs. The first time I don't know what kind of currency I was changing. After changing it, I gave the money back to the person who gave it to me. After receiving the money that person vanished. I don't know where. I can't put a name to that person. When you [the police] ask me why Gillon was unable to do it himself, my answer was that he was short of time. Gillon needed money here for gambling, as a professional gambler. I also heard he wanted to buy a golf course. The money originated in casinos and from Gillon's dealing in horses.

Thomas Gorst endorsed his wife's lies and described 'Gillon' as a stud-farm owner in Ireland. The international drug trafficker told his interrogators:

> I have nothing to do with drug trafficking or money laundering. Gillon said he would have exchanged the money himself but it was a better rate for a Belgian national to do it. I am sure the money was for a legitimate purpose. I have never seen Gillon since January of 1995.

In the same interview he implied that his wife and Gilligan had been having an affair:

> I first met Gillon in a bar in Antwerp with Mariette. I know that John and Mariette saw each other four or five times after that. To what extent this was a friendly relationship or something more I can't tell you.

In early December the Belgian detectives contacted the gardaí in Dublin requesting assistance in identifying a 'John Gillon or McGillon'. On 7 December Garda Headquarters replied:

> Based on details supplied by you there is no such person known to our records. There is a person named Gilligan who has numerous convictions for larceny and burglary offences. He is considered dangerous. In order to confirm identity can you supply a set of fingerprints of the subject?

But the Belgians didn't have Gillon's fingerprints. Gilligan had no idea how close he came to drawing heat on himself. There was no more follow-up by the Irish police. The Belgian police, however, charged the Gorsts with money laundering. Two years later, on 17 January 1997, they were both given six-month prison sentences for the offences.

Rahman's other henchman, Martin Baltus, had been cleared of the firearms charge from his arrest in March 1995. The State could not prove he had prior knowledge that the bag he had been given on that date contained the Agram machine pistol. He continued to work for Rahman and in April 1996 took delivery of a bag containing £30,000 (€60,000) from Russell Warren. It was the last recorded occasion that Baltus exchanged money for the Gilligan gang. Around the same time, Gilligan began supplying Rahman with a combination of both forged and genuine Irish driving licences and passports. He also had counterfeit dollars.

Forged documents are the stock-in-trade of international drug trafficking, and an Irish passport is particularly popular. It tends to arouse less curiosity at the point of entry in most countries, especially the drug-producing ones.

Rahman appreciated the quality of the Irish documents and dollars. These were being churned out by Dutchy Holland through a small printing business he had in Dublin. The counterfeit documents were the only saleable goods that Holland had produced since setting up the print shop after his release from prison. His attempts to print legitimate publications had failed, but the business was still useful for hiding his drug money.

Other documents were being sourced through the gang's Northern Irish and English underworld links. The forged documents could be sold or bartered for guns or drugs. A typical international drug trafficker could have as many as twenty passports in different names to avoid attention. Rahman's violent sidekick, Johnny Wildhagen, used a number of Gilligan's fake Irish passports and licences to travel between Europe and Africa.

Gilligan reckoned that the documents would burnish his reputation with his European counterparts. He had tried to model himself on Rahman, the sophisticated international criminal and by now was on first-name terms with some of the heaviest criminals in Europe. The psychotic little godfather's ambitions had broadened far beyond the boundaries of the Irish underworld – he wanted to emulate his Mafia hero, John Gotti.

Ireland's Teflon Don, however, was loathed and mistrusted by Rahman and his cronies. They tried but failed, to keep a safe distance from 'De Klein'. Rahman and Baltus were impressed with the forged dollars and let their guard down. They began passing them off through various international contacts. Rahman used them as part payment to African and Eastern European gangs for drugs and other contraband shipments.

Gilligan posted more samples of the dollars to the Bilderberg Europa Hotel in The Hague's coastal resort of Scheveningen. The envelopes containing the fake bills were addressed for the attention of Simon Rahman and were collected by the addressee without a hitch.

On 10 April another sample consignment of thirty $20 bills was posted to the hotel. When Rahman didn't turn up, Gilligan instructed Carol Rooney to make several phone calls to the hotel enquiring if the envelope had been collected yet.

There were so many calls that the hotel management became suspicious and called the police. On 18 April 1996 Rahman received a call from Gilligan reminding him about the envelope. Rahman sent Baltus to collect it for him. When he arrived in the hotel Baltus was arrested. It was discovered that similar notes had also been found in the home of his son several months earlier.

In a follow-up investigation, Simon Rahman's home was searched and more of the counterfeit notes were found. Rahman calmly informed the police that Baltus had given him the notes. In a statement the drug trafficker claimed without a hint of irony:

> Martin Baltus gave me those notes. I knew they were counterfeit and I threw them in the direction of the wastepaper basket. When I threw them, they must have missed the basket and ended up in the press.

In one of the calls which led to the arrests, Carol Rooney had left an Irish telephone number for the hotel staff to call in the event that the envelope remained uncollected. On 30 May the Dutch police sent an official request to Dublin to trace the telephone number. It led back to Rooney and Gilligan. The Irish connection was about to be exposed.

The heat now bearing down on Rahman as a result of his relationship with Gilligan also touched on Johnny Wildhagen. Rahman and his organization considered Wildhagen a potential weak link if he was arrested. His cocaine habit combined with his violent nature made him a loose cannon. He was mad enough to spill the beans not only on Rahman but on several other arms and drug traffickers, including the 'hash farmer' and Havid. When the Dutch police went looking for him, Wildhagen had disappeared. International alerts were issued to Interpol for information on his whereabouts. Bulletins were also sent to Europol, the relatively new law enforcement organization for the European Union. Consisting of officers from all member states, it had been set up under the Maastricht Treaty in 1992 with the objective of pooling police resources and intelligence.

Several months later, when the police discovered that he was using Gilligan's false passports, searches for a Peter McMann or Peter de Mann also drew a blank. Johnny Wildhagen was never seen again.

The police suspected that he had been murdered by his own mob who saw him as a liability, especially to Simon Rahman. It was a course of action of which Gilligan would wholeheartedly have approved.

Exactly a month before the arrest of Baltus, Gilligan's crude money laundering methods had also brought him to the attention of the Dutch authorities. On 18 March Gilligan, Meehan and Baker visited the Scheveningen Casino, The Hague. Meehan exchanged 250,000 guilders, the equivalent of €157,000, for tokens at various gambling tables. None of the trio played and after an hour Meehan went to the cashier's desk. He asked to have the tokens cashed and the money transferred by the casino to a Dutch bank account.

Security staff in the casino had been monitoring the criminals on CCTV and immediately recognized a money laundering scam. Staff refused either to transfer the money to a bank account or to lodge it in the casino account for Meehan. Under strict money laundering laws, the staff explained, they could only transfer or lodge sums of money that had been won on the premises. And the casino staff made it clear they had proof that the men had not made any money in the casino.

Meehan was following Gilligan's instructions, hoping to have documentary proof that the cash had come from gambling and was therefore legitimate. Gilligan had done the same thing many times in the past. He also had his cherished bookies' cheques that he kept for whenever the police or Customs stopped him.

Gilligan and Meehan had become agitated and aggressive by the refusals. Had the casino been in Dublin or Cork, the pair would have adopted their normal approach and threatened to murder the staff and burn the place to the ground. But this was the Netherlands and they couldn't resort to intimidation quite so easily. Surrounded by several burly security officers Meehan and Gilligan decided to accept the situation. Meehan's tokens were cashed, and the money returned to him. Unlike most other customers, they left angry that they still had their money.

Through sheer arrogance and stupidity they had attracted unwanted attention to themselves as the casino later reported the incident to the Dutch Office for the Disclosure of Unusual Transactions. The money laundering agency began investigating the backgrounds of Meehan and Gilligan and scrutinized their financial affairs in the Netherlands. The Dutch authorities had also downloaded the CCTV footage of the three Irish men in the casino.

Before the end of April they had contacted the police in Dublin about the casino incident and the information was passed to the fledgling Money Laundering Unit (MLU) which was then part of the Garda Bureau of Fraud Investigation (GBFI). It had been established under the 1994 Criminal Justice Act which made money laundering an offence, but its powers were completely inadequate to combat the new era of organized crime ushered in by Gilligan.

The MLU were told that if they required the tape for evidential purposes, they must request it through official channels within a certain number of days. When the Dutch didn't hear from the Irish force the tape was erased in compliance with the law. MLU detectives eventually went looking for the deleted tape and realized that in future they would have to be quicker off the mark.

Nevertheless, the events in March and April, and the arrests of the Gorsts in Belgium the previous year, would eventually provide vital evidence to help smash the Gilligan gang. But by then his European partners were experiencing more bad luck.

In April Thomas Gorst's brother, Eric, was arrested by British police when they swooped on his drug distribution network. He was caught taking delivery of hundreds of kilos of hash. It had been shipped from the Netherlands in large cardboard boxes purporting to contain machine parts. This arrest again led back to Simon Rahman.

The global drug dealer was already known to the British authorities. The pieces of the international crime jigsaw were gradually falling into place.

Back in Dublin, circumstances were slowly beginning to change for the worse for Gilligan and his ilk. The then Garda Commissioner, Paddy Culligan, and his deputy, Pat Byrne, had been working hard to modernize the force and create new specialist units to respond to the changing criminal world.

The gardaí had realized that crime was no longer confined within national borders. In order to catch the bad guys, the authorities would have to work closely with law enforcement agencies worldwide and use the latest technology available. John Gilligan, George Mitchell and the rest of the big Irish mobs had already gone international. The gardaí were playing catch-up with the criminals, but at least they were in the game.

Culligan was credited with being one of the first garda commissioners to push back against political interference when it came to promoting senior officers in the force. He pursued a strategy of elevating only the most qualified people and appointing them to areas where their talents could best be utilized. This new breed of dynamic cops included Tony Hickey and Kevin Carty.

By 1996 Tony Hickey had been promoted to the rank of Detective Chief Superintendent and given command of the Central Detective Unit (CDU) where he had worked for most of his service with the Serious Crime Squad. A native of County Kerry, he was a recipient of the prestigious Scott Medal for bravery in the line of duty. Detective Chief Superintendent Hickey was one of the most experienced and respected detectives in the gardaí who over two decades had been involved in the investigation of scores of high-profile crimes.

He was given the task of completely overhauling the existing unit and transforming it into an FBI-style, serious crime agency called the National Bureau of Criminal Investigation (NBCI). The NBCI would provide a large team of experienced detectives to work on serious crime cases throughout the country. It would support local divisional units, providing expertise and extra personnel during major enquiries. One of Hickey's key objectives was targeting organized crime.

Another organizational change in response to the flourishing drug trade was the creation of the Garda National Drug Unit (GNDU) to replace the old Drug Squad. The GNDU would be a national and international unit. Detective Chief Superintendent Kevin Carty, Hickey's predecessor in CDU, was transferred to head up the new national drug agency. A Special Branch intelligence officer for most of his career, Carty had swapped chasing terrorists for targeting drug traffickers. Like Hickey, Carty had also been decorated for his gallantry on the streets. He had been chairman of the Drugs and Organized Crime Group during Ireland's stint as European President. The body initiated far-reaching, cross-border, anti-crime measures. He also spent a term as An Garda Síochána's representative with Europol.

Detective Chief Superintendent Carty and his second in command, Detective Superintendent Austin McNally, set up a number of operations to target major criminals. They focused on intelligence gathering, realizing that criminal gangs had been overlooked for several years. The lack of information was one of the main reasons John Gilligan had become such a dangerous gangland threat.

In their first months McNally and Carty notched up notable successes through the use of a new network of informants and electronic surveillance. One of those complex operations was the targeting of George 'the Penguin' Mitchell's organization. The GNDU busted a large ecstasy factory capable of churning out millions of pounds worth of the drug every week. The investigation also uncovered Mitchell's involvement in the Brindle hit leading to Boyle's arrest in London.

The GNDU made history a few months after the arrest with the seizure of 13 tons of hashish as part of a major international investigation involving the US Drug Enforcement Administration (DEA) and the Canadian police. The shipment was destined for the UK and European markets. It belonged to an international consortium of Dutch, UK, American and Canadian drug traffickers. George Mitchell's gang had been tasked with providing the transport for the dope which had been landed off the Irish coast. If the international consortium had come to Gilligan then he believed they would still have their drugs. It also suited him that the Penguin was at the top of the police most wanted list.

But Gilligan and Traynor's success had been noticed. The Coach's dealings in the second-hand car business and his new-found wealth were a source of intense interest to the police on the ground. Gilligan's attack on Veronica Guerin, the subsequent death threats he made against her, and the publicity afterwards had put the little man in the limelight as well.

Then there was a flood of reports coming into headquarters from exasperated officers wondering, like Guerin, how Gilligan could afford Jessbrook, not to mention his racehorse. The intelligence gathered also outlined suspicions that the pair was involved in drugs and guns.

Across town Meehan and Peter Mitchell were arrogantly making fun of the police and bragging about the money they were making. It was impossible to ignore them any longer. Action had to be taken.

In late April 1996 Carty launched a top secret investigation codenamed Operation Pineapple. The main targets were: Traynor, Gilligan, Meehan, Derek Baker, Dinny Meredith and Carol Rooney. The GNDU, with assistance from Hickey's people at the NBCI, and the MLU, set out to compile information on the gang's membership and the extent of their wealth and criminal activities.

A trawl of garda intelligence and sightings reports from units in Counties Dublin, Meath and Kildare placed Gilligan in the company of Traynor, Meehan and Mitchell on several occasions. Then there was the English police investigation which had caught Gilligan on tape with other drug dealers in Brighton, and the cash seizures in Dublin and Holyhead. The investigation expanded to include more police units and representatives of the Customs and the Revenue.

Nora Owen, the then Justice Minister, had been drafting legislation to organize a united, multi-disciplinary offensive against organized crime. She was anxious to break down the traditional boundaries and a silo mentality among the security forces.

Intelligence reports and requests for assistance were arriving on Carty's desk about Irish links to organized crime syndicates in Europe. The bulk of the intelligence came from the Netherlands where the Dutch Office for the Disclosure of Unusual Transactions had been compiling information on the financial transactions at the Bureau de Change in Centraal Station, Amsterdam. In the Netherlands the police set up a team to operate in tandem with the Irish investigation and officers from the MLU and GNDU flew over for meetings.

By May 1996 Operation Pineapple began in earnest. Unfortunately the investigation concentrated on compiling a paper-driven picture of Gilligan's operation and gang structure. If, instead, physical surveillance had been placed on the gang members it is likely that it would have quickly led the team to the centre of the distribution operation. After all Gilligan was running an industrial-scale operation with deliveries and pick-ups happening like clockwork in plain view on several days of the week. Meetings were taking place between the main players and huge sums of money were being collected and then transported out of the country. Dozens of people were involved.

When Pineapple was launched it was to be a long-term investigation into a criminal gang. There was no urgency. The fact that the gang's supply and distribution operation was not exposed until the following October – four months into the Guerin murder investigation and six months into Operation Pineapple – illustrated the airtight security shield Gilligan had constructed.

As the gardaí were limbering up to go after the mob boss one of the darkest plots in Irish criminal history was in an advanced stage of planning.

CHAPTER FIFTEEN

PRELUDE TO MURDER

'Who does that fucking bitch think she is?' Gilligan erupted when he received a summons ordering him to appear at Kilcock District Court on 14 May. Derek Baker recalled Gilligan flying into a violent rage when he learned that he was to be charged with assault and causing criminal damage to the journalist's clothes.

Gilligan was still obsessed by Veronica Guerin and the threat she posed to his ambitions of becoming Ireland's Teflon Don. He had no idea that the gardaí were preparing to come after his gang. The police were the last people on his mind.

Despite his bravado that he would win the case, Gilligan still wasn't prepared to gamble on the court outcome because the stakes were too high. If he lost he was going to jail and he had no intention of allowing that to happen. The only law he had any confidence in was the law of the underworld.

The 'Guerin problem' had exposed how the money and power had completed Gilligan's transition to an avaricious psychopath. Like the celluloid drug trafficker Tony Montana, in the classic movie *Scarface*, the narcissistic Gilligan talked only about money and himself. In his mind he was smarter and better organized than all the other 'Muppets' in gangland. His default position on most issues was to issue threats to kill or maim anyone who crossed his path. Associates described him as being like a man possessed. It was one of the reasons why Baker and Meredith backed away from him.

Gilligan's rage against the journalist scared Carol Rooney. She had witnessed his furious diatribes and heard the threatening phone calls he made to the journalist, which chilled her to the bone. The naïve youngster knew that her misogynistic lover was an exceptionally dangerous man.

She later told the police, in the weeks and months following the attack:

> He was all wound up about the case and he was getting more irritable and angry all the time. He would say 'no one messes with my family or my business'. John didn't like that she was intimidating him, especially a woman.

Veronica Guerin was the main topic of conversation at the monthly gang meetings in Leixlip between Gilligan and his inner circle, Meehan, Traynor, Holland, Fatso Mitchell and the Ward brothers. The gang discussed ways that the journalist could be convinced to drop the charges. Gilligan ordered the Coach to get this done. Rooney recalled:

> He told John Traynor that Veronica Guerin was not going to get away with what she was trying to do to him or else he would have to kill her. He said Traynor was responsible for the problem and needed to sort it out. He said: 'She'll get what she deserves if she doesn't leave my fucking family alone.'

Rooney also witnessed Gilligan discussing the issue with Holland. The hit man agreed that his boss was the victim of an egregious injustice. In the eyes of the impressionable teenager the fifty-seven-year-old assassin was far too old and gentle to be the bogeyman she heard the gang gossiping about behind his back. But the gang knew better and were afraid of Holland. Behind the genteel image he projected to the world lay a cold, callous creature who would kill anyone as long as the price was right. It was never personal, always business with the hit man.

Gilligan and the gang demonstrated their esteem for the oddball loner by avoiding crude language or expletives in his company because he disapproved of profanity, especially taking the Lord's name in vain. The prudish killer also disliked the fact that Gilligan and Baker were cheating on their wives. Rooney recalled:

> John was terrified of Paddy Holland because he said he [Holland] could easily put a bullet in his head if the price was right. The others were also afraid of him. He [Holland] was the one man John never gave out to and was also respectful towards. Paddy was always soft-spoken and courteous. But when he was not around, the lads would talk about all the people he was supposed to have murdered.

By April 1996 the gang's 'market share' was going through the roof. The average consignment was now around 400 kilos every few weeks, which netted the mob boss a profit of over €590,000 per shipment. If Gilligan went to prison it would have a detrimental effect on the fortunes of all the gang members, including Holland. It was in everyone's interests for the assault charges to go away, either one way or the other. His cronies wholeheartedly agreed. 'Who the fuck does Guerin think she is?' was their refrain.

As the weeks passed Gilligan came to the decision that there was only one course of action open to him – murder.

————————

On 14 May Veronica Guerin travelled to Kilcock Court with her husband, Graham, and a colleague, Michael Sheridan. Sheridan, who

Garda mugshots of notorious gangster John Gilligan in his factory-robbing days

John and Geraldine Gilligan pose for a photo with former boxing world champion Prince Naseem

A young John and Geraldine Gilligan in happier times

Tracey Gilligan

Darren Gilligan

Gilligan with Brian 'the Tosser' Meehan (top) and Peter 'Fatso' Mitchell (far right) and Meehan's mother (front centre) in St Lucia

John and Geraldine in the Sandals resort in St Lucia

John 'the Coach' Traynor

Patrick 'Dutchy' Holland

Brian 'the Tosser' Meehan

Peter 'Fatso' Mitchell

Paul 'Hippo' Ward

Derek Baker

Brendan 'Speedy' Fegan

Denis 'Dinny' Meredith

George 'the Penguin' Mitchell

Christy 'Dapper Don'
Kinahan

Martin 'the General' Cahill

The palatial family home and equestrian centre (above and below) that Gilligan built from the proceeds of crime

Gilligan poses in a wax works museum with Benny Hill

John Gilligan leaves Portlaoise Prison in 2013 (far left) and appearing in court numerous times

A rare photo of John Gilligan living it up with trusted sidekick John Traynor

Veronica Guerin

Veronica talks to John Traynor

Veronica Guerin's grave

The author with his colleague, Liam O'Connor, at the murder scene

A garda ballistics expert examines the angle of the bullets fired into Veronica Guerin's car

Veronica with her son Cathal

In hospital after the first gun attack in 1995

John Traynor driving the racing car, which he crashed on the day Veronica was shot dead

Members of the Lucan investigation team with Veronica's mother, Bernie (fourth from right), at the unveiling of a monument in Dublin Castle

Pat Byrne

Fachtna Murphy

Tony Hickey and Todd O'Loughlin

John O'Mahony

Prosecutor Peter Charleton

Felix McKenna

CAB Chief Legal Officer Barry Galvin

Members of the Lucan investigation team at a social gathering

Gilligan's mistress Carol Rooney

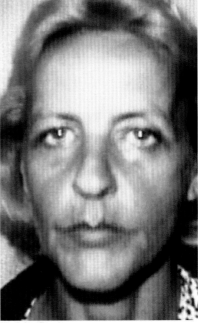

Mariette Gorst

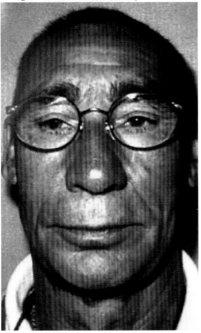

Thomas Gorst

Gilligan's drug supplier Simon Rahman

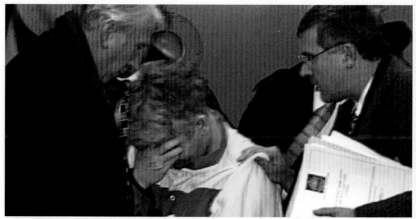

John Gilligan is formally arrested by detectives Bernie Hanley and Todd O'Loughlin after his extradition from London in 2000

Brian 'the Tosser' Meehan is escorted by detectives Fergus Treanor and Noel Browne off a military flight following his extradition from Holland

Patrick 'Dutchy' Holland (centre) after his arrest with detectives Sean O'Brien and John O'Driscoll

Irish Independent

METRO EDITION

IRELAND'S BEST-SELLING DAILY NEWSPAPER   www.independent.ie   **Monday 17 March 2014**   €2.00 (£1.25 in Northern Ireland)   R

40 PAGES OF SPORT

Schmidt: We wouldn't have won it without Brian

DAVID KELLY, RUAIDHRÍ O'CONNOR, VINCENT HOGAN, GEORGE HOOK, TONY WARD & BILLY KEANE ON THE BIG WIN

HEALTH & LIVING FREE INSIDE
David Coleman: Dealing with problem eaters

+ **EUGENE McGEE:** HOW CLUB CHAMPIONSHIPS UNDERLINE WHAT GAA IS REALLY ALL ABOUT SPORT P26-27

Gilligan flees country after his driver is gunned down

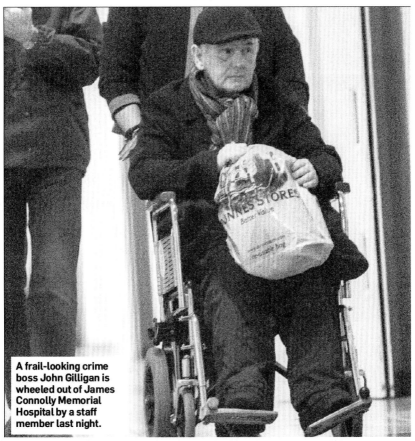

A frail-looking crime boss John Gilligan is wheeled out of James Connolly Memorial Hospital by a staff member last night.

Frail and scared: John Gilligan leaves hospital to flee the country in March 2014

Weapons and ammunition seized by gardaí during the Guerin investigation

Bugs concealed in 'Dutchy' Holland's shoes

One of the crates in which Gilligan's drugs were smuggled from Holland

The case containing the cash Gilligan was arrested with in Heathrow

The grave where Gilligan's arsenal was buried

Gilligan is arrested by Spanish police in 2020

Prescription drugs found in a search of Gilligan's property in Spain

Police locate a Magnum revolver, which they initially believed was the murder weapon

Gilligan pumping iron behind bars

went on to script a movie *When the Sky Falls* and write a book in her honour, recalled how she was frightened at the prospect of facing the man who had assaulted and threatened to kill her with such chilling malice.

As she stood outside the health centre which doubled as the local court, she tried to suppress her nerves. Gilligan arrived in a convoy of jeeps and cars with an entourage of henchmen and Geraldine, his 'estranged' wife, by his side.

The scene epitomized Gilligan and what he had become. The Irish John Gotti wanted to appear strong and dangerous the only way he knew how – with a show of force and menace. His goons crowded around him, talking on their mobile phones and eyeballing the crowd. Gilligan wanted everyone to know that he was a godfather who no one should fuck with.

Around the same time one of Gilligan's bagmen was on his way to the Bureau de Change in Amsterdam with a bag full of cash. Records later showed that he changed Irish punts and sterling pounds worth €250,951 into guilders at 11.52 a.m. An hour later he played the tables at the casino in Schiphol Airport before catching the return flight to Dublin. The following day records showed that Gilligan's brother, Thomas, exchanged £122,050 (€240,000) into guilders to buy more hash. Gilligan was determined for business to carry on as usual.

As soon as he got out of his jeep in Kilcock, Gilligan caught sight of his nemesis, the person threatening his legal and illegal enterprises. He probably had to restrain himself from running over and throttling her again. There were just too many witnesses.

Gilligan knew that the case would be adjourned for at least a month because of a legal technicality. He spoke briefly with his solicitor, Michael Hanahoe, and continued to stare at Veronica as he walked up the steps, but Geraldine couldn't keep her distance.

She sauntered across to where Veronica's group was standing with a sarcastic grin on her face. She did a twirl in front of Veronica and said: 'You won't forget me in a hurry.' Then she tottered back to her husband's side. Judge John Brophy adjourned the court hearing until Tuesday 25 June.

It was later suspected that Gilligan's lackeys went to the court to see what the reporter looked like, what kind of car she was driving and if she had police protection. The conspiracy was already being pieced together. Another incident that occurred around this time showed how Gilligan was trying to cover all the angles.

A member of Brendan 'Speedy' Fegan's Northern gang later confirmed to this writer how he'd heard 'preparations' were being made for something 'big'. The source didn't know the details. At the beginning of May, the gang member drove Fegan and his partner Paddy Farrell to Dublin for a meeting with Gilligan, Meehan and the rest of the Dublin mob. Fegan and Farrell were now major business partners of Gilligan's.

A car picked up the Northern drug traffickers from a city centre pub leaving Fegan's driver to wait. The henchman later revealed:

> I knew something heavy was going down but I knew better than to ask any questions. A few hours later Gilligan dropped Speedy back to the pub. All he [Fegan] said was that he would have to be in Dublin more often over the next few months.

A week later Meehan rang Fegan and asked him to travel to London for a meeting with the little man. Fegan and an associate flew to Heathrow where they were met by Meehan in a stretch limousine. They were driven to a plush hotel in central London where Gilligan was waiting. Carol Rooney was there, too. Gilligan had a strange request for the Newry drug dealer. Fegan's associate recalled:

> He asked Brendan to pose for a number of pictures of him with Carol Rooney, to make it look like they were boyfriend and

girlfriend. Gilligan told Fegan that the picture would be hung up in Rooney's apartment to give the impression that Speedy was her boyfriend. He said that something was going to happen which would have the cops crawling all over everyone in Dublin and he didn't want Rooney getting caught up in it. We were amazed that such an ugly little old guy like Gilligan could have such a young, attractive girlfriend. She was no more than twenty. I think Brendan fancied his chances with her, anyway. Gilligan told Fegan that he was in control of the underworld in Dublin and implied he had an arrangement with the Provos. He said: 'No one messes with us. You have nothing to worry about from the Provos.'

On Friday 7 June Russell Warren and his friend, Paul Cradden, spent the day drinking. They fell out of the Speaker Conolly pub in Firhouse, south Dublin, around closing time. Cradden had mentioned a powerful Kawasaki 500cc motorbike his employer kept in a lockup garage in Dún Laoghaire. The two drunks decided to upset him by stealing it. Warren drove his van to the coastal suburb, parking in a lane beside the lockup. The bagman jumped over a wall and broke into the garage. They staggered as they heaved the large motorbike into the back of the van, giggling as they drove away.

But the pair had a problem. They hadn't a clue what to do with the bike. Warren called another pal who had a lock-up garage in Terenure. They told the friend that they had repossessed the bike and he agreed to store it for them. When he sobered up Warren tried to sell the bike and put the word around. A few potential buyers, unconcerned by the provenance of the bike, viewed it, but no one bought.

Less than a week later Warren picked Gilligan up at Jessbrook to drive him around on business. Warren was at Gilligan's beck and call and was treated with utter contempt by his boss. A born bully, Gilligan delighted in exploiting the weakness, and fear, of others. To him Warren was just another piece of property bought and paid for with his growing mountain of dirty money.

During the trip Warren told Gilligan about the motorbike that he was considering dumping. He wondered if the nasty godfather might have some use for it.

Gilligan was interested. He asked what size it was and where it was being kept. 'Don't dump it, just keep it. Don't do anything with it. I may need it,' he grunted.

On 20 June Gilligan telephoned Warren and asked if he still had 'that bike'. He wanted to see it. He arranged to meet his hapless bagman at the Terenure House pub car park later that day. He told Warren he wanted him there alone as Brian Meehan was coming with him and neither of them wanted to be seen.

Despite being banned from driving for up to forty years each, the two hoods arrived in a car driven by Gilligan. They wanted to know whether the motorbike was suitable for the project they had in mind. The Tosser was just as accomplished driving a getaway bike as a car. The bike would do the job. Gilligan ordered Warren to do whatever was needed to make it roadworthy.

Meehan said he would be back to test drive the motorbike when the work was done. The three left the garage and got into Gilligan's car. Before he started the engine to drive back to the pub car park where Warren had left his van, Gilligan turned around and stared at the bagman. It was the kind of bloodcurdling glare that sent a chill down Warren's boneless spine. Gilligan spoke in a low menacing tone that left no room for misinterpretation.

> I was told not to trust you, but I will. If you ever make a statement
> or say anything to anyone about me, I will kill you. Your mother
> and father, brothers and sisters, you and your wife, and the rest

of your family will be shot. I am just tellin' you to keep it in your mind. Don't think I want to do this but, no matter where you are, I'll get you.

Meehan sat in silence looking forward as Warren reassured the boss that he had nothing to fear. Gilligan held his menacing stare on the bagman for a few more seconds and then turned around and drove the car to the pub. He reminded Warren about the work that had to be done to the bike. There was no mention of paying the bagman for the bike or the work, and Warren knew better than to ask.

Around the same time Veronica Guerin had a new project in mind. She declared to her friend and news editor Willie Kealy that she was going to name and shame all the bosses in the criminal underworld.

Guerin began putting pressure on Traynor to come across with more inside information about the Mr Bigs. She particularly wanted to dig deeper into Gilligan's empire and the source of his money. Then she played her ace card by telling the Coach she intended writing a story exposing his own involvement in the drug trade. She was aware of Traynor's links to Gilligan but, like the police, did not know the sheer scale of the operation.

Relations between the reporter and the con man deteriorated dramatically. He threatened to seek a High Court injunction against her. Veronica responded by repeating her threat to expose him. It was a dangerous game of psychological jousting, but not unprecedented between a journalist and source in the murky world of crime reporting. The argument between Traynor and Guerin, however, was more personal than most and, indeed, confusing.

It seemed that Veronica knew at that stage that the Coach was behind the attempt on her life in 1995 and the shooting less than four months earlier. Adding fuel to the flames she told him that his name had featured in a police investigation of a Liverpool-based heroin gang and there were strong suspicions that he was a heroin dealer. She said she understood a contract had been placed on his head. Veronica was putting one last squeeze on the arch manipulator.

A criminal associate of Traynor later recalled his reaction to the exposé threat: 'Veronica had Traynor in the horrors. He was terrified that she was going to write about him being a drug dealer. John preferred to stay out of the limelight.'

She met the Coach on a number of other occasions to discuss the allegations but adopted a less confrontational approach. She was hoping to record Traynor admitting his involvement in narcotics. Short of a verbal admission she would not get the story past the newspaper's libel lawyers – or his face on the front page beside Gilligan's.

On one of the tapes Veronica could be heard discussing her assault case against the little man: 'Even last week when you were saying about Gilligan and what he's capable of, and trying to stop me going to court, it makes me more determined. It's the way I am.' Traynor replied: 'If he never done anything, at the back of your mind, you know what he's capable of.'

It was during one of these meetings that Veronica sealed her fate. She let slip the fact that she was due to appear in Naas District Court on a speeding fine on 26 June, the day after the assault case was to come up again. The speeding case was on her mind. Veronica had been prosecuted so many times for speeding that she was genuinely worried that she might lose her driving licence and the mobility necessary for her work.

It was just innocuous small talk as she tried to prise more info from the Coach. But the cunning crook had gleaned much more from the conversation than she had.

———

On the morning of 7 June 1996 an IRA gang murdered Detective Garda Jerry McCabe during a botched armed robbery in the village of Adare, County Limerick. McCabe's colleague, Detective Garda Ben O'Sullivan, was left critically injured when a member of the gang blasted them with an AK-47 at close range. The appalling crime sent shockwaves through Irish society.

That morning this writer was leaving Dublin to cover the story with a photographer when Traynor phoned. A bizarre conversation followed. He enquired if I had heard anything about a threat on his life that he said Veronica was aware of. I said I hadn't heard anything because I had only just returned from a three-week holiday abroad.

Traynor, who was always affable and talkative, told me about his problems with Veronica. He had complained about her on several occasions in the past but that was only because he was trying to play one competitor off against another for his own ends. This time, though, he was concerned that she was going to expose him as a drug dealer, something which he vehemently denied. He said that he was going to seek legal advice later that day about a possible injunction. I dismissed the whole thing as nothing more than Veronica winding up the Coach.

Later that same morning Veronica phoned Traynor and told him that she wasn't satisfied he was a heroin dealer and was postponing the story. He cancelled his appointment with his solicitor.

That afternoon Veronica and I both attended a press conference in Limerick about Detective McCabe's murder. We exchanged greetings across the room but didn't get a chance to speak. The callous terrorist attack on the gardaí was a huge scandal that had plunged the country into a political crisis. It was Friday afternoon and both of us were after an angle for the front page. Saturday morning is the final deadline for a Sunday newspaper reporter. It was the last time we ever met.

Veronica returned to Limerick to cover the funeral of Jerry McCabe. The whole incident upset her greatly. Later she told her husband, Graham, that she would like the hymn 'Be Not Afraid' played at her funeral. The hymn had been sung during the detective's funeral Mass.

On Monday 10 June, Veronica met Traynor again in Dublin on her way back from Limerick. The Coach later claimed she told him she now knew he was selling hash and ecstasy but not heroin. Three days later Traynor swore an affidavit about his dealings with Veronica in order to obtain an injunction against the *Sunday Independent* preventing it from publishing the allegations.

It was a masterpiece of the Coach's lies and half-truths. The philandering drug dealer expressed fear for the safety of his family. An article would put them all in danger from vigilantes. They would have to move over the shame of it. He described himself as a struggling used car salesman. Traynor's affidavit read:

> I have never dealt in, touched, seen or been involved in anything to do with drugs. I have never invested any money with anybody involved in drugs and do not know or have not been in company with any of the people mentioned by Veronica Guerin at the time of writing this.

The following day Traynor's counsel, Adrian Hardiman, obtained an interim ex-parte (one side only) injunction blocking the publication of any story about his client. Lawyers for the newspaper informed the court that such a story was not imminent.

On 24 June the lawyers gave a further undertaking that the story would not be published in the following Sunday's edition. The case was adjourned to 1 July. Veronica was due to swear a responding affidavit by then. She had an appointment with the *Sunday Independent*'s legal advisers for the afternoon of 26 June – after her appearance in Naas on the speeding charge. Traynor had got himself some breathing space.

By then the die had been cast. Charlie Bowden would subsequently tell gardaí that the first time he realized there was 'hassle' with the crime reporter was in early June at one of the gang's weekly meetings in Meehan's apartment. Bowden stated:

These discussions were about the impending court case where Gilligan was charged with assaulting Veronica Guerin. I was already aware of this assault from the newspapers. Meehan, Mitchell and the Wards discussed with me the fact that John Gilligan was upset over this, and how he had said to them he wasn't going to go to prison for anyone, and that he wasn't going to let her get away with it.

Meehan said that Gilligan had all the contacts for the hash in the Netherlands. If he was inside, then the operation would 'fall apart'. Bowden did not pay much heed to what he was hearing. Gilligan and his henchmen were always talking about killing someone. 'It was the way they went on,' Bowden later explained.

A few days later Bowden, Mitchell, Meehan and Paul Ward were driving through the Strawberry Beds beside the River Liffey. As usual all the talk was about guns, drugs, money and the problem with the meddling crime journalist. Meehan asked Bowden about the .357 Magnum Rahman had sent them in January. Meehan said he and another gang member couldn't find it when they had gone to the cemetery to collect it. Bowden explained that they had been importing so much weaponry that he had been using more than one grave to store them. He told the police:

This was the first time I was aware that they were planning to shoot Veronica Guerin. I was aware that she had been shot before to warn her off and I thought at that time that this would be a similar attempt to warn her off. This was all that was talked about.

On 18 June Bowden met Meehan and Mitchell and brought them to the Greenmount lockup. The previous day Bowden had collected another consignment of 423 kilos from John Dunne's courier at the Ambassador Hotel, County Dublin. As they checked the merchandise, Meehan told the armourer that they were planning to shoot Guerin.

Bowden later said in a statement:

> Brian Meehan told me that himself and John Gilligan had
> planned to shoot Veronica Guerin. He told me that he had offered
> to do it himself but that Gilligan had decided that 'the Wig', who
> I now know as Paddy [Dutchy] Holland, should do it, because
> he owed Gilligan a favour and that he had a proven track record
> as a hit man. Meehan said that a lot of hits in the town, that had
> been put down to Derek Hutch [the brother of Gerry Hutch,
> the Monk], had actually been carried out by 'the Wig', and he
> specifically referred to the murder of Paddy Shanahan.

Gilligan had turned Meehan's offer down because of his dismal
performance in the Foley hit.

Traynor had given them the information about Guerin's court
appearance in Naas on Wednesday 26 June. It would be the best
opportunity to get her, somewhere on the road between Dublin and
Kildare. Bowden wondered if she would have a police escort as a result
of the earlier attacks. But Gilligan and Meehan had it all worked out
– they would have the journalist under surveillance.

Bowden also recalled another occasion when Meehan discussed
the motive for the attack on Guerin:

> I recall Brian Meehan saying to me that Veronica Guerin deserved
> what was coming to her, because she was an interfering bitch and
> that if John Gilligan was locked up over her, the whole operation
> would stop because only John knew the full ins and outs of it.

At the same time, from the activity at the safe house, Carol Rooney
was also beginning to suspect that something big was afoot. In the
two weeks leading up to the court appearance she recalled that there
were more meetings about Guerin with Meehan, Mitchell, Traynor
and the Ward brothers. Gilligan became more secretive, ordering her
to leave the room when the subject came up.

On 25 June Veronica Guerin made a second trip to Kilcock District Court. Again she would have to face Gilligan. This time he behaved less ostentatiously and arrived without his goons in his solicitor Michael Hanahoe's car. The hearing lasted a few minutes. It was adjourned to 9 July when the case was scheduled to go ahead.

Before he left, Gilligan spotted two detectives, who were attached to the Investigation Branch at Garda Headquarters, keeping an eye on proceedings. Gilligan walked over to the two cops. 'She's a fucking stupid bitch. This case will never get off the ground,' he snarled before walking to his solicitor's car.

Hanahoe drove Gilligan back to Jessbrook in order to familiarize himself with the layout of the place for the forthcoming case. Gilligan asked him for a lift to Dublin Airport, as he was catching the afternoon flight to Amsterdam.

As Veronica Guerin drove back to Dublin and Gilligan made his way to the airport, Brian Meehan phoned Russell Warren. He wanted to meet at the garage to test the motorbike. He told Warren to make sure no one was around. Sometime later Meehan met Warren in the car park of the Terenure House pub. He was being driven by Peter Mitchell.

They went to the garage and Meehan took the bike for a test drive. Ten minutes later he returned, satisfied that it was working well. As he was leaving, Meehan turned to Warren and asked him if he knew who Veronica Guerin was. Warren didn't know. The bagman later recalled in a police statement:

> He said that she was between thirty and forty years old, small build and I think he said greyish short hair. I didn't know who she was, and he didn't mention anything about her being a journalist or anything to do with the papers.

Meehan said he would show Warren a picture of her later that evening. The meeting didn't take place. Meehan rang Warren instead and told him that he wanted to pick up the bike the next morning at 9 a.m. and he would talk to him then.

The same evening Gilligan rang his bagman, who was due to fly to Amsterdam the following morning to deliver money to him. The mob boss told Warren that the trip was off and that he was to stay put as Meehan needed him in Dublin.

Warren knew there was something happening but didn't know what. But whatever it was, it was big enough for Gilligan to warn him not to 'fuck it up'.

That afternoon Meehan and Mitchell met Bowden at a pub in Harold's Cross. He drove them to the Greenmount lockup. Shay Ward had retrieved the Magnum and twelve rounds of ammunition from the graveyard. Bowden cleaned the powerful weapon and loaded it. He left six spare rounds alongside the gun on a bench. There was tension in the air and this time Bowden knew that the murder plot was no longer just coke-induced talk.

The ex-soldier could have picked up a phone and made an anonymous call to the police telling them the journalist was in mortal danger, but he did nothing. Instead, Bowden was more worried about protecting his own skin and began to think about setting up his alibi. The ex-soldier would later claim that he wasn't sure if the gang was going to 'shoot at her or shoot her'.

Gilligan met Carol Rooney around 8 p.m. in the Hilton Hotel, Amsterdam, where he had booked a suite. She had taken a separate flight earlier that day. They met Thomas Gorst who had rented a house for Gilligan near Aalst in Belgium. Gilligan had called him some weeks earlier and told him he wanted to stay in Belgium for at least a month. He planned to take his mistress there the following day.

The same afternoon Thomas Gilligan changed another £150,000 (€290,000) at the Bureau de Change in Amsterdam. It was still business as usual for the gang.

Rooney later recalled how Gilligan seemed to be 'on edge' when they went back to the hotel. He paced the floor making phone calls. Then he turned to his paramour and smiled. He told her that he was expecting good news the following day, saying: 'After tomorrow all my problems will be over.'

In reality they were just starting.

CHAPTER SIXTEEN

———

THE HIT

On Wednesday 26 June 1996, Ireland awoke to glorious sunshine. It was the kind of ideal summer's day that made people feel good to be alive. But by the time the sun had set, the day would be etched in a nation's memory as one that had witnessed a terrifying crime.

Veronica Guerin had breakfast with her husband, Graham, and six-year-old son, Cathal. He was going to work with his dad for the day while his mum was answering the speeding summons in Naas.

The previous December she had been caught by traffic cops driving her distinctive red Opel Calibra car at 103 mph on the Naas dual carriageway (M7 motorway). She had also been charged for not having her tax displayed and failing to produce her driving licence or insurance.

Veronica, who loved driving fast, had been fined before and was in fear of losing her licence. After the court case she was due to meet the *Sunday Independent* lawyers to draft a responding affidavit to Traynor's threatened injunction.

That evening the soccer-mad fan was looking forward to watching England play Germany in the Euros with her family. The following day she was due to fly to London to participate in a forum entitled 'Journalists Under Fire: Media Under Siege'. She was scheduled to contribute to a discussion under the topic 'Dying to Tell a Story: Journalists at Risk'.

At 9.30 a.m., as she was preparing to leave, Brian Meehan phoned Paul Ward, who was at his home in Walkinstown. He told his pal that he had to 'bring the kids to school' which was code to notify Ward and his brother Shay that the job was on.

The brothers were to wait and listen to the police frequencies on a scanner. Meehan and Holland had finalized their murder plan and would drive to the Wards immediately after the hit. The brothers' job was to dispose of the murder weapon and the motorbike.

Around 9.45 a.m. Meehan arrived at the garage where Warren was waiting for him and examined the motorbike again. He said he would be back later for it.

Meehan then asked Warren to drive to Naas in his van and look for a red Opel sports car with a KE (Kildare) registration. It would be parked somewhere in the vicinity of the courthouse. When he spotted the car the bagman was to call Meehan. There was no mention of Guerin's name.

Warren drove to Naas and parked his red van outside the local social welfare office, which he mistakenly took to be the courthouse. When he discovered his mistake, he drove down the town and asked a uniformed garda for directions.

At the same time Gilligan was pacing the floor of his room in the Hilton Hotel, constantly checking his watch and making phone calls. Carol Rooney sat in silence and listened. She particularly remembered his threatening and abusive calls to Russell Warren. He was calling his bagman a 'gobshite' and 'a bollox' and warning him 'not to fuck things up'.

Back in Naas Warren had parked the van and walked to the courthouse, all the while being bombarded with phone calls from Meehan and Gilligan. The boss was anxious to know whether he had located the red car. He said he hadn't. Gilligan told Warren that a second man was also in Naas, watching for the car from a rooftop.

Veronica had arrived in Naas early and after parking her car she had a coffee before her court appearance. She met her solicitor, Brian Price, on the steps of the court at 10.40 a.m. He told her that the police were happy that her documentation was in order so she should get off with a fine.

Shortly before 12.30 p.m. Veronica's case – one of 225 listed for the day – was called before Judge Thomas Ballagh. Mr Price told the judge that his client wanted to apologize to the court for the offence and would stay within the limit in future. With a straight face he assured the court that Veronica's driving was improving – this time she was going a mile slower than the previous time she had been caught speeding! Veronica was fined £150 (€300) for the speeding offence. The case was over in a few minutes. Hugely relieved that the judge had been lenient, she walked to the door of the court and thanked her solicitor.

Veronica returned to her car and set out for Dublin. It was now just after 12.30 p.m. and the day was getting warmer. As she drove off mobile phones were crackling with activity between Naas, Dublin and Amsterdam. Predatory eyes had spotted the red Opel Calibra heading towards the motorway.

Russell Warren was walking towards the courthouse when he spotted the car. He phoned Meehan, who was sitting on the motorbike parked down a side road off the Naas dual carriageway. Holland was his pillion passenger. He had the powerful .357 Magnum tucked inside his leather jacket. Meehan checked she was the only one in the car and told Warren to follow her and report on the route.

Warren tailed Guerin, staying about four cars behind her on the road. As she passed near the village of Rathcoole he phoned Meehan to tell him. 'OK, I see it,' Meehan shouted back and begun weaving through the traffic, stalking the red car. The bike sped past Warren's van and stopped behind Veronica's car. There were two other gang cars in the traffic monitoring her movements. One of them was driven by Peter Mitchell.

As usual Veronica was constantly on the phone in the car. At 12.50 p.m. she called her mother, Bernie, with the good news of her near escape.

'Mum I got off! I was only fined £100 and won't lose my licence,' she said cheerily. She was too preoccupied to notice the motorbike bearing down behind her.

At the junction of the Boot Road and Naas Road Veronica stopped for the red light. She rang a garda friend to tell him about the good news from Naas court. At that moment the bike drew up beside the car.

Holland had already pulled the gun from his jacket and was clutching it in his right hand. He put a foot down on the road to balance himself, reached over and smashed in the driver's window, sending shards of glass over the journalist.

Veronica was leaving a voice message on the policeman's answering service. 'Hi. I did very well...eh...fined a maximum of 150 quid ...alt...' In the chilling recording the cheerful voice suddenly disappeared with a sharp crack. Then there was the sound of a phone key being pressed and another crack. Then silence. It was timed at exactly 12.54 p.m.

Dutchy fired two shots at point-blank range hitting her in the chest. Veronica slumped to her left, across the passenger seat. The gunman reached in and fired another four shots into her body, hitting her in the back.

The powerful bullets tore through her body causing devastation. Meehan shouted to his accomplice: 'That's it...that's enough.' Holland sat back on the bike, casually put the weapon back in his jacket and they roared off into the traffic. Two other cars pulled out and drove at speed behind it.

In one of her rare interviews about that fateful day Bernie Guerin would later recall: 'Three minutes and 48 seconds after we spoke... she was dead.'

When the lights went green none of the vehicles stopped near the red Opel Calibra moved. Their drivers and passengers sat in shock, staring at the car, its engine still running, as they tried to assimilate the violent scene they'd just witnessed. They'd all seen similar scenarios in the movies but never anything so horrifying in reality.

One of the drivers, a nurse, ran to the car. She pulled Veronica back into her seat and felt for a pulse. There was none.

Veronica Guerin, wife, mother, courageous journalist and the sworn enemy of John Gilligan and John Traynor, was dead. Organized crime had just set a new precedent in depravity.

———————

Warren had witnessed the horrific incident. The hapless bagman had become an accessory to murder. Traffic was at a standstill as more shocked motorists got out of their cars and ran to Veronica's car. Warren drove off as people were frantically phoning the police and emergency services. He was in shock. 'I froze. I went to get out as if I could help. I just stopped. It was like slow motion. I realized what we were after doing,' he told police months later. Further down the road he got out of the van and threw up. He had several missed calls from Gilligan. When he regained his composure, he rang his boss back.

'Are they gone? Did they get away?' Gilligan demanded as he answered the call. Warren replied that the pair on the bike had just shot somebody. 'Are they dead?' Gilligan asked. Warren was still in shock. He said that the person in the car had been shot six times. 'The same thing will happen to you and your mate [Paul Cradden] if you do anything about it,' Gilligan warned Warren before hanging up. The stunned bagman went to meet a friend for a drink as he'd realized he needed an alibi.

Meehan and Holland sped to the Wards' house in Walkinstown, using back roads which have long since been gobbled up in the city's urban sprawl. They arrived at the garage within minutes of the murder. At the same time Peter Mitchell was spotted by an off-duty garda driving at speed towards Walkinstown, coming from the general direction of the murder scene.

Paul and Shay Ward were waiting in the house when Meehan and Holland arrived. The Tosser was pumped up with adrenalin and the lines of cocaine he had snorted before going on the deadly mission. He began jabbering on about how the hit had gone down with military precision – it had been a perfect job.

Holland on the other hand was totally calm and in control. He left the gun on a table to be disposed of and washed his hands. He complimented Ward on the great job he was doing renovating the house. It was as if nothing had happened. The motorbike was also left in the garage for disposal. Holland soon departed, getting a lift down to Crumlin Village where he collected his unemployment assistance payment.

Shay Ward, meanwhile, brought Meehan to the Greenmount lockup, where he quickly changed his clothes to get rid of any forensic evidence. Ward later took the clothes away in a bag and burned them. He dropped Meehan to Aungier Street, in central Dublin, at 1.30 p.m., where he was spotted by Detective Sergeant John O'Driscoll, the head of the North Central Divisional Drug Unit, who noted the sighting.

Meehan then met Mitchell. The pair walked across town to Bowden's hairdressing salon on Moore Street. On the way Meehan called Paul Ward to check if he had disposed of the gun. Ward was already on his way to do so, sitting on a bus. He was petrified that he might get caught with the weapon. The .357 Magnum Colt Python revolver was never recovered.

Bowden had been in the shop all that morning and through lunchtime. It was to be his alibi. Sometime before 2 p.m. Bowden met Meehan and Mitchell nearby.

Meehan told him what had happened. He said it was a 'good job this morning'. As if he was talking about the winning score in the Euros, he added:

> I thought Paddy was only going to fire one or two rounds at her.
> I was surprised at how cool he was. He emptied it into her. Fair
> play to him.

Back in his Amsterdam hotel room Gilligan's phone was 'hopping'. He got a quick call telling him to look at his TV for the first reports of an assassination in Dublin. He was delighted with the day's work. It appeared that everything had gone to plan.

Carol Rooney witnessed the entire drama unfold through Gilligan's conversations with his minions. She later said she became sick with fear realizing that Gilligan had not been making idle threats over the previous nine months.

Her immature mind swirled uncontrollably in a state of panic as she tried to comprehend the horrific situation in which she now found herself. Rooney was trapped in a nightmare with a real-life beast. She was too terrified to even speak. 'I knew that he was involved in the murder – I couldn't imagine him being so evil,' she would later tell gardaí.

She heard Gilligan phone Dutchy Holland. He was laughing and joking. 'Did ya hear the good news?' Gilligan asked. 'I hear you put a smile on her face.' Rooney said that Holland gave him a quick report on how the shooting went down, like he was describing a walk in the park. Gilligan also spoke to Meehan several times.

'Ah well, that's that. She [Veronica] wasn't going to get away with it. I wonder what criminals she will be writing about and investigating now she is in heaven,' the little man laughed. Gilligan wasn't quite as loquacious, however, when Geraldine then phoned demanding to know if he had anything to do with the murder. He swore on his children's lives that he hadn't. He has maintained the same line for the past twenty-five years.

After the call he turned his attention to his terrified girlfriend. He reminded her that she and her family would be harmed if she ever opened her mouth. Rooney later said he threatened her in much the same way he had menaced Russell Warren and Veronica Guerin.

Gilligan told the teenager that Veronica had cancer and 'was going to die anyway'. It illustrated how delusional the gangster had become as he tried to conceive a warped logic for the atrocity. Veronica had been in perfect health before her life was so brutally ended.

Despite the drama unfolding back in Ireland, it was business as usual for Factory John. By 2.30 p.m., one hour and thirty-six minutes after the murder, Carol Rooney was paying a visit to the Bureau de Change in Centraal Station. She exchanged £40,000 (€78,000).

Gilligan's business partner Speedy Fegan and his associate were driving between Newry and Belfast when a news flash came on the radio reporting the murder of the high-profile journalist in Dublin. He later recalled:

> The minute it came on the radio, Fegan said in a matter-of-fact way: 'That was the Dublin lads. They got her. I didn't think they would. There'll be a lot of shite flying now.'

———

John Traynor had also carefully concocted an alibi for the time of the murder. As the shots were fired Traynor was in one of his racing cars at Mondello Park, a few miles from Naas. Before he had finished his first lap, he overturned the car on a hairpin bend known as the 'Coca-Cola' corner by racers.

When people rushed to the car they saw that he was shocked but uninjured. It was suggested that he should go for a check-up to Naas General Hospital. He was in the accident and emergency ward when he received the call that Veronica had been murdered. According to eyewitnesses he appeared stunned at the news although that was probably deliberate to build his alibi. Traynor knew that his life would never be the same again. That afternoon he went on a booze binge with his fellow fraudster Sean Fitzgerald and a number of London crime associates.

About an hour later the young guns had put the murder behind them and went on a marathon drinking session in the Hole in the Wall pub on Blackhorse Avenue, not far from Bowden's new home beside the Phoenix Park. They drank and watched the Euros – the same match Veronica Guerin had been planning to view that evening.

The group included Bowden, Julie Bacon, Mitchell, Meehan, his girlfriend Fiona Walsh, and other friends of Bowden. Later that night Meehan got in a physical fight with another drinker in the pub toilet. The Tosser was still keyed up after the murder.

At closing time the raucous group went back to Bowden's house for a party. Bowden's neighbour, Senan Molony was the crime reporter at the *Irish Star*. He had spent the day covering one of the most distressing stories of his career. Molony had been to the scene of the murder and saw his colleague's body in the car. He felt sick and distraught. The murder had sent shockwaves through every newsroom in the country – journalists were now targets of organized crime.

When Molony arrived home that evening he noticed trays of alcohol being brought into Bowden's home. Bowden had been a neighbour from hell ever since he bought the house from a garda in October 1995.

The journalist later told the Special Criminal Court:

> Mr Bowden lived by night. He was constantly active and moving around at night. He often had people back to his house, five or six times a week. There was always incessant, blaring 'techno' music coming from the house.

That night the party went on till around 5 a.m. and Molony was sure that the mob were celebrating the murder.

The following morning the gang went back to work, distributing hash and collecting cash to be sent to Gilligan to organize yet another shipment.

Meehan later bragged about the murder to a friend of Bowden's, shop assistant Julian Clohessy. On 11 July Clohessy was out with Bowden, Meehan and the rest of the gang in the POD nightclub in central Dublin. Clohessy was stunned when Meehan, who was stoned on cocaine and booze, gloated that he had been involved in the murder.

Meehan claimed that before she was shot Veronica had pleaded with him. 'She said, "Please don't shoot me in the face",' said Meehan, as if he was recalling something as mundane as crossing the road.

'I said, "Fuck you, you bitch",' Meehan boasted.

CHAPTER SEVENTEEN

———

PRIME SUSPECT

For most Irish citizens the abiding, indelible memory of 26 June 1996 is one of shock: the kind of debilitating shock that feels like an out-of-body experience. People remember where they were when they heard the news of the execution of Veronica Guerin. It was Ireland's JFK moment.

Coming so soon after the murder of Detective Garda Jerry McCabe in Limerick by the IRA, it created a public perception that the country was in a state of lawlessness and chaos. It also sent a shudder of fear through the Establishment. Anyone who could interfere with the workings of organized crime was justified in believing they could be the next target. And in the mind of John Gilligan they were all certainly fair game.

It was just before 1 p.m. when this writer's mobile phone rang in the *Sunday World* newsroom. It was a detective friend who was in no mood for small talk. He bluntly told me that Veronica had been shot. I laughed and told him that he had heard a sick joke.

'I'm sorry...She has just been shot...She's dead...I'm standing beside the car now on the Naas Road. It happened about five minutes ago.' He spoke in a short, staccato burst. 'Look, for your own sake, just stay in the office or go home. Don't come up here,' he advised.

Within a few minutes I had made my way to the scene of the outrage. As news began to filter out, the phone started ringing and didn't stop. Colleagues were asking in disbelief if the news was true. Other garda contacts were calling to say what had just happened. Everyone was stunned.

Squad cars hemmed in the red sports car and the area was being cordoned off with crime scene tape. Detectives and uniformed officers who had arrived at the scene seemed to be as bewildered as everyone else. Ashen-faced cops came over to commiserate. A senior detective began organizing officers to start interviewing eyewitnesses and keep the crime scene clear.

A few feet away my closest professional rival, a friend, was lying in the driver's seat of her car, dead. Her body was full of bullets and her clothes were drenched in blood. It was a dreadful sight, a memory that has never faded with time. Five years later those same emotions came rushing back when another colleague and friend, Martin O'Hagan from the *Sunday World*, was also executed by a criminal gang.

Paramedics had confirmed that Veronica was dead. The scene was being preserved for forensic examination. In the quest to bring her killers to justice every bit of evidence, no matter how small, was gathered and preserved.

Veronica's execution was one of the biggest crime stories in Irish history. But then a gut-wrenching reality suddenly struck home. I, like Veronica, had been threatened and had received intermittent police protection. I had been advised about personal security and taken precautions. Nothing had happened. No one actually believed that the criminals would step across the line and fire fatal shots.

I was convulsed with fear and shock. My mouth went dry, my legs felt like jelly. I was throwing up. Tears streamed down my cheeks. The whole world had gone completely fucking mad. I lost it for a while, until a colleague and a detective friend brought me away to gather my thoughts and composure. Life would never be the same. A lot of lives changed for ever that afternoon.

Crime reporting was no longer a 'game' in the way that we had understood it to be. The fine line in a modern democracy that explicitly protected a free press from criminal or terrorist reprisals no longer existed. This was the equivalent of a criminal coup – a barbaric attack on the foundations of Irish society. It was another act of narco-terrorism, similar to the car bomb attack on Dr James Donovan fourteen years earlier.

Tony Hickey, the garda officer who would lead the subsequent investigation, remembers how the attack shocked even the most experienced cops:

> Despite the fact that there had been an attack on Veronica's house, and she had been shot, I don't think that anybody would visualize a situation prior to the 26th of June that anyone would have thought of assassinating her.

Within twenty-four hours of the atrocity, people began placing flowers outside the Dáil in Kildare Street. It followed a suggestion by Joe Duffy on his Radio One show the next morning as he reflected the sentiment of the vast majority of Irish people. His idea galvanized the nation.

Soon there was a virtual wall of flowers, symbolizing the feelings of the people. Thousands of notes and prayers pinned to the bouquets expressed sorrow, demanded action and asked God to mind the woman who overnight had become a modern-day martyr in the eyes of the Irish people.

The politicians knew they had to act decisively. Decades of neglect and inaction had created a monster that now threatened the security of the Republic. Organized crime had issued a spine-chilling threat and society demanded justice.

Apart from Veronica's family and friends, the murder came as an earth-shattering blow to her colleagues at the *Sunday Independent*. Willie Kealy, her news editor, was one of the last people to speak with Veronica. He could barely verbalize his sense of grief.

A book of condolences was opened in the office of the Middle Abbey Street headquarters of Independent Newspapers and was signed by thousands of people, including church, political and business leaders. Among the signatories was Gerry Hutch, the Monk, the man Traynor and Gilligan had tried to blame for the previous attacks on Veronica. In a hugely symbolic gesture Hutch quietly took his place in the queue. For a high-profile criminal godfather to publicly register his revulsion at a crime was unprecedented. He was sending a message to the culprits that, in the eyes of a dying breed of so-called ordinary decent criminals, the murder was an egregious breach of unwritten protocols.

Hutch knew the identity of the prime suspect as did most cops and reporters. It didn't take the deductive abilities of Sherlock Holmes to work it out. John Joseph Gilligan had the motive and the brutal capacity.

But knowing that he was responsible and proving it were very different propositions. Fear had always been his weapon of choice and now he had taken it to a new level. It would strengthen the wall of silence around him. However, he had thrown down the gauntlet and the State had no choice but to pick it up.

The morning after the murder, the *Irish Independent*'s front-page headline summed up the feelings of frustration: 'We know who killed her – and he's untouchable.'

Factory John had become Ireland's Public Enemy Number One.

In his detached state of mind Gilligan genuinely believed he was invulnerable, as did the likes of Meehan and Mitchell. They reckoned the Guerin investigation would go the same way as the increasing numbers of gangland murder cases, none of which had been solved. All they would have to do was bide their time before it fizzled out.

After the murder Gilligan and Carol Rooney went to lie low at the rented house in Aalst which had been sourced through Thomas Gorst. He was visited there by Holland and Meehan for a fuller debrief on the 'good job'.

On the following Friday afternoon this writer tried to contact John Gilligan. Geraldine sounded angry and put out when she answered the phone at the equestrian centre. She had plenty to be angry about.

In the two days since the murder Jessbrook's thriving business had collapsed. Pictures of the multi-million-euro equestrian centre had been published next to stories describing how it had been built by Gilligan even though he was officially unemployed. The huge showjumping arena was almost completed and several major events were already booked to take place there. Overnight, all work stopped, and the events were cancelled.

In the wake of the horrific crime, the people whose patronage Geraldine wanted would not set foot in the place. Her dreams were shattered. On the phone Geraldine was anxious to point out that she was separated from Gilligan and that he didn't live at Jessbrook: 'Do you want his phone number? Because he doesn't live here, so I don't know why everybody keeps ringing me. Thank you, goodbye.'

Gilligan answered his mobile phone almost immediately. I introduced myself and announced that I wanted to discuss Veronica Guerin's murder with him. He needed little encouragement to talk about the case. 'I was terrible sorry to hear about that and I had nothing to do with it' was his opening remark.

The following is an edited extract from the transcript of the forty-five-minute telephone conversation that ensued. It is a classic example of Gilligan's lies, obfuscation and dissemblance.

Williams: Do you know that they are putting your name around a lot, John, for doing it?

Gilligan: The only ones putting my name around is the newspapers. Terrible, terrible sorry to hear it. I had nothing to do with it. I had nothing to worry about the [assault] case. I'd have had the case over and done and won. It's only a Mickey Mouse case.

Williams: Yeah?

Gilligan: Six months is all it'll take at the very worst [in prison] and I've no problem. I had it won, it's home and dried and I certainly wouldn't have got time.

Williams: Well, who do you think would have it done, John?

Gilligan: I don't know, Paul, and that's telling you one thing. I don't know, I don't know, I didn't do it, I didn't get it done. Not in a million years did I get it done. I'm very sorry for her. I don't deal in drugs.

Williams: But you are not in the country at the moment. It seems a bit suspicious that you left the country on Tuesday night, the day before the murder?

Gilligan: I wasn't in the country when anything happened [to] that lady.

Williams: Well, we know that you left beforehand. It all looks very suspicious, John. This stuff isn't being made up by the papers. Even your old cronies in the underworld, they're saying that it is you who organized the murder of Veronica Guerin.

Gilligan: I'm telling you one hundred per cent I don't believe the police are doing this, saying I did it. It's the fucking newspapers.

Williams: So you are saying, John, that the newspapers just want to set up John Gilligan?

Gilligan: I am, yeah, I think that's what they are trying to do. They're trying to get me in trouble.

Williams: I work in the same business as Veronica and was friendly with her. We are all absolutely gutted over what has happened. Do you understand that?

Gilligan: Well, so am I. I like Veronica.

Williams: Why did you fucking beat her, then, if you liked her?

Gilligan: I didn't beat the shit out of her.

Williams: You gave her a fair few digs. I saw her afterwards. We talked about it. Jesus, John, beating up a woman?

Gilligan: No, I don't beat up women. Before I go any further, I don't beat up women. I had no problems with the case. She lied and she went home and changed her clothes. I don't know who beat her up. All her statement was lies. It's a terrible thing to say about the lady, she's dead. Lord have mercy on her soul.

Williams: But what about the statement you made after the assault when another *Sunday Independent* reporter phoned you? "I'll fucking kill you and your family, my old flower..." You think you are a hard man, you're well known in the villainy business as a hard man.

Gilligan: I'm not hard. I believe in Ireland.

Williams: Who do you think did this, John, because whoever it was really stitched you on it?

Gilligan: That's right, they stitched me. Very cute, very cute, now. Let's ask you a question and answer honestly, do you think I done it or got it done?

Williams: I don't know if you got it done or not, John. It is hard to know what is going on when someone on a motorbike pulls up and shoots a woman like that. Everyone I know in the underworld seems upset by this.

Gilligan: I'm pissed off about it, too. I'm well pissed off, too.

Williams: You have to see how it looks. You go away and twelve hours later Veronica is murdered. Did the guards contact you at all since you went away? Will you come home to talk with them?

Gilligan: Sure, the last time I was away after the assault, the alleged assault, I was in contact with the cops daily and as soon as they wanted me to come home I did. I don't know, they must know who was shooting Veronica. Sure, it's not the first time she was, I don't know it's a terrible loss of life for her. There's only one person that we know didn't shoot her and that was herself.

Williams: You tell me then, John, who do you think would have done something like this, with your extensive knowledge of the Dublin crime scene? You tell me.

Gilligan: I don't know. Some cunt, sleveen bastard.

Williams: Veronica didn't do you any favours by getting killed?

Gilligan: No, she didn't do me any favours, that's for sure. She didn't do me any favours in coming and causing me grief and looking for stories when I had none to give...She got killed, that's the worst thing that could ever happen, I'm sorry for her, I'm sorry for her family, I'm sorry for her child and her husband, I am sorry, believe me, I am sorry. If I wasn't sorry, I would say I don't give a bollocks. I am genuinely sorry. I had the case won.

Williams: But did you have the case won? It looked that you could get up to three years for the assault.

Gilligan: Paul, on my children's lives, right? Lord have mercy on Veronica's life and on her grave, I was going to win the case one hundred per cent. I don't like to talk about the deceased as a liar because she cannot defend herself, but I can't defend meself either…I had me case won, one hundred thousand million per cent…trillion per cent!…My record was putting a hole in a factory wall with nobody in it, going in, stealing out of it and if I got away, I got away, if I got caught, I went to jail. That was the end of that.

Williams: What are you doing now? What are you earning a living at now? I hear you're one of the biggest cannabis dealers in the country.

Gilligan: Have you? I don't believe you. I have nothing to do with drugs.

Williams: Can you imagine the amount of heat that is going to come down on everyone in your line of work as a result of this murder?

Gilligan: Yeah, well, what can I do for them? There's nothing I can do, there's enough on me and I didn't do it. Someone put it down to me, so I don't know. I can't do anything other than face the court or the police or face anybody. If somebody wants me I'll be there, there's no problem…I hope they find the fuck who done the murder and then I hope when they catch him, that you will write and say you blamed John Gilligan in the wrong.

Williams: What are you working at, what would you describe yourself as now, for the purpose of a story? A retired criminal, a businessman, are you employed anywhere?

Gilligan: You can put me down as what you want.

Williams: But what are you? I am a crime correspondent, that's what I do now, what do *you* do?

Gilligan: I'm the main suspect in something I know nothing about, that's what I am.

Williams: I know that. Describe what you do, then, for a living. You don't work in the equestrian centre, you don't own the equestrian centre, you're not registered as being employed anywhere, so what do you do? Are you a businessman? Are you a drug dealer? I have to describe you as something?

Gilligan: A small little fella...I don't think you're upset over Veronica at all 'cause you are laughing and all.

Williams: I'm not laughing and joking about Veronica Guerin being shot at. It's not a laugh and a joking matter. I'm laughing at the fact that your only answer to me when I'm asking you a straight question is a smart arse remark, when I'm trying to find out your side of the story, when you're accused of one of the most brutal murders in this State...Do you not think I am entitled to an answer, John? You say you are no longer a criminal and you are not a drug dealer. Then what are you, apart from being a small, little fella with a line in smart arse commentary?

Gilligan: I breed horses, yeah, I'm a registered breeder. I am, yeah, I am.

Williams: Oh, so where do you base your activities as a horse breeder?

Gilligan refused to say where he operated as a horse breeder. Questioning returned to the murder.

Gilligan: I swear to you I had nothing to do with it. If I hated her, I wouldn't do that to her. I would scream and shout at her on the spur of the moment but to go and ask people to do this and do that is just madness.

Williams: Did you hear that the Independent Group are offering a reward of a £100,000 (€200,000) for helping to catch Veronica's killers? Would you help the guards if you could?

Gilligan: I've never grassed in me life before. That's all I'd say, I hope they catch who done it. Paul, is there something I can do for her family, like, I didn't do anything, but if there is anything I can do because I am genuinely sorry it happened, it's a terrible tragedy...I'm sorry that...I'm sorry she's not around. I don't know, maybe I should be pissed-off even saying it, but ring me back if you think I can do anything.

He ended the call on that note and hung up before he could be asked any more questions.

A few hours later the removal of Veronica's remains took place to the Dublin Airport church. It was the same church where she attended Mass every Sunday morning with Graham and Cathal. The celebrant, Father Declan Doyle, a close family friend, said of the journalist: 'She raised questions of Church, State and institutions, often awkward, difficult, even embarrassing, but ultimately important questions.'

Her little boy was confused by all that was happening around him. He touched his mummy's coffin and waved as if he could see her as the congregation sang the hymn 'Be Not Afraid'.

The following morning the President of Ireland, Mary Robinson, and leaders of Church and State mingled with several hundred friends, colleagues, police officers and ordinary citizens in a deeply sad funeral ceremony. Before the service ended, Graham Turley got up to speak about his beloved wife. Graham's voice was calm and gentle as he said:

> The best day I ever had was on 21 September 1985, the year myself and Veronica promised to love, cherish and honour each other 'til death do us part. We also promised each other that we would have fun. And we really did, believe you me, we had a lot of fun. Then we were rewarded seven years ago with Cathal. After that we were one small group together that no one could get between. I am also saying goodbye today to my best pal.

As he walked back to his seat the congregation stood and applauded a man whose courage was deeply moving in the face of such overwhelming despair.

During the Mass, gifts which encapsulated Veronica's life were offered on the altar: the cherished picture with Manchester United star Eric Cantona, her sports medals, her wedding picture, a football, Manchester United gloves and the FA Cup semi-final programme. Veronica's sister Claire read from Veronica's own Bible, reciting 'Over wisdom, evil can never triumph.'

Little Cathal followed his mother's coffin, clutching a spray of lilies with a red rose at its heart. Graham lifted him to kiss the coffin. The picture became an abiding image of the tragedy. Cathal wrapped his arms around President Robinson's neck, hugging her like an auntie. 'You did her proud,' the President reassured his brave dad.

At Dardistown Cemetery Veronica Guerin was laid to rest on Saturday 29 June. Cathal prayed the 'Hail Mary', while his father crouched beside him at the graveside. When the prayers had finished the little boy blew a kiss into her grave, saying, 'Goodbye Mummy.'

The following day Graham and Cathal visited the gates of the Dáil to see the mountain of flowers and messages of support which had been placed there by thousands of angry and fearful citizens. The Irish population's tolerance for John Gilligan and his kind had evaporated.

On Monday 1 July 1996, at 1 p.m., the country came to a standstill. In factories and farms, offices and on the streets everywhere, people stood and observed a minute's silence for Veronica Guerin. Earlier that morning in the High Court, John Traynor had succeeded in blocking Veronica's article about him. Graham Turley attended the hearing as a show of solidarity with the *Sunday Independent* editor Aengus Fanning. Traynor had instructed his lawyers to continue their efforts to stop the *Sunday Independent* running a story about his drug trafficking operation. In reality there was no need – the only person who knew the details was now dead.

In Traynor's affidavit Veronica was portrayed as unstable, irrational and threatening. Traynor claimed that Veronica had admitted that her story about him was false. It was all in accordance with the letter of the law. As one observer recalls, it was like watching a boxing match in which only one boxer can throw the punches. Veronica was depicted as an aggressive liar, as first they murdered her and then they tried, unsuccessfully, to tarnish her reputation.

It was a victory for Traynor when the court granted the injunction prohibiting the *Sunday Independent* from publishing any story stating he was involved in the sale or supply of drugs.

A week later it was John Gilligan's turn to benefit from the murder of Veronica Guerin. On 9 July, two weeks after the murder, a large group of reporters arrived at Kilcock District Court. Veronica's former colleagues were still reeling from the shock of her murder. Garda sniffer dogs were brought in to check the courtroom for a bomb, something which had never been seen at the local court before. It underlined the continuing sense of threat.

Neither Gilligan nor his lawyer was anywhere to be seen. There was no need for them to attend. In the stuffy health centre, which had taken on the monthly role of courtroom, Judge John Brophy took his seat at the bench.

A number of cases had to be processed before the *D.P.P. v. John Joseph Gilligan* came up for mention. The packed courtroom fell silent as the court clerk announced Gilligan's case.

Superintendent Brendan Quinn, who was handling the case for the State, rose to his feet. 'Is Mr Hanahoe in court?' Judge Brophy asked about Gilligan's solicitor. There was no reply.

Superintendent Quinn told the court his instructions were to have the case struck out because the State's only witness, Veronica Guerin, was dead.

Judge Brophy explained the legal process as he wrote the words 'struck out' on the copies of the court summons in front of him. 'The reason it cannot go ahead is because there is no effective evidence that can be offered in a court of law because of her untimely death within the last two weeks,' he said.

He then took off his watch, placed it in front of him on the desk and asked the court to stand with him to observe a minute's silence in memory 'of the lady who was the principal witness in this case'.

When the minute's silence had ended, the judge described the murdered reporter as a 'crusader in her own right'. He urged the media to continue to expose the godfathers:

> Remember the hymn at Dublin Airport church, 'Be Not Afraid'. If you are afraid, then the barons and the major gangland people in this country will take away your rights and freedoms which this country has fought for over many decades. Ms Guerin lost her life as a result of what she did. I hope that other people in the media will follow on in her tracks.

As the judge was speaking, in Dublin the government announced the appointment of a new Garda Commissioner, Pat Byrne. Veronica's friend had trained with the FBI and Scotland Yard and had spent much of his career in the anti-terrorist Special Branch. Noel Conroy, the former head of the Serious Crime Squad, who was by now an Assistant Commissioner, was promoted to the rank of Deputy Commissioner in charge of operations to replace the vacancy left by Byrne. Their priority was to lead the counter-offensive against organized crime.

The Justice Minister Nora Owen, also a friend of Veronica, announced a package to alleviate the immediate difficulties in the criminal justice system. Most significantly, there was also a commitment to establish a 'special unit' to go after the proceeds of crime. It would be headed by the police but would comprise officials from the Revenue and Social Welfare.

One of Pat Byrne's first tasks as Commissioner was to advise the then Taoiseach, John Bruton, and Nora Owen about the new unit. The government had planned to put it in the control of civil servants, but Byrne argued that it should be led by the police.

'If you don't do this, then in a year you will come back and say that it was a mistake not to put the gardaí in charge. Organized crime knows we won't be bullied,' Byrne urged Bruton, winning their agreement.

Legislation on the disposal of criminal assets was also in the process of being drafted, based on a private member's bill put forward by the then opposition Justice spokesman, John O'Donoghue. The legislation would reduce the standards of proof required to seize a criminal's assets.

The Dáil achieved an historic record when, in the space of just four weeks, in July 1996, it passed a tough raft of anti-crime legislation. The *Irish Bar Review* described it as '...the most wide-ranging proposals for change in Irish criminal law and procedure since the foundation of the State'.

Six new Acts of Parliament were passed on the night of 25 July, the eve of exactly one month after Veronica's murder. The package of laws was tailor-made to provide statutory mechanisms for identifying the proceeds of criminal activity and empowering officers of the State to question where the money and assets came from and seize them. The new laws laid the legislative framework for the Criminal Assets Bureau.

John Gilligan, the gangster whose swift rise had changed the face of organized crime, had also single-handedly dragged Irish law enforcement into the twentieth century.

The fightback had begun.

———

CHAPTER EIGHTEEN

THE INVESTIGATION BEGINS

John Gilligan planned to wait in his Belgium hideaway while the dust settled on the furore raging back in Ireland. He reckoned that Veronica Guerin would soon be forgotten. In time his impregnable wall of silence would kill the investigation. And the cops were already swamped investigating the murder of Jerry McCabe. It was merely a waiting game.

He assured Geraldine, distraught over the sudden boycott of Jessbrook, that he had nothing to do with the crime and everything would be back on track soon. He would be cleared of all suspicion and everyone would realize he was an innocent victim of the gutter media.

Gilligan was confident that there was no way the cops would ever get the evidence to charge him or bring down his drug business. The murder had been too well planned. The drug operation was in the safe hands of his trusted lieutenants who were all rock solid. Anyway, no one would ever dare give up him or the gang. If anyone did he would have them dealt with. He was the master of gangland.

But Gilligan's extreme confidence was the product of his hubris. The mobster didn't possess the cognitive capacity to understand that he had taken a step too far. The killing was compared to the assassinations in Sicily of two senior prosecuting magistrates, Giovanni Falcone and

Paolo Borsellino four years earlier. The judges died in bombings, three months apart, atrocities which were carried out on the orders of the head of the Corleonesi Mafia, Salvatore Riina. It proved to be a watershed in the history of Cosa Nostra as it impelled the Italian State to launch an unprecedented counter-offensive to take them down. The same scenario was about to be played out in Ireland.

The murder of Veronica Guerin would prove to be a major miscalculation. Over the following few months 330 individuals were arrested, 1,500 were interviewed without arrest and 3,500 statements were taken. A large quantity of drugs, guns and cash were also seized. It was the biggest search and arrest operation ever mounted in the history of An Garda Síochána.

Tony Hickey was happy for Gilligan to continue labouring under his delusions and remain in Belgium. The wily Kerryman was on holiday in Portugal when he overheard two Irish people talking about the murder. His phone started to ring and he was quickly brought up to speed on the events unfolding in Dublin. Pat Byrne, who was then in charge of garda operations, knew Hickey was the ideal person for the difficult task ahead and told him:

> They've [criminals] crossed the Rubicon, this is a step too far. They [government] realize now the threat they pose to society so there won't be a problem with resources. We want you to take charge Tony, this is your investigation. You do what you have to do...whatever you want, just ask.

Hickey never got excited in a crisis. From when he first became a cop he was known as someone who considered all the options before reacting. In many ways his demeanour resembled the contemplative, unflappable Chief Superintendent Christopher Foyle, the central character in the TV detective drama *Foyle's War*. Hickey spent the last three days of his holiday plotting his strategy and making calls to Dublin.

Lucan garda station had been chosen as the base for the investigation just after the incident. The nearest station to the scene of the crime, Clondalkin, was too small to accommodate the number of officers required.

Over the first twenty-four hours after the murder there was chaos in the incident room in Lucan. Officers from specialist squads and district units all over the city were being called in. Everyone had a theory and wanted to play a part in the investigation. An army of angry officers turned up to volunteer for duty. One member of the investigation team recalls:

> There was sheer bedlam. We were trying to get a structure and a focus on the situation. There were so many gardaí coming into work, the place was literally jammed. The scene of the crime had to be forensically analysed and statements taken from eyewitnesses to build a picture of what happened. Everyone was stunned at the murder coming so soon after the murder of Jerry McCabe. There was a sense that this just couldn't go on.

Detective Inspector Jerry O'Connell and the local district officer, Superintendent Len Ahern, took charge of organizing the incident room and co-ordinating the investigation. Detectives from the old Central Detective Unit, now called the NBCI, were drafted in. O'Connell knew of the mammoth task ahead. No one could afford to screw up.

Hickey returned from Portugal on the following Saturday, dropped his bags at home and drove the short distance to Lucan station. He began sifting through the various statements and reports and was briefed by his officers on the scene.

A graduate of the FBI Academy in Quantico, Virginia, Hickey had also been trained to use the Scotland Yard template of organizing a major crime enquiry. He knew the Gilligan investigation needed control, direction and focus.

On Monday morning Hickey and O'Connell began putting together the group who would become known as the Lucan Investigation Team. They were hand-picked gardaí Hickey and his senior officers knew and trusted. Detective Inspector Todd O'Loughlin, an accomplished investigator who was attached to the Investigation Branch at Garda HQ, was brought in. So, too, was quiet-spoken Detective Sergeant John O'Driscoll. He was a trusted confidant of Hickey's who had spent most of his career as a member of the surveillance squad attached to the CDU. For almost twenty years he had been involved in keeping tabs on all the major gangland players, including the Monk and the General.

The senior officers then selected officers from divisional detective and uniformed units across the city and also from specialist squads at Garda HQ. The team included experienced investigators and younger cops who they reckoned were up to the task ahead.

Within a week of the murder, Hickey had a team of around a hundred officers working on the case. The actual investigation team consisted of a core of thirty detectives. They were also supported by the gardaí's specialist units.

The enquiry team was broken into two smaller teams. The group, headed by O'Connell, would collate all available information about the crime and run the nerve centre of the investigation. They would gather the forensic evidence and all other relevant information. O'Driscoll was given the time-consuming job of analysing every call made by every known suspect in and around the gang. He co-ordinated with the Crime and Security Branch (C 3) in the Phoenix Park, who provided phone taps, and the National Surveillance Unit (NSU).

The other team, under Todd O'Loughlin, would compile and investigate a list of potential suspects. Information, such as recorded sightings of the various players, was gathered from collators in every district in the city, C 3, CDU and Special Branch.

Within days the list included over 200 names of known criminals and members of the IRA and the INLA. All the gangs in the city were targeted. Every criminal Veronica had ever written about or threatened to write about was scrutinized. It was a trawl of massive proportions.

Hickey ordered that each suspect be individually approached and asked to account for their movements on 26 June 1996. Every known criminal and terrorist, no matter where they stood in the underworld hierarchy, was to get a visit. The approach was to be robust and uncompromising. Gangland was about to be turned upside down.

Sitting at the top table of the incident room, Hickey told his team that he wanted the investigation to be methodical and proceed on a broad front. It would be slow, systematic and strictly by the book. The poker-faced chief would not allow the enquiry to be compromised by pressure from either the media or the politicians. There would be no short cuts or quick fixes.

Hickey was acutely aware that he and his team were in the full glare of public attention, but there would be no rush to assuage the public with a result. He told them: 'I will deal with the media and the politicians – you focus only on the case.'

Everyone in the country knew the names of the prime suspects as John Traynor and John Gilligan became household names overnight. Gilligan had already acknowledged that he was the man in the frame in interviews with the *Sunday World* and the *Sunday Tribune*. In an interview with *Sunday Tribune* crime correspondent Liz Allen, Gilligan actually admitted that he had threatened to murder Veronica and kidnap and rape her son Cathal.

Despite this, Hickey did not want them rounded up. To successfully smash the gang responsible he would need hard evidence that stood up to rigorous examination in court. Pulling Gilligan in for questioning now would be a waste of time. If he and his gang were involved, then they would be prepared for a 'pull'. They were all hardened criminals. The fact that Gilligan had removed himself to the Continent was a distinct advantage. In his absence, Hickey wanted the gang's weakest links identified, isolated and then exploited to the maximum.

In the previous two years there had been twelve gangland murders in Dublin alone and none of them had been solved. Hickey had been involved in most of those investigations and, while the police had identified the hit men and their motives, the problem was putting together a case that would survive in the courts. In each investigation there had been people who secretly gave information but refused to testify. In the absence of an outright confession from the killer, there was nothing to sustain a charge. Several files on gangland murders had been sent to the Director of Public Prosecutions recommending that individuals be charged. Each time the State's criminal law officer decided not to prefer charges because there simply wasn't enough evidence.

Organized crime was protected by a wall of silence. Its foundations were fear and violence and the more cases that went unsolved, the higher and harder the wall became. Gilligan, who had created an airtight organization and was the most feared godfather around, had the biggest wall of all.

Hickey knew that breaking down that wall required a wholly new and revolutionary approach. It would have to be dismantled brick by brick. Members of the actual murder gang held the key to success. But there was no mechanism in place, such as a witness protection programme, to encourage individuals to come clean in safety. Without protection, families and witnesses could be easily got at. Like everything else in the Irish criminal justice system, the people on the ground would have to improvise and Hickey resolved to cross that obstacle when he came to it.

A team member recalls Hickey's strategy. He would say:

> 'OK, Gilligan is our main suspect because he had the motive and was capable of the crime.' But he said this had to be a thorough

and professional investigation. We had to work from the outside
and move inwards, like the ripples on a pond. We had to peel away
each layer to get to the next and all the time pick up information
and evidence. If Gilligan's gang was responsible, then they would
only emerge from a process of elimination and not speculation.

Hickey was a great leader. So, too, were O'Loughlin and
O'Connell. They never panicked or got excited. Hickey
brought out the best in everyone because he had such energy
and conviction. One day, after we spoke to an associate of John
Traynor's, one guy at a conference told the chief that the criminal,
who was also an informant, said we were going the wrong way
about the enquiry, that we should be looking at such and such.
Hickey never loses the head, but you could see he was angry. 'It
would be a bad day when a fucking thug is going to tell us what
we should be doing. *We* are in charge of this investigation,' he
said. That was a turning point for everyone. We all thought,
'Yeah, Hickey's right.' From then on everyone on the team was
determined that we would solve this one.

Hickey also could not rule out the possibility, however slim, that
Gilligan's mob was not responsible. He did not want a miscarriage of
justice in the rush for vengeance. The killing could easily have been
a devious plot by a rival organization, designed to set Gilligan up.
Another theory was that the gang couldn't be so stupid and arrogant
as to organize a murder and think that there would not be major
repercussions – or could they?

The intelligence that had been gathered on Gilligan and his gang
by Kevin Carty's Operation Pineapple team proved invaluable. It had
collated the names of known associates of Gilligan, such as Meehan,
Mitchell and the Ward brothers. Lists of telephone numbers, addresses
and bank accounts had also been identified giving the investigation
a kick-start. But nothing was yet known about Bowden or Warren,

or how the gang operated. No one suspected the kind of money that was actually involved.

Officers were dispatched to Naas in the hope of finding out whether Veronica was being followed on the day of her murder. It was too well planned an attack to have been opportunistic. Hickey's attention to detail paid off.

At least one eyewitness recalled seeing a man who matched the description of Russell Warren, and a caretaker discovered that a roof tile had been dislodged on the court building. Three months later these seemingly innocuous observations provided corroboration when Russell Warren began to talk and claimed Gilligan had told him another person was watching from a rooftop. The witness could place him in the vicinity of the courthouse when Warren said he was there.

At the same time O'Loughlin's team went to work on the underworld. Unlike most gangland investigations, the criminals approached by the team were prepared to co-operate. Any villain with half a brain had by now realized that someone had gone too far. When he queued to sign the book of condolences Gerry Hutch had sent an unequivocal message that the underworld disapproved of the murder. Criminals were witnessing the unprecedented public outrage and the authorities' rush to introduce a raft of tough new anti-crime legislation. Whoever pulled the trigger had screwed them, too.

One investigation team member described the underworld trawl:

> In other cases you would expect to be told to fuck off, but the vast majority of them told us where they were and how we could check out their alibis. We talked to the criminals. We'd ask: 'What do you think about the murder? Do you know that this is going to fuck everything up for the lot of you?' The criminal fraternity was genuinely upset by the whole thing and didn't want to be seen to be suspects. It was bad for business. We started getting a lot of information which kept going back to Gilligan and his

outfit. The gangsters wanted us to know that they had nothing to do with it and that's why they talked. We also got information about other serious crimes which was passed on to other units.

We made huge connections with the underworld, which had never been done before because there hadn't, I suppose, been a good enough reason or the resources there to conduct such a campaign. When we called to see suspects we demanded that they talk to us. We weren't prepared to leave without some information. After about three weeks or so the list was getting smaller. The intelligence was pointing all the time at Gilligan. Former members of the old Factory Gang began talking because they no longer wanted to be associated with him. Every day we were making progress.

From the list of suspects Gilligan's henchmen stood out as the least co-operative. On 21 July Detective Sergeant Fergus Treanor and Detective Garda Andy O'Brien called to see Brian Meehan at his apartment. When they asked about his movements on the day of the murder, Meehan said he couldn't remember. Then he paused and said: 'I was with me father, Kevin, at his workplace.' When O'Brien asked if anyone else had been there that day to verify his story, Meehan replied, 'No,' and shut the door.

Three days later the same officers visited Peter Mitchell. O'Brien asked him where he was on 26 June. 'Probably doing what I normally do, driving around the place gettin' stopped by the fuckin' guards,' Fatso replied aggressively. Then he said he had probably been on Moore Street talking to his mother Eileen, a street trader, when they heard the news of the murder around 2 p.m. O'Brien tried to ask him another question, but Mitchell told him to 'Fuck off', climbed into his sports car and drove off at speed.

When he was approached, Paul Ward claimed that he had been at home looking after his heroin-addicted niece, helping her through withdrawals. His girlfriend, Vanessa Meehan, could corroborate his story.

Dutchy Holland was also asked to account for his movements. He politely told the officers that he had been with a friend, an elderly man, in Finglas. The same man, coincidentally, had provided Holland's alibi after the murder of Paddy Shanahan in 1994.

About three days after the murder a man out walking along the banks of the River Liffey at the Strawberry Beds saw what looked like a motorbike in the water. He had heard the appeals for information after the Guerin murder and reported it. A uniformed officer made a half-hearted effort to locate the bike but didn't find it. The tip wasn't reported to the Lucan team.

A week later the same man noticed the bike again and decided to pull it out himself. Ironically, this time he was spotted 'acting suspiciously' and someone rang the gardaí. Members of the investigation team rushed to the river and found the man with the bike. It was later claimed that Paul Ward had dumped it at that spot two days after the murder. With the help of another criminal, he had cut the bike up and brought it to the river in a van.

The motorbike was taken to the Garda Technical Bureau and rebuilt. At that stage it wasn't known if it was the right motorbike, but Hickey wondered why else someone would go to such lengths to cut up a bike and then dump it. Obviously, the bike held a clue.

It was a promising development.

CHAPTER NINETEEN

—

BLACKMAIL AND DIRTY TRICKS

As the garda investigation was picking up pace, Gilligan's operation continued to flourish and expand – as a direct consequence of the murder. Every other drug dealer was keeping his head down, but Gilligan's men showed no fear and enthusiastically filled the void, increasing the size of their shipments. The supply of hash would have dried up in the country in the first few months after the Guerin murder had it not been for Gilligan.

Operating between Belgium and the Netherlands, Gilligan organized nine shipments of cannabis during July and August 1996. In total 2,283 kilos were estimated to have arrived along the normal route. His personal profit was worth over €3.5 million.

The drugs were still being picked up as usual from the Ambassador Hotel and brought to the Greenmount lockup, from where Shay Ward and Charlie Bowden made their deliveries.

The supplies were getting larger. At times the two criminals were driving around Dublin with anything up to 100 kilos in the back of the van. All it would have taken was one eagle-eyed cop at a road traffic checkpoint and the largest drug trafficking operation in the State would have been rumbled.

A nervous Warren, who had been deeply disturbed by the murder, continued to work as their bagman. In the weeks following the killing he recruited his parents, his sister and her husband to begin counting the huge sums of money rolling in. His parents' house became the equivalent of a gangland bank, where huge piles of cash were sorted, counted and packed. Russell wasn't very generous to his folks and paid them only £50 (€100) each time they counted the dirty money. In July and August alone they counted over £2 million (€3.9 million) in cash which Warren then transported to Gilligan in Belgium. As the operation continued to spiral, Warren was too afraid to try and extricate himself.

Gilligan's primary concern now was keeping tabs on the Lucan investigation. Through the gangland grapevine and the media he could see that the crime was being pursued with unprecedented vigour. Arrogantly, he and his lieutenants still believed they couldn't be caught.

While Gilligan still expected the enquiry to run out of steam after a few months, he was determined to do everything he could to divert it away from him. He ordered his henchmen to conduct their own investigations into the police and try to plant false leads where they could.

Two days after the murder a young, uniformed cop named Rory Corcoran arrested Brian Meehan when he caught him driving despite having been disqualified for forty years. When he brought Meehan back to the Bridewell station to process him, Meehan offered to help the cop recover guns and get information on who had killed Veronica Guerin.

Corcoran was all ears, but he was clever enough to inform his detective inspector of the offer. Meehan arranged a number of meetings with Corcoran, which were attended by the senior detective. It quickly turned out that Meehan was looking for more information than he was actually giving. The cop was told to keep Meehan on side and feed him a few false lines about what the police knew.

Meanwhile Gilligan's men decided to cash in on their 'investment', Garda John O'Neill. 'We've paid O'Neill enough money, so it's time that he started earning his keep,' an underworld source overheard Paul Ward saying to Brian Meehan in early August. Ward had just had O'Neill pull a warrant for Meehan's girlfriend, Fiona Walsh, relating to casual trading offences.

A few days later Meehan and another associate met the decorated officer in Crumlin. They were sitting in a BMW car when O'Neill arrived and sat in the back seat. Meehan had no fears about coming to the point and told O'Neill that he was putting him on the 'payroll' at £500 (€970) per week. For that sum he was to 'look out' for Mitchell, Ward and himself. Meehan wanted him to report back anything he heard being said about the gang or any intelligence documents going through his Tallaght station about them.

He also wanted to know if they were under surveillance. O'Neill was to continue 'looking after' outstanding warrants and court summonses and, when required, to process passport applications.

Buffalo O'Neill didn't suffer moral qualms that he was betraying everything he stood for as a garda. For him it was all about the money.

Meanwhile in Lucan, forensic reports revealed that the bullets used in the murder were unusual in that they were reloaded bullets. Reloading bullets is the illegal practice of recycling old, used bullets. It is done mainly by deer hunters because the ammunition required is so expensive.

Operations Mauser 1 and, later, Mauser 2 were launched in Lucan in a bid to locate the individual who had made the rounds. Gun enthusiasts and hunters throughout the country were visited while others were arrested and questioned. The vast majority of the people lifted were respectable professionals. While it didn't lead them to the person who made the bullets used to kill Veronica, it did glean other results.

The hunt for the reloaded bullets resulted in the seizure of over eighty illegal firearms, including assault rifles, pump-action shotguns and automatic pistols. Twelve people were arrested and charged with firearms offences. A weapon used in the unsolved murder of a biker in County Wicklow was also traced by the Lucan Investigation Team.

The motorbike find was a more solid breakthrough. Detectives had compiled a list of all stolen motorbikes in the greater Dublin area. When the bike was pieced together, the gardaí were able to trace it to its owner, who had reported the bike as stolen shortly before the Guerin murder.

The in-depth analysis of the phone traffic between the known gang members had also thrown up the names of several other persons of interest to the investigation. Detective Sergeant O'Driscoll cross-referenced numbers to identify the gang members and build up a picture of their activities. Of particular interest was the volume of traffic between at least four phones on the day of the murder. Unfortunately, due to the fact that the cell sites were down on the day of the murder, the gardaí were unable to identify the locations where the phones were being used. But at the time there were no ready-to-go burner phones so each phone owner was profiled and checked against the huge bank of intelligence information the Lucan team had compiled from all branches of the system. Russell Warren and his friend Paul Cradden, who worked for the owner of the stolen motorbike, were among those identified. It was clear Warren had been in regular contact with Gilligan and Meehan. 'It was more evidence that Gilligan and his gang were the right people,' a member of the team recalled.

A phone belonging to a 'Paul Conroy' was also featuring prominently on the lists, but by late August he still had not been identified. Subsequently they discovered that Conroy was the false name given by Charlie Bowden when he was registering his phone.

Through Cradden's connection with Warren and the theft of the bike, the Lucan team now had a potential link connecting the bike with Cradden, and Cradden in turn with Warren. Things were progressing in the right direction.

Warren was approached by the team and asked to account for his movements on the day of the murder. Like the other gang members, he lied. But the approach left him seriously spooked that he was in the frame. The detectives reported back that the bagman was definitely the weak link.

Warren's details were passed to the National Surveillance Unit and he was put under watch. His phones were also bugged, and a tracking device was secretly attached to his car.

In the meantime Gilligan and Traynor were doing their best to control the public narrative – and silence another irritating journalist in a bizarre blackmail plot. Their target was this writer.

———

On the Monday night following the murder I was a guest on a late-night radio show on FM104 in Dublin. The programme encouraged people to call in and get things off their chests and that night we were discussing Veronica's murder. After about half an hour of debates with listeners, a guy claiming to be the Coach came on the line. John Traynor was drunk and emotional. Live on the air he pleaded:

> I thought the world of that girl and you know that's true, Paul.
> I want you to ring me after that show and meet me. You know
> that I am telling the truth.

I reminded Traynor of the warnings he had given me over the past year about Gilligan and what he said he would do to Veronica.

Traynor denied that he ever made the comments. I put it to him, still live on the air, that he had staged the accident in Mondello as part of his alibi, an accusation that he also denied.

The next day we had a long conversation on the phone about the murder. Traynor was distraught and refused to meet now that he was sober. He said he made the decision after seeing a picture of himself talking to Veronica which had been surreptitiously taken by the *Sunday Independent*. He didn't want to be set up again. A few days later Traynor left the country and went into hiding in France.

On 12 July Traynor phoned again, claiming that the INLA was about to issue a statement which would clear his name. He was clearly trying to size up the pros and cons of doing a face-to-face interview – and controlling the narrative that he was an innocent man.

The following weekend the *Sunday World* exposed the relationship between Gilligan and the INLA, especially his friendship with Fergal Toal and Dessie O'Hare in Portlaoise Prison. The INLA issued a statement from Belfast, which Garda Headquarters interpreted as a serious threat, condemning me for the story.

INLA thug Declan 'Whacker' Duffy approached me while I was out with my family and made threats over the story, leading the gardaí to search my car for a suspected boobytrap device and place armed patrols at the family home. The same day the story appeared Traynor called me about meeting him. He was concerned about the story and said the INLA had 'nothing to do with Veronica's murder'.

On 17 July I met the Coach in Lisbon, Portugal. Traynor looked hassled. His face was grey and he seemed genuinely worried. He constantly chain-smoked and answered calls on his mobile phone. At the time I had no idea that the caller was John Gilligan. Over two days I interviewed Traynor in Lisbon and in nearby seaside resort Costa da Caparica.

He consistently denied any knowledge or involvement in the murder. Traynor claimed it had been the work of two men he named as having been involved in the murder of Gilligan's old friend John Bolger in 1994. Significantly, the two men Traynor referred to had fallen out with the INLA gang in Dublin. They were fair game for his accusations.

He kept trying to divert attention away from the terrorists and then suggested that I was still in some danger from them. Traynor was playing mind games.

'I'll do you a favour in relation to that,' he said, adding that he had just received a phone call 'from some of my people saying that they are planning to approach you and talk to you. I told them not to lay a finger on that man because he is helping me while he is out here,' he claimed.

His cack-handed attempt to manipulate the situation was visible a mile off but we wanted to keep him talking. At this stage, the murder was only three weeks old and there was little information about the Coach's involvement in the drug trade or the extent of the gang's operation. Everyone was seeking answers.

It was clear he was scared of someone. He didn't say who, but it later became obvious that it was Gilligan. Whenever I tried to bring the conversation around to Gilligan, Traynor simply refused to discuss him. He claimed that there was 'no way Gilligan would do anything like that'.

He was more talkative as he tried to contextualize his relationship with Veronica. His whole motivation was self-preservation – distancing himself from the outrage and getting his alibi into the public domain:

> Despite the fact that we had fallen out, I still had a deep regard for Veronica and have been genuinely, deeply saddened by her murder. I considered her a good friend. She had a warm, bubbly personality and I got on with her from the moment we met until she revealed to me that she was going to write a story about me.

> I liked her from the minute we met. Veronica was full of life. She was very intelligent and had a nice manner. She always had a

twinkle in her eye and I suppose I was mesmerized and fascinated with her. I admired her for her courage and eagerness to get a story, especially being a woman. I considered her a good friend and we regularly met for coffee.

Since I came out of prison in 1990, I had tried to put my criminal past behind me and had begun socializing with decent people. If a story like the one Veronica was writing appeared about me, it would make them think I was some kind of animal. The week before Veronica was murdered my legal team told me that they were almost one hundred per cent sure that I had won my case and that no story would be appearing about me. On the day of the murder I was the happiest man in the world that morning as I headed off with my two boys to Mondello. If I had been planning to kill Veronica, Naas would have been the last place in the world I would have gone to.

People say the accident was staged, but I was lucky to get out of that car alive. I was in shock and covered in glass and I had hurt my shoulder. Anyone who saw the accident will say that I could easily have been killed. When I came out of the X-ray room in Naas hospital, one of my sons who had my phone said that someone had been shot. My daughter had passed the scene where Veronica was shot about five minutes after it had happened.

Within the space of five minutes I had several calls telling me that someone had been killed. When I was told that it was a woman in a red Calibra, I knew it was Veronica. I was very upset. I said to the nurse who was looking after me: 'I knew that person who was shot...She was a good friend of mine.' I got a lift to the garage I owned in Naas and got a car and drove my sons home.

I went around by Saggart because I just could not face driving by the murder scene, I couldn't stomach it. Veronica and I had fallen out but I still had a lot of respect and feelings for her. I was feeling very, very sad. In the following days the press started hounding me and then the injunction hearing came up and I was in every paper in the country. I was astounded that people began to look at me as if I did it. I don't believe Veronica would have wished this kind of damage on me in a thousand years. My home was besieged by photographers and my family started to get threatening phone calls. I left because my nerves couldn't stand it any more.

That weekend the *Sunday World* ran a front-page story and four pages of Traynor's interview inside. He had even posed for pictures. It was, the story emphasized, his version of events which would be tested by the findings of the ongoing investigation.

There was then a bizarre and unexpected sequel when Gilligan decided to get in on the act.

On 24 July I received a call from someone with a Dublin accent purporting to be a friend of John Gilligan's. I later discovered it was Brian Meehan.

'John Gilligan is concerned that you are being threatened and blackmailed by Traynor not to write about him [Gilligan]. Mr Gilligan would like to talk with you, if that is alright, on the phone,' Meehan said.

I agreed to take the call. About five minutes later the phone rang again. This time John Gilligan was on the line.

'Traynor is a very dangerous man,' Gilligan immediately said, setting out his stall. He continued calmly:

When you left Lisbon, he [Traynor] rang me and said he had threatened you not to write any more stories about me. He is blackmailing you with compromising pictures which he showed you before you left Portugal. The pictures are of you with a woman and I wouldn't like to be in your shoes dealing with that man.

The little godfather again denied any involvement with the murder and then turned menacing:

> I hate to say it, but I hate that fucking woman now for all that she has done to me and my family. But if I were you I would be very careful because Traynor might put those pictures in the papers.

I replied angrily:

> If you do come across any pictures of me, send me some for my family album, you sleazy little bastard. It's clear to me that you organized Veronica's murder and this is your fucking game.

Gilligan appeared to be taken aback:

> Now, I don't want you to be upset with me. I just don't want to be involved between you and Traynor, do you understand me? Now, this conversation never took place, is that alright?

It was an obvious attempt to stop me writing about him. From his tone it was clear that he believed Traynor was actually blackmailing me. I told him he would be reading a lot more about himself in the *Sunday World* and hung up.

I phoned Traynor and asked what was going on. The con man sounded scared as the preposterous stunt was revealed:

> Before you came to meet me in Portugal, Gilligan told me to set you up and get pictures of you. He told me: 'Set that man up with a few slappers and then we'll have him on side and shut him up.' While you were with me Gilligan kept ringing, asking had I done it. When you left I told him that I had set you up and had pictures in my possession. I am scared of Gilligan and he is so volatile at the moment that I was afraid at what he would do to me if I refused. The easiest way out was just to say that I had

done it. When he [Gilligan] phoned you, he thought he had you in his hip pocket.

A few days later Traynor was on the phone again. He claimed that Gilligan was intensely angry with him because he had been made to look a fool. Traynor said:

> He told me that he was sending people to get me...You don't understand, you don't say no to Gilligan and hope to get away with it. He is a very bad man. I have a family in Dublin and he has a big network of people.

In a moment of truth Traynor admitted that Gilligan had ordered the murder. From my extensive dealings with the gangster, I believed what he was saying.

Traynor claimed that he had no knowledge of how Gilligan had planned the murder or who he hired to do it. But events would show that he did know that Veronica was going to be shot and he could have easily tipped off the police. Her so-called friend was equally complicit in the crime.

The unfolding situation at the time was so febrile that it was decided not to publish the blackmail story because of fears for the safety of Traynor's family. They were, after all, innocent victims. But I contacted the Lucan garda team and made a full statement. The police, who had the gangsters' phones bugged, were already aware of the bizarre plot. It was another small piece of the jigsaw.

CHAPTER TWENTY

LOOSE ENDS

By the end of July, several weeks into the investigation, there was no sign of a let-up in the relentless onslaught being spearheaded by the investigation nerve centre at Lucan station. The underworld was being pummelled from all sides as the police waged war. Gilligan and his associates were increasingly concerned that it was bad for business.

Brian Meehan was incredulous when he phoned a friend after yet another group of people had been lifted in a swoop by the Lucan team. 'The cops aren't still fucking chasing after us? I thought that would be over ages ago,' Meehan said, sounding genuinely surprised.

In August gardaí received intelligence of a secret meeting in the Netherlands between Meehan, Gilligan and George 'the Penguin' Mitchell. Mitchell wanted to see the status quo restored and, like the rest of the criminal fraternity, blamed Gilligan for the mess. He advised Gilligan and Meehan to murder a garda to divert the heat. The police were involved in two massive enquiries already, the murders of Guerin and Detective Garda Jerry McCabe. A third high-profile investigation would stretch the cops beyond their limits, leaving the drug traffickers alone. Mitchell was reported as advising:

Anywhere in the country, set one [garda] up and riddle him, using machine guns. There'll be so much hassle with that investigation that they'll put all their good men onto the cop murder. If it's done right, then they'll think it's the Provos. Anyway, they have murdered cops before. The Guerin thing will be forgotten in no time.

When the intelligence was analysed by the Crime and Security Branch, the potential threat posed by Gilligan was classified as credible. He was a capricious, unintelligent psychopath with a ruthless gang of like-minded killers at his disposal. Gilligan was the only major criminal player who would have no compunction about waging war against the police. The information was passed on to the head of the investigation.

Tony Hickey decided to step up security around the investigation and ordered his officers to be extra vigilant about their personal security and to wear their firearms at all times. Two detectives armed with Uzi sub-machine guns were placed on around-the-clock duty at Lucan to protect the always-open incident room. Extra armed patrols were put in place in and around Lucan Village to watch for suspicious activity in the vicinity of the station house. Bomb and fireproof safes were specially imported, and part of the station was refurbished to accommodate them. The potential of Gilligan launching an attack had to be taken seriously. Nothing was being left to chance.

Hickey summarized what the gardaí and the CAB were up against during one of the many subsequent court appearances connected with the case:

We know from intelligence that the people concerned [Gilligan gang] have the resources, the money and the firearms and will resort to anything to maintain this wall of silence which they believe is necessary to protect themselves.

By mid-August, after a painstaking process of elimination, Gilligan and his henchmen had been officially categorized as the prime suspects in the murder conspiracy. The investigation was now focused on two objectives: to bring Gilligan and his gang to justice and to smash his operation.

The long hours of plodding investigative work were paying off but there were still large pieces of the underworld puzzle missing. Gilligan, Traynor, Meehan, Mitchell, Paul and Shay Ward, Meredith, Paul Cradden, Derek Baker and Warren were all now in the frame. Paddy 'Dutchy' Holland's name was also beginning to feature prominently in information spilling from the underworld and in the trawl of phone records. Hickey had a major interest in Holland, whom he had jailed twice in the past. Holland's name had also featured on the list of suspected hit men. Bowden had not yet been linked to 'Paul Conroy', although he had been mentioned by detectives from the North Central Divisional Drug Squad as an associate of Meehan and Mitchell.

In a different approach from that used in previous investigations, as the team homed in closer to the gang, the friends, relatives and associates of each suspect were interviewed under caution or arrested. Each suspect had someone in whom they confided and Hickey's team was determined to find out what those confidants had been told.

The smallest morsel of information could give the investigators a new lead. Each group of individuals targeted for arrest was lifted in large, co-ordinated swoops. The strategy was to play hardball as the team tore down the protective layers the gang members had erected around themselves.

Horrified civilians found themselves being ordered out of bed and arrested in the early hours of the morning by armed detectives. Some of them had never before received so much as a parking ticket and now they were in a garda interview room, looking into the grim faces of experienced interrogators.

They found themselves answering blunt questions about a loved one or friend in relation to a heinous crime that horrified them, as it did the rest of the nation. An arrest, or even an approach, by detectives in connection with the Veronica Guerin enquiry was a source of stigma and shame.

The murder investigation became a template for future complex serious crime enquiries including the notorious Kinahan and Hutch feud which broke out in 2016, twenty years later.

One team member recalls:

> Once a target group was picked, intelligence on the whole group was collated and analysed for what they might be able to offer or should know. Team leaders organized arrest and search parties. Various stations were selected where prisoners were to be taken and interrogation teams picked. Extra manpower would be summoned from across the city as well as specialist armed backup from the Emergency Response Unit. The National Surveillance Unit would have been in position for days beforehand and could pinpoint the locations of those who were to be pulled in.

> Before a raid, everyone involved was required to meet in the incident room for a briefing on the identities and locations of the various targets. It was decided that reinforcements should be treated on a need-to-know basis, simply to avoid loose talk. Searches were slow and meticulous. We were told to search for evidence and clues that could be used for potential leads and during questioning. Unlike in the past we were also told to seize any documents relating to money or property.

> If there was something illegal there to sustain a charge, it would be considered a bonus. Practically everyone who was arrested was run for the full length of their [statutory maximum] 48-hour detention period. We used the full scope of our powers. The

majority of prisoners gave us some information. The tactic was very successful and had the added effect that when people were released from custody the word spread like wildfire that we meant business. In the weeks after the murder the tables had changed – we, the police, were dictating the agenda.

The Lucan Investigation Team worked all day, every day, for most of the first six months. Adrenalin and sheer determination kept everyone going. The morale of the team was boosted in September when Commissioner Pat Byrne promoted Hickey to the rank of Assistant Commissioner. Breaking with normal practice, Byrne decided that Hickey would remain head of the Guerin investigation. By then detectives were gearing up to make a direct attack on the Gilligan gang.

The Guerin murder was the first time that comprehensive phone records played a pivotal role in an investigation. Detective Sergeant O'Driscoll had produced a detailed analysis of the gang's calls on and around the day of the murder. The conspirators had used the phones like walkie-talkies and the times and length of each call showed a structure.

Flowcharts mapping out what was known about the gang and its structure were placed on the wall at the top of the incident room. So too was a montage of pictures of the individual members. The room was also overlooked by a picture of Veronica Guerin, which Hickey had pinned up during the first week of the investigation.

No matter where anyone stood in the large room, they met Veronica's smiling face. A team member recalls:

> It was as if she wouldn't allow us to forget what all this was about. It was what she had died for, exposing evil bastards like Gilligan and his outfit. People from the various forces who had been asked for assistance in the investigation were brought to Lucan and given a full briefing about the murder and the gang. They also

saw the picture of the victim. It was a poignant reminder about what this was all about.

The Lucan strategy was working.

———

As the momentum continued to build in Ireland, things were not running so smoothly for the gang in the Netherlands. In early July further requests were made for assistance by the Departments of Justice and Foreign Affairs to the Dutch side of Operation Pineapple.

The local force organized Operation Setter, named after the Irish red setter dog, targeting Martin Baltus and Simon Rahman. Baltus had already begun to talk to the Dutch police about his association with Gilligan following the seizure of the counterfeit dollars. When Rahman had told police that the notes belonged to Baltus, his sidekick felt betrayed by his former partner in crime. He suspected that his arrest in March 1995, in possession of the machine gun, might have been set up by the drug trafficker.

Operation Setter began trawling through Rahman's myriad companies to track down his criminal empire. From his base in Belgium, Gilligan was ordering larger shipments of hash. Rahman never refused a deal as long as there was hard cash coming. With Baltus in prison, and Johnny Wildhagen officially 'disappeared', Rahman was forced out into the open.

In July he shipped just under 1,000 kilos to Cork. To fill Gilligan's orders, Rahman was forced to buy up stock from the other major traffickers based in Amsterdam. Without his henchmen, Rahman had no one he trusted enough to pick up and pack the drugs for shipping to Ireland.

On 1 August an undercover surveillance team watched Rahman

as he drove to meet one of his associates at a McDonald's restaurant in Zoetermeer, north of Rotterdam. Rahman was in a hurry to fill one of Gilligan's orders. He took his associate's car and drove to his secret warehouse at Wiltonstraat. He didn't trust his associate with knowledge of the location. The police couldn't believe their eyes when they actually saw Rahman carrying bags of hashish to the car.

As he drove off, they moved in. Rahman was arrested with over 200 kilos of hash and with counterfeit currency. The global drug dealer had finally been caught with his hands on the drugs.

A further 15,000 kilos of hash were recovered in a search of the warehouse. At his house police found two receipts – for over £100,000 (€190,000) each – from the Bureau de Change at Centraal Station, Amsterdam, in the name of John Gilligan.

During an interview Rahman admitted that he knew Gilligan but claimed that he had never done business with him. Rahman was subsequently convicted, sentenced to two years in prison and fined the equivalent of €38,000. He had got off lightly. He would never do business with John Gilligan again. After Rahman's arrest the Operation Setter team began investigating the supply route to Ireland.

Following the murder Carol Rooney had remained with Gilligan at the safe house in Belgium. She returned briefly to Leixlip to clear out the safe house on Gilligan's instructions. She would later tell detectives that she was too terrified of him to make a run for it. Gilligan's mistress had witnessed his growing obsession with Veronica Guerin and had heard him orchestrating the journalist's murder. She was convinced that the same could happen to her.

Gilligan grew wary of his young lover. He knew Rooney's knowledge could bring his whole world crashing down around him. She was a weak link and needed to be neutralized. But instead of killing her, the godfather decided it was in everyone's interests that she move offside, far out of the reach of the police back in Dublin.

Rooney didn't need much encouragement when he suggested that she go to Australia to live with a relative. She was being freed at last. Gilligan gave Rooney £8,000 (€15,000) and paid for a one-way flight from Heathrow to Sydney on Monday 12 August.

The day before Rooney's flight the *Sunday Business Post* published an interview with Gilligan. Like Traynor he was trying, without much success, to control the public narrative and paint himself as the innocent victim of a pernicious conspiracy. His comments made him look even more suspicious. He told journalist John Mooney:

> Anyone can get anyone killed if they have the money. You don't have to be a criminal. I could have ordered her death but I didn't. I had no hand, act or part in it. One part of me hopes that they find the murderer because that will take the heat off me, but in all honesty, I'm a criminal. Part of me hopes they will get away so that no one will go to prison. Is the public going to say sorry if they catch someone else? No, I'm still a drugs baron and a factory robber in their eyes. I have been dragged into this because I threatened her before she died. If I was going to kill her I would hardly have advertised it by threatening her. I mean that's not the way things like that are done.

Although his claims in the interview had no credibility and he portrayed himself as a lying fool, Gilligan actually thought he had cleared his name.

That evening he turned up unexpectedly for a surprise farewell at the London hotel where Carol Rooney was staying before her flight the next morning. He was accompanied by Dutchy Holland who had been playing a much bigger role in the business since the murder. Gilligan wasn't there for sentimental reasons. He reminded Rooney of what would happen to her family if she ever broke the code of *omerta*. Then he left her alone with Holland. Rooney later related how the hit man smiled as he urged the petrified young woman: 'Get yourself a new boyfriend over in Australia, forget all about John and forget about everything you've seen and heard and everyone will be alright.' She knew that it was a thinly veiled threat from a cold-blooded killer.

The following morning she boarded her flight to Australia, planning never to see John Gilligan again.

Anxious to maintain control Gilligan wanted to find out first-hand what was happening on the ground back in Dublin. Although no one had said it to his face, John Gilligan had become a pariah in the underworld and many of the big players had shunned him. It made him even more paranoid and aggressive than normal. He decided to do the one thing that no one expected him to do – return to Dublin to remind everyone that he had not gone away.

On 14 September he slipped back into Ireland through Rosslare, on the ferry from Roscoff, France. As a precaution he travelled around Dublin in taxis and stayed in different houses. He met Meehan, Mitchell and Ward to find out exactly what was happening with the police investigation.

They reassured him that their man on the inside, John O'Neill, would tip them off if there were any big breaks in the case. Gilligan also attended a small birthday celebration for Geraldine at Jessbrook. After the party Geraldine again confronted him about his mistress and they had a row that resulted in him beating her.

Two days after Gilligan's return, his old friend John Cunningham absconded from Shelton Abbey open prison in County Wicklow. Cunningham had been serving the last two years of his sentence for organizing the kidnapping of Jennifer Guinness.

He had been spotted drinking with another convict, Eamon Daly, a member of the General's mob, and a prison officer in a pub near the prison in contravention of the rules. As a result the officer was suspended and Cunningham and Daly were about to be sent to an enclosed prison as punishment. Cunningham had also lost a temporary release to attend his daughter's wedding a week later.

Unwilling to face it, he ran. Gilligan organized for him to stay in Russell Warren's house on 17 August, the night before he left the country on a truck driven by an associate of Meredith.

Once in the Netherlands, Gilligan helped Cunningham to get set up in the drugs trade in partnership with Christy Kinahan, the Dapper Don. Between them they went on to build one of the biggest drug trafficking operations in Europe.

The Lucan team was aware of Gilligan's arrival in Ireland but did not want to lay hands on him just yet. It was better if he returned to Belgium. The absence of his intimidating presence would inevitably loosen his stranglehold on his gang, giving the police the opportunity to get the hard evidence they needed. Hickey's team was working closely with the Dutch, Belgian and British police to keep tabs on his movements.

When the time was right they would know where to find him.

The Criminal Assets Bureau officially came into existence on 31 July, although it would have no statutory powers until the Criminal Assets Bureau Act was made law on 15 October 1996. Chief Superintendent Fachtna Murphy, who had spent most of his career investigating fraud, was appointed as Chief Bureau Officer. Financial and taxation fraud was a highly specialized area and few garda officers had Murphy's expertise.

Nothing like the CAB had ever been tried before in other

jurisdictions. The proposed powers and structure were an exciting and innovative departure that was much more advanced than similar units in Europe. Nevertheless, its success would depend on how it was organized and run. Like Hickey, Murphy knew that the agency could not be seen to fail.

The State Solicitor for County Cork, Barry Galvin, was brought in as the CAB's Chief Legal Officer. For several years Galvin had been a source of embarrassment to successive governments over his public claims that Ireland was being used by international crime syndicates to launder drug money. Four years earlier he had famously appeared on RTÉ's primetime chat show, *The Late Late Show*, to expose the fact that several major international traffickers were running their drug empires from luxury homes in the south-west of the country. Galvin demanded that new powers be introduced to target these criminals and seize their assets. But he was derided by the justice minister at the time, Padraig Flynn, as an over-zealous solicitor who fancied himself as some kind of Eliot Ness. Politicians believed that the drug empires Galvin was describing simply didn't exist and he was exaggerating the problem. Gilligan had vindicated the solicitor's position.

Veteran serious crime squad officer Felix McKenna, now a detective superintendent, was appointed as the new bureau's second-in-command. The officer who had broken the Factory Gang and secured Gilligan's longest stretch in prison was about to become a thorn in the little man's side once more.

A team of gardaí was hand-picked for the new agency, as were investigators from Revenue, Customs and Social Welfare. One of them was Brian Purcell, the social welfare officer who had been shot by Martin Cahill. The key to the subsequent success of the CAB lay in Pat Byrne's insistence to Taoiseach John Bruton that the government place the agency under the control and protection of An Garda Síochána. Byrne subsequently commented:

Our experience always showed that criminals were more ruthless with those who were not members of An Garda Síochána because they had no fear of civil servants. They knew that we were not afraid of them. When a man or woman joins the gardaí they know that they may have to risk their own lives in the course of their duty. They are trained for it and have the backup of 12,000 colleagues. I said that it would be wrong to expect civil servants to take on these dangerous individuals. That had already been illustrated when the General shot a social welfare inspector in 1989. John Gilligan had also openly threatened other public servants and there were many other cases of intimidation that we had been aware of for years but were powerless to do anything about. The bottom line was that we had the people, the resources, the authority and the guns to fight fire with fire.

As a result of Byrne's intervention, for the first time ever, the relevant government departments would work together as one unit. The new agency would ensure that there would be no more intimidation of civil servants. The days of John Gilligan and his ilk telling Revenue officers to fuck off were over.

As soon as news broke about the Proceeds of Crime Act several crime figures rushed to clear out their ill-gotten gains and left the country. George 'the Penguin' Mitchell was one of the first godfathers who fled Ireland when the CAB came into existence. He established permanent residency in the Netherlands. For the gangsters it was the most severe repercussion of the Guerin murder, for which they bore no responsibility – and everyone blamed John Gilligan.

The mob boss was also quick to react. In the space of a week, from 24 July to 31 July, Geraldine Gilligan withdrew over £200,000 (€390,000) from four Bank of Ireland accounts she held at the branch in Lucan Village. In an ironic twist it was across the road from Lucan garda station where the Guerin murder investigation was being co-ordinated.

In August, over a number of weeks, Brian Meehan began clearing out his bank accounts. Meehan and his father then opened deposit accounts in the Creditanstalt Bank in Vienna, Austria, lodging a total of £619,491 (€1.2 million) there. John Traynor also arranged to have large amounts of cash delivered to him from Ireland.

From the moment Murphy, Galvin and McKenna were selected for the mammoth task ahead they knew who their first target was going to be: John Joseph Gilligan.

At one of the first meetings of CAB staff Felix McKenna gave them a brief on what they could expect to encounter on the road ahead. His words would prove to be prophetic:

> They [criminals] and their lawyers will test us at every opportunity and they will make sure that they do not lose face. Gilligan especially uses every legal avenue he can to frustrate the system. It's quite possible that we will be retired by the time we get our hands on the likes of Jessbrook.

The first major multi-agency investigation conducted by the CAB was to raise an initial tax assessment for Geraldine and John Gilligan. Kevin Carty's Operation Pineapple team's analysis of the financial documentation they'd seized when they raided Jessbrook was handed over to the CAB on the day it came into existence.

Gilligan was also of help in calculating the tax due. In his interview with the *Sunday Business Post* he did an extraordinary volte face. Having essentially murdered Veronica Guerin for asking him awkward questions about the source of his wealth, Gilligan actually bragged about it.

> I don't know where they [gardaí] get their figures from but I'm not far off £15 million (€29 million). Most of this is invested in offshore companies, I'm not mad enough to trust anyone and invest it in Ireland.

Combined with data from seized documentation and banking records, the CAB raised a tax demand at the beginning of September. It was calculated that between them the husband and wife owed over £3.4 million (€6.6 million) in unpaid income tax, including interest, for the year 1994–1995. Interest was being added to the bill for every week that it remained unpaid. When the assessment was drawn up, none of the tax inspectors assigned to the bureau would sign the document, for justifiable fear of reprisals.

In the absence of an inspector's signature the assessment could not be served. To get around the problem Barry Galvin officially became an inspector of taxes. It was a bold move which characterized the courageous Corkonian. He also became the first and only legal official to be issued with a police firearm for his own protection. He signed the documents and sent them to Jessbrook.

The tax demands were delivered to Geraldine Gilligan on 17 September – almost a year to the day since Veronica had called to Gilligan's house and was savagely beaten.

When Geraldine informed him of the State's encroachment into their lives, the mobster lost his head with rage. He called a friend in a state of fury which was picked up on a police intercept. 'Who in fuck do these pricks think they are...Are they fucking mad? It's daylight robbery, that's what it is!' he ranted. In the call Gilligan mused about having a revenue official shot in a bid to scare them off.

But time was running out for the gangster.

CHAPTER TWENTY-ONE

GANG BUSTERS

Around the time that Gilligan left the country again in September 1996, the police decided to place Russell Warren under full-time surveillance. They were still unsure of the true nature of his dealings with Gilligan but were confident that he would provide the key to getting inside the gang's operation. Information coming from the Dutch police showed that Warren was involved in the exchange of huge sums of money.

Warren had also given them just cause to arrest him because his alibi for the day of the murder had not checked out. He claimed that he had been shopping with his wife, Debbie, at the crucial times and then went drinking in a pub in Rathgar. A check showed no record of the purchases he claimed to have made and the people he named said he hadn't arrived in the pub until after 3 p.m. He was hiding something.

At the same time the mysterious 'Paul Conroy' was finally identified as Charlie Bowden. In Lucan the available intelligence on Bowden was studied closely, including his army record. It was believed that, like Warren, he was not a hardened criminal of the same calibre as the rest of the mob. The duo represented the weak spot in Gilligan's security.

Detective Inspector Todd O'Loughlin later explained the strategy that was adopted:

> One of the first things we noticed was the extent of the operation and the size of the pyramid that Gilligan had created. In a two-year period we conservatively estimated that his organization had smuggled in cannabis worth over £200 million on the streets. We had never seen a gang making such profits before and it opened our eyes to the true extent of organized crime.
>
> It took 400 arrests before we finally got a full picture of the size of this pyramid. The people who served time with him in Portlaoise wouldn't talk and they remained loyal right to the end. But because of the size of the operation he also recruited people who were not hardcore criminals like Charlie Bowden, Russell Warren and John Dunne. When they were taken into custody they had remorse, which none of the other guys had, and through this then we were able to obtain details of the entire organization, and this was how we dismantled it from within.

The unrelenting arrest operations were making Gilligan and his lieutenants edgy and nervous. Almost daily there was news of more arrests or developments in the Guerin investigation in the media. Meehan, Mitchell, and the Wards began keeping their heads down and staying out of sight. On 23 September Meehan was given a week's respite from the stress of it all, courtesy of the State. He was jailed for indecent behaviour, from when he'd masturbated in front of gardaí in the Bridewell station.

Judge Gerard Haughton was not impressed with Meehan's performance. 'His conduct was disgraceful and I would have no hesitation in jailing him for six to twelve months if that penalty was open to me,' he declared.

As Meehan lay in his cell the money was still flowing in. Two more shipments, totalling 760 kilos, arrived in Cork from Amsterdam and were then transported to Greenmount for distribution.

Since Veronica Guerin's murder, Gilligan had instructed Russell Warren to bring the money to him by ferry via England and France. He delivered the bags of cash to his boss in London, Dover and Calais. His friend Paul Cradden travelled with him on four occasions.

On Sunday 29 September, Gilligan phoned Warren in Dublin and hurled abuse at him for not having collected a bag of cash from Dutchy Holland the previous evening. Warren regularly met Holland to collect cash from his end of the drugs operation. About half an hour later the hit man called Warren and arranged to meet him near O'Connell Bridge in Dublin.

Holland gave him a carrier bag with over £70,000 (€135,000) in cash. Warren brought the money back to his parents' house for sorting. The following day he was to collect more cash from Meehan and then fly to Schiphol Airport. Meehan then told him that the money wouldn't be ready until a day later.

That same afternoon a conference was held in Lucan station to decide the next major step in the investigation. The surveillance operation on Warren had gleaned a huge amount of intelligence which justified making a move on him, members of his family and some of his associates.

A search and arrest operation was planned, involving dozens of officers. The team was about to make its first strike close to the heart of Gilligan's gang.

Later that evening Warren and his wife went to a pub in Rathgar, south Dublin, to meet some friends, including the man who had unwittingly stored the getaway motorbike in his garage. As they sat in the bar, several of the anonymous punters around them were members of the surveillance team.

At 9 p.m. the detectives from Lucan arrived in the bar to make their arrests. Warren had just finished relieving himself at the urinal in the pub toilet when two detectives arrived either side of him. The bagman was informed that he was being arrested under Section 30 of the Offences Against the State Act 1939 on suspicion that he was in possession of information relating to a scheduled offence, namely the possession of a firearm at the Naas Road and Boot Road on 26 June 1996.

Warren was speechless and the blood drained from his face. The bagman nodded that he understood what he had been told. He was searched and his hands were cuffed behind his back. As he was being taken out of the toilet, his wife and their friend were also being placed under arrest.

At the same time Paul Cradden, Derek Baker, Warren's parents, Patrick and Yvette, his sister Nicola, her husband Brian Cummins and a number of other associates were also being arrested and their homes searched. The officers found Holland's bag of cash.

Warren was held for questioning for two days during which he was asked about his involvement with the Gilligan gang. Hickey and his team believed that the nervous bagman was the key to cracking Gilligan's wall of silence. They had made the right call.

While Warren was careful to deny any knowledge about the murder or the motorbike, he detailed his activities as Gilligan's bagman. He also admitted knowing and collecting money from Brian Meehan. He refused to explain the telephone traffic between him and the other Gilligan gang members on the day of the Guerin murder.

One of his interrogators, Bernie Hanley, a vastly experienced detective, had made a connection with Warren and persuaded him to talk. The first major breakthrough came when Warren agreed to make a statement on 1 October.

> When I first started collecting money for Gilligan there used to be £20,000 or £30,000 in it. This figure would be the lowest amount. It would go as high as £160,000 sometimes but most

of the time it would be around £70,000. At first I was told this money was from betting and the sales of smuggled cigarettes and tobacco. As time went by, I got more involved. I realized that this was money from the sale of drugs. I was only involved in looking after the money for counting and delivering it to him [Gilligan]. Meehan is very closely connected with Gilligan. I think he looks after his drug business for him. I am sorry for getting my family [involved] in all of this.

At the same time Warren's family members, who had never been in trouble with the law in their lives, gave statements describing Russell's connection to Gilligan and how he'd recruited them to count money. They were horrified at being implicated in the criminal conspiracy. Patrick Warren, his father, said: 'I am disgusted that he [Russell] has got me and my wife into this position. He will never get us into it again.'

When asked if he thought his son was involved in Veronica Guerin's murder, Patrick Warren replied: 'I don't think Russell would have the guts to pull the trigger because behind it all he is a coward at heart.'

The arrests rattled Gilligan and the rest of the gang but they would have to wait until their release to find out what had been said – and what the police knew. They were still confident that even if anyone gave the cops a statement it would never amount to anything as no one would dare testify against them.

In the interim they had a much more pressing issue to deal with – keeping the money moving. Meehan summoned Charlie Bowden to Paul Ward's house. He said Warren was in custody, so 'everyone will have to lend a hand'. When Bowden arrived, Meehan, Mitchell, Paul Ward, Brendan 'Speedy' Fegan and an associate of his from Newry were already busily counting and wrapping the large bundles of used notes.

Meehan told the other hoods that they'd have to hurry because Holland was due to collect the cash for delivery to Gilligan in

England. The cash had to be sorted with the notes facing up, in batches of £1,000, wrapped with elastic bands at the ends. Sterling was sorted separately.

By the time they had finished counting and sorting, there was over £300,000 (€580,000) which was then placed in two holdalls. Later the gang members went to a local pub, where they handed the bags to Holland. It demonstrated the sheer arrogance and avarice that drove Gilligan and his minions. They were focused on increasing their business and their cash flow at a time when they knew the police were circling around them and getting too close for comfort.

––––––––––

Gilligan was staying in a hotel at Russell Square in London when he heard about the arrests. He was particularly concerned about Warren's detention. He knew the bagman was weak and liable to spill the beans.

Holland arrived on the ferry and took a train to London to deliver the cash. They discussed what kind of action they would have to take if Warren, or, indeed, any of the others did decide to talk. Dutchy advised his little boss to order Warren over to England, interrogate him and 'put the fear of God in him'. He pointed out that Warren's statement to the police would mean nothing when he refused to get into the witness box. The bagman should be left under no illusion of the dangers inherent in becoming a tout. There was no witness protection programme in Ireland to hide informants. If all that failed, they always had the cleaner option of killing him. Gilligan was in complete agreement.

At the same time in Lucan Warren's 48-hour period of detention was running out. The team met to discuss progress. They had made a breakthrough, but they felt that Warren knew a lot more. In the meantime there was enough evidence in the statements to sustain charges against Warren and his family under the new legislation for laundering the proceeds of drug trafficking.

The connection between Warren, Cradden and the motorbike had still not been explained. Neither Cradden nor Warren had given any indication that they knew anything about the bike, but the Lucan team now suspected that Warren had been one of the gang's lookouts during the murder. The structure of the plot had been deciphered in John O'Driscoll's phone analysis.

It was decided to release Warren and his family and later send a file to the Director of Public Prosecutions recommending suitable charges. It would buy time for Bernie Hanley to work on Warren and, when the time was right, the gardaí would lift him again.

On Wednesday evening, 2 October, Warren left Lucan station in a taxi. As soon as he switched on his mobile phone, Gilligan rang. The Crime and Security Branch in Garda HQ had the phone tapped. 'Can you talk?' he enquired. Warren said no, but he would be at home within twenty minutes and Gilligan could call him back then. Gilligan impatiently rang another three times before Warren got home.

As soon as Warren arrived at his house, Gilligan was on the phone again. Gilligan demanded to know everything that was said while Warren was in custody, hissing:

> I'm now telling you, you're dead and your family is dead and everyone around you will be dead. I want the truth, tell me exactly what was said and what your family said.

Warren told him about Holland's money that had been found in his parents' house. Gilligan was furious and berated Warren for not collecting the money earlier. Warren said he hadn't had time.

'When I tell you to do something, you do it,' Gilligan retorted and then demanded to know again what was said in Lucan.

'Get on a plane first thing in the morning and meet me here in London,' Gilligan ordered.

'I can't. Everyone here is upset after the arrests,' Warren pleaded.

'Come over here or I'll go over to ye and I'll kill ye all,' the little man snarled and hung up.

The following morning at 8 a.m. Gilligan was on the phone to his bagman again. 'Why aren't you over here? If you're not fucking over here I'm going over to you and I'll kill you, and I'll kill you if you tell me lies,' Gilligan raged.

Warren could only respond that he had no money to travel. Gilligan told him to call Meehan and he would give him the money.

Later that day there was further evidence that the police were stepping up their offensive. Officers attached to the Money Laundering Unit and the Criminal Assets Bureau visited the office of Gilligan's solicitor. It was the first time that gardaí used the new CAB legislation to enter a lawyer's office armed with a search warrant and the power to seize a client's legal file. In a previous age such a move was considered unthinkable, with client privilege sacrosanct. Gilligan's actions on 26 June had brought about this fundamental change.

That evening Warren met Brian Meehan who gave him £1,000 (€1,900) to cover his travel costs to London. The Tosser was much calmer than Gilligan. He asked Warren what had been said while he and his family were in custody. He particularly wanted to know how much the cops knew about the motorbike. The bagman reassured Meehan that no one had said anything.

By now Russell Warren was teetering on the edge of a nervous breakdown. He was sandwiched between the police on one side and Gilligan on the other. One group could probably put him and his family in jail for a long time, the other could have him and his family wiped out. Either way he was in a tight corner.

After the murder Warren hadn't been able to sleep or eat properly. He wasn't cut out for running with gangland's most dangerous killers.

Warren flew to London on Friday afternoon, 4 October. Before leaving he told his wife, Derek Baker and another friend that he was meeting with Gilligan. He wanted them to know his plans in case Gilligan decided to make him 'disappear'.

The bagman arrived in Heathrow and was instructed by Gilligan to take a train to Russell Square in central London. When he arrived there a man with an English accent, who Warren had never met before, walked up to him and asked if he was 'Russell'. The man led Warren to Gilligan's hotel room. Warren was shaking with fear as he sat down.

Gilligan paced up and down the room as he began his inquisition. He opened proceedings like he always did, with a threat.

> You and your family are dead, and Debbie, no matter how long it takes, I'll get you all. I want the truth. Now put the words 'I'm going to be killed' in the back of your mind. You have to answer questions for me and don't tell me lies.

Over the next few hours Gilligan bombarded his bagman with questions and threats. But Warren somehow held firm, convincing his boss that he had only been asked about the money and to account for his movements on the day of the murder.

He had not made a statement and anyway, a lot of people were being arrested and asked the same questions. He persuaded the little man that he was telling the truth. Once Gilligan was satisfied, it was back to business.

Gilligan's arrogance and stupidity blinded him to the effect of the new laws back in Ireland. His priority was to reclaim the cash seized from Warren, even though there wasn't a chance of that happening. Gilligan wanted to know exactly how it had been wrapped and packed, so that he could identify it when it came to claiming it. Before that he had another job for Warren.

'I want you to bring money to Calais this evening for me,' Gilligan demanded. Warren said he couldn't travel because he didn't have a passport with him as the police had taken it. Gilligan paced around the room fulminating about the intolerable interference with his business. Then he turned and pointed to a silver case in a press:

> There is £300,000 (€580,000) in there and who is going to bring it for me now? I am the fucking boss around here and you're working for me. You should be doin' this, not me. I'll just have to do it meself!

In a further statement to the Lucan team, Warren said that he had somehow plucked up the courage to ask Gilligan about the Guerin murder.

> I said to him something like, if you knew it was going to cause all this trouble, would you still have gone through with shooting Veronica Guerin. He said: 'Are you joking? I even tried to ring Brian [Meehan] to call it off, but I couldn't get through to him.'

Gilligan repeated the lie he had already used on Carol Rooney, telling Warren that Veronica had cancer.

That evening Warren returned to Ireland – feeling lucky to be alive. The next time he and Gilligan met would be across the chamber of the Special Criminal Court in Dublin.

The same day that Russell Warren travelled to London to meet Gilligan, 4 October, Brian Meehan was having problems of his own. He was due to appear in the District Court that morning for driving while banned.

By this stage the *Sunday World* was also aware that Meehan was a key member of Gilligan's gang and one of the prime suspects in the murder. We had been building up background information about him and his associates but we needed to get a picture of him.

At the court session I sat in the back row of District Court number five watching out for him to arrive. Outside, two photographers, Padraig O'Reilly and Liam O'Connor, were in place.

When he walked into court, Meehan spotted me. Even though he was in a packed courtroom he immediately assumed that we were there specifically for him. He walked over and stood, staring menacingly into my face for several seconds while I smiled back at him. He didn't seem to care that the room was full of police officers watching him. The encounter exemplified how the thugs still believed they were invincible and capable of threatening anyone and everyone.

Meehan's arrogance failed him badly. He and Mitchell left the court covering their faces but the photographers caught them in their lenses. A week later the *Sunday World* ran a front-page story about Meehan. He couldn't be named at the time for legal reasons on the grounds that he might sue for defamation. Instead he was called 'the Tosser' because of his indecency charge. This was the first time that the media spotlight had come so close to the murder conspirators. Soon Meehan would have no reputation to defend.

By the time the story was published the fortunes of the Gilligan gang had taken a dramatic turn. The Lucan team was making preparations for another series of arrests and searches. The intense work of the past fourteen weeks had been building to this moment. Special Branch, the Emergency Response Unit and scores of other reinforcements were being mobilized. The operational plan was to first hit Charlie Bowden and his group of associates, followed by a swoop on Paul Ward's group, then the Meehans, Mitchells and, finally, Traynor and Gilligan.

The team's plans had to be brought forward when a tap on Bowden's phone revealed that he was planning to fly to London the following morning, Saturday 5 October. He was heading off with his mistress for the weekend, behind the back of his girlfriend Julie Bacon. The team feared that Bowden might also be planning to go into hiding.

They weren't prepared to take any chances. At 5 a.m. on Saturday a large group gathered in Lucan. Bowden's plans for a dirty weekend were going to be rudely interrupted.

An hour later armed officers took up position around Bowden's home. Detective Sergeant Fergus Treanor pounded loudly on the front door. When Bowden answered six detectives, their guns drawn, piled in on top of him. He was spreadeagled against the wall of his hallway and handcuffed.

Detective Garda John Roche formally arrested the ex-soldier in connection with the murder of Veronica Guerin. When asked if he had anything to say, Bowden calmly replied: 'I don't know what you are talking about.' He was taken away in a squad car to Lucan garda station.

Bacon was also arrested and taken in a separate car. In a search the officers found cocaine and a large amount of cash. An hour later Bowden's brother, Michael, called to bring his brother to the airport. He, too, was arrested.

In a search of Michael Bowden's home, he gave the police a bag containing £5,000 that he had been holding for Charlie. Michael Bowden was then brought to Cabra station for questioning. At the same time two other friends of Bowden's, Julian Clohessy and Paul Smullen, were also lifted.

Initially Charlie Bowden claimed he knew nothing about the murder. He protested that he was a hard-working hairdresser struggling to make a living. For most of the day Bowden refused to budge.

One of his first interrogators, Detective Sergeant Des McTiernan, was frustrated by Bowden's denials and decided to give him some food for thought. He slammed down photographs of Veronica's body in her car on the table in front of the prisoner. Bowden would later claim that he had an epiphany when he viewed the shocking images.

Either Bowden wanted to save his own skin or he had genuine remorse. Whatever the motivation the former soldier was about to blow the Gilligan gang apart.

At 9 p.m. detectives Bernie Hanley and John O'Mahony walked into the interview room. The experienced interviewers immediately put Bowden on edge. He would later recall that despite psyching himself up for an arrest for months, the arrival of Hanley and O'Mahony blew his strategy out the window.

'When I saw these two guys coming in suited and booted, I knew that I was in trouble. I was fucked. They seemed to know everything about me,' Bowden recalled.

The interview proceeded:

O'Mahony: I am putting it to you, Charlie, that you know Brian Meehan, Paul Ward, Shay Ward and Peter Mitchell, and you were in contact with some of them by telephone on the day that Veronica Guerin was murdered.

Bowden: OK, OK, I know them. I know them through Peter Mitchell. Look, I want to tell you about the money you found. I know nothing about the murder. I would have nothing to do with anything like that, it would scare me shitless. I have been working with Meehan, the Wards, Mitchell – and that's where the money is from. If I was talking to them on the day of the murder, it was only about business.

Hanley: What business would that be, Charlie?

Bowden: Selling drugs, that's my involvement with them.

The blunt answer would prove to be the turning point in the investigation. The interrogators had found the chink in Bowden's armour. He was prepared to talk about the drugs but was determined to distance himself from the murder. Warren had adopted the same posture.

At first Bowden gave them a concoction of truth and lies. As the hours wore on, the untruths were being gradually whittled away. O'Mahony and Hanley had found their opening and began breaking down Bowden's protective shield.

The officers were stunned at Bowden's reply when they asked him how much money he made from selling drugs for Mitchell and Meehan: 'I don't know, a lot. Lately I couldn't handle the amounts. It was getting on top of me. I will show you where I have it hidden offside.'

At 10 p.m. Bowden was brought in a squad car to show the investigators his shop on Moore Street, in the city centre. He also disclosed the address of a friend's apartment on Mespil Road in south Dublin where he had hidden cash. An hour later Detective Inspector O'Loughlin and a search team raided the apartment and recovered £100,000 (€190,000) in cash hidden in a holdall.

While sitting in the back seat of the police car, sandwiched between O'Mahony and Hanley, the tough ex-soldier began to talk – and couldn't stop. He said he hadn't told the full truth about how he got to know Mitchell and he described his drug dealing activities.

The officers tried to hide their astonishment when he blurted out how the gang had built the empire. He explained Gilligan was the boss and how the system worked giving money to him. He talked about Russell Warren. Every sentence he came out with provided another lead and another piece of the jigsaw.

When they returned to the station Bowden was placed in his cell for the night. The detectives couldn't write up their notes of the conversation quickly enough. But the ex-corporal was still being highly selective about what he was telling. He'd said nothing about his role as the gang's manager and armourer or about the lockup where the drugs were stored.

The investigators knew that he was holding out. And Bowden's hand was about to be forced. One of the other prisoners arrested in the same swoop described how Bowden once brought him to the Greenmount lockup. The gang's quartermaster had broken his own strict rule of never bringing anyone other than gang members there.

A search warrant was obtained and surveillance teams dispatched to watch the place overnight. The following Sunday afternoon a search team moved in, using a sledgehammer to break down the door.

Inside they found 47 kilos of hash, false drivers' licences, a substance for mixing cocaine, weighing scales and the cardboard boxes used to ship the drugs from Holland. The boxes still had the false shipping labels placed on them by Martin Baltus and Simon Rahman.

The most significant discovery was Bowden's weekly delivery sheet. On it were the names of the gang's customers, the quantities they had ordered and what they owed. It was a who's who of the drug trade. Everyone on that list was arrested in the follow-up investigation. They were also targeted by the CAB.

There was also a direct connection established between Bowden and the warehouse. Keys found in the search of his house matched the locks on the doors of the Greenmount lockup.

At 1.50 p.m., armed with the information about Greenmount, Hanley and O'Mahony rejoined Bowden in the interview room. The pair had struck up a good rapport with Bowden and their strategy was to be patient and make the ex-solider feel comfortable.

They asked him about the murder again.

Bowden: I am not involved in the murder. I am not a heavy. I just do the drugs for Meehan and Mitchell for the money.

Hanley: Where did you get the drugs?

Bowden: They were delivered by Meehan or Mitchell.

O'Mahony: Do you know where the drugs are stored, Charlie?

Bowden: No, I don't.

Hanley: Do you know where they come from?

Bowden: No. I don't ask questions. I just deliver the hash to the list of customers given to me by Meehan and Mitchell.

Hanley: Charlie, the gardaí have located a warehouse at Greenmount Industrial Estate and they are searching it. They've discovered a large quantity of cannabis and other suspected drugs.

At that moment, Bowden realized the game was up. There was no longer any point in diluting the truth. What was left of his protective facade had been shattered. Bowden wilted.

Bowden: Have ye found it? I should have told ye last night. Fuck it. I was going to tell ye when we were driving back from Mespil Road. Now you have found it, I will tell you everything I know. I am sorry for not telling ye about it already.

O'Mahony: All we want is the full truth. We want you to tell us all you know about the drugs operation and give us whatever information you have regarding the murder of Veronica Guerin.

Bowden: I will tell you everything. I am scared. If Gilligan hears that I have ratted, I am dead.

The former soldier then gave the two detectives a detailed statement about his involvement in the drugs operation and how the system worked.

He dropped bombshells which took them totally by surprise, candidly describing how large amounts of weaponry had come with the drugs and offering to show the location of the gang's hidden arsenal.

To their amazement, Bowden also began describing the gang's attack on Martin Foley the previous February. The police had no leads on who had been responsible for the second attack. Bowden explained how Foley's hit was planned, the weapons used and what happened afterwards.

Bowden: They [Meehan and Ward] made a bollocks of it and he got away. Meehan couldn't handle the gun.

Then came the final piece of the puzzle.

Bowden: In January of this year another sub-machine gun and a .357 Magnum with twelve rounds came in.

Hanley: Where is the .357 Magnum now?

Bowden: I know that is the gun you are looking for – for Veronica Guerin's murder.

Hanley: How do you know what type of gun we are looking for?

Bowden: I got it wrapped up and put it in the graveyard, too.

The ex-soldier then described Dutchy Holland as the man he believed was the actual hit man.

O'Mahony: How can you be sure that the .357 is the one used to murder Veronica Guerin?

Bowden: Because I cleaned it and got it ready before the murder. There were refill bullets in it. Brass with silver heads, the tops were turned in, rather than coming to a point.

Bowden agreed to make a full statement. It took almost three hours to dictate his terrifying story of drugs, guns, money, greed and murder. His account blew the lid on the secret underworld.

But just as Bowden was beginning to spill gangland's dirty secrets, there was an even more dramatic development across the Irish Sea.

CHAPTER TWENTY-TWO

—

CLOSING IN

John Gilligan was now classified as one of the most dangerous criminals in Europe although as yet there was no warrant for his arrest. Law enforcement agencies in the UK and across the Continent were circulated with an alert from Europol and Interpol that included his picture and passport details. Similar alerts were issued for the other key members of the mob. In particular, police and customs in the Netherlands, Belgium, France and Britain were now secretly monitoring his movements. Each time he or other known members of the criminal cartel passed through an airport or ferry terminal they were flagged and the reports were funnelled through official channels back to Lucan.

Although he was extremely paranoid, Gilligan was still blissfully ignorant of the amount of attention he was attracting. Ironically, he had finally achieved his ambition of becoming a top international gangster.

On the morning of Bowden's arrest, Gilligan took the 8.30 a.m. KLM flight from Heathrow to Schiphol, clutching a case of money. After Warren's arrest he had no bagman and the gang's supply chain had been severely disrupted. With the increasing heat coming down from the police in Dublin, the gang could not find a quick replacement to move the cash directly to the Netherlands. Gilligan had to be his own bagman. That night he returned to London.

The next morning Gilligan met with Michael Cunningham, John Cunningham's brother. Michael brought a parcel of cash to him and planned to travel on to the Netherlands with Gilligan. This was a risk for Cunningham because he was wanted in the UK for questioning in connection with the killing of a police officer during an armed robbery in West Yorkshire in 1985.

As a result of intelligence from Ireland, he had also been flagged as a suspected drug trafficker for HM Customs' attention. At 9.55 a.m. the two men booked seats on the 1 p.m. flight to Amsterdam. The Club Class tickets were one way.

Over the next two hours there was frantic telephone activity between HM Customs and Lucan garda station. The incident room was already a hive of activity as officers prepared to raid the gang's drug depot. Hickey, O'Loughlin and O'Connell anxiously waited for news from Heathrow.

In the CAB Fachtna Murphy and Felix McKenna had also been apprised of the development. There was a possibility that Gilligan could be carrying drug money. If he was, then the British would require assistance putting together a case to show that the cash was the proceeds of crime.

Customs and armed police officers drifted into the departures lounge of Terminal 3 to discreetly watch over the two underworld pals who had started their criminal careers together as kids on the streets of Ballyfermot.

Ten minutes before the flight was due to depart, Gilligan walked up to the boarding gate with his passport and ticket. He was carrying a large, silver, metal case in one hand and a briefcase in the other. At that moment back in Dublin, the Lucan squad had literally smashed down the door to his drug empire.

HM Customs had long memories when it came to John Gilligan and were happy to oblige their Irish colleagues. Detective Garda Pat

Bane, who co-ordinated the investigation from Lucan, had been in contact with senior customs investigator Roger Wilson in Manchester all morning.

Wilson had been working closely with Hickey's officers since the murder investigation began. He had not forgotten his previous encounter with Gilligan and the death threats after he had seized the mobster's drug money at Holyhead in December 1994. This time Wilson wanted to ensure it was Gilligan who would be placed under armed guard. Wilson had instructed his colleagues in Heathrow to intercept Gilligan when he presented at departures.

The West Yorkshire police had also been informed of Michael Cunningham's arrival in the jurisdiction and they were making arrangements to take him into custody.

As Gilligan approached the boarding gate Roger Wilson was sitting by his phone in Manchester. Customs officer Andrew Booth stepped forward as the mobster passed through Gate 16, saying: 'Hello, sir, can I see your passport, please?'

Without speaking, Gilligan handed over the document. 'How long are you going to Amsterdam for?' Booth asked, as he scanned the pages, as though it was a routine enquiry. The Q&A session continued as Gilligan replied:

Gilligan: A couple of weeks.

Booth: What is the purpose of your travel? Is it business or pleasure?

Gilligan: Business.

Booth: What sort of business is that, then?

Gilligan: Racing.

Booth: What sort? Horse racing?

Gilligan: Yes, and property.

Booth: Do you own horses?

Gilligan: Yeah, I do.

Booth: Whereabouts?

Gilligan: In Ireland.

Booth: Is the trip to Amsterdam for racing, then?

Gilligan: No, for property. I'm looking at property there.

Booth: Are you buying property there?

Gilligan: Yeah.

The mob boss was growing weary of all the nuisance questions. He was anxious to get on board his flight. The questions grew more searching as Booth asked:

Booth: Do you have any money with you to buy that property?

Gilligan: Yeah, I do. In the case.

Booth: How much do you have?

Gilligan: I've £300,000 (€583,000). It's all legal and above board. Look.

Gilligan produced a document headed 'statement of affairs' from his briefcase as Booth asked: 'Who does the money belong to?'

He was growing ever more impatient as he replied: 'Me. It's mine. It came from the bank. Here's the receipt. Look, what's the problem? It's OK to take the money out, isn't it?'

The last passengers for the flight rushed past him. At the same time Cunningham had also been taken aside.

The customs officer explained that large movements of cash were considered suspicious and that such an amount might be detained if it was believed to be linked to drug trafficking or other criminal activities.

The diminutive godfather suddenly found himself standing in a circle of customs officers and policemen carrying Heckler and Koch sub-machine guns. He was asked to sit down while further enquiries were made. In the meantime his flight departed.

The police arrested Cunningham and took him away to West Yorkshire for questioning about the 1985 murder. He was subsequently released without charge.

Booth returned at 1.20 p.m. and informed the little man that he wasn't under arrest but that Customs wanted to make further enquiries about the money and would appreciate his assistance.

Despite everything that had happened over the past week, Gilligan decided to brazen it out. Warren had been arrested and questioned, Gilligan's files had been taken from his solicitor's office and Bowden, the gang's quartermaster, had also been lifted but the little man was not losing his money. Gilligan could have walked away and said he would return for the money. But he had beaten Customs before and he was confident he could do it again and no one was taking his money. In a holding room Gilligan was asked to open the silver case.

Inside, the officers found a pillow, some clothing and a large bundle of cash in bubble wrap. 'How much is in it?' asked the customs officer.

'£330,000 (€640,000) and there is a receipt in the briefcase,' Gilligan replied.

In the briefcase the officers found an assortment of photocopies of bookmakers' cheques, a copy of a receipt for the return of the money seized by Roger Wilson in 1994 and what turned out to be a bizarre loan agreement for £4 million between John and Geraldine Gilligan and a mysterious Lebanese businessman called Joseph Saouma. An electronic gadget for detecting bugging devices was also found in the case.

A customs officer phoned Roger Wilson to update him on developments. 'Arrest him now. Don't let him out of your sight. I'm on my way,' Wilson said urgently. John Gilligan had finally been caught.

As he raced to London, Wilson called Pat Bane in Lucan to inform him that their number one target was in custody. There was jubilation in the incident room but everyone had to act fast.

Fachtna Murphy and Felix McKenna met with Hickey in the flurry of activity that followed. The main objective now was to ensure that Gilligan remained in custody where he could not influence the rapidly changing events back in Dublin.

It was decided to send Felix McKenna and Detective Garda Bernard Masterson from the murder investigation to London to liaise with the UK agencies. The Irish evidence would be crucial to prove Gilligan's money was the proceeds of drug trafficking.

A combination of hard work, Gilligan's hubris and good luck had finally paid off. In Heathrow John Joseph Gilligan was formally arrested at 2.06 p.m. by HM Customs on suspicion of laundering the proceeds of drug trafficking. He was held there for questioning.

At that same moment Charlie Bowden had just started coming clean about the inner workings of the gang.

At 10.30 p.m. that evening Roger Wilson walked into an interview room and sat across the table from the man who had threatened to kill him almost two years earlier. When Wilson introduced himself, and jogged his memory, Gilligan knew he was in trouble.

Masterson and McKenna then arrived from Dublin. Gilligan spotted them walking past the room where he was being held and the penny finally dropped. In the space of less than forty hours his criminal empire was crumbling down.

McKenna waved at his old adversary and gave him a smile that had 'Gotcha!' written all over it. It was the first time the cop and the robber had seen each other since McKenna's evidence had put Factory John away for four years in November 1990. The last time 'Felix the Cat' had smiled at Gilligan was when he was being led to the prison van on his way to Portlaoise Prison.

Gilligan tried to put on a brave face but he knew he had been outsmarted and trapped. He had seriously underestimated his foes. He never dreamt that they would come after him this way. Gilligan smirked and told one of the customs officers: 'Tell Felix I said hello.' A few minutes later McKenna popped his head around the door and, with a wide grin on his face, told his old enemy: 'How are you, John? I'll see you, John, in about fourteen years – if you're lucky.'

By now the incident room in Lucan station resembled the command centre of a battle. Phones were ringing, statements and evidence were being filed and catalogued, search and arrest warrants were being processed, and teams were being organized to interview suspects, make further arrests and carry out searches.

As Gilligan was being questioned in Heathrow, Charlie Bowden finished giving his initial statement to O'Mahony and Hanley. He concluded:

> The only regret I have is that I didn't let someone know what I knew was going to happen. I would like to sincerely apologise to Veronica's husband and son for my part in her murder. I am full of remorse and am glad to have told you the truth.

Late that night, under cover of darkness, Bowden showed the detectives where the gang's arsenal was hidden in the Jewish graveyard on Oldcourt Road, Tallaght. It was decided not to carry out a search until daylight. Shortly after midnight on Sunday, Bowden was returned to his cell.

A Lucan team member recalled the tumultuous events of that day:

After almost three months suddenly everything began to fall into place...By midnight on 6 October we had the guns, we had the drugs, we had the supply route, we had the mechanics of everything that had happened before and during the murder, and Gilligan was out of harm's way in custody in England. Technically, the case had been solved.

The investigators worked through the night collating the huge bank of information they had gathered. The following morning the car park of the Ambassador Hotel was placed under surveillance. A new consignment of drugs was expected to be delivered that day from Cork.

Another crew was dispatched to Cork to investigate the involvement of John Dunne, whom Bowden had named, as managing the other end of the gang's supply route. The Criminal Assets Bureau was called in to work on the Cork connection, which would provide proof of Gilligan's drug trafficking activities for the UK investigation. It would also support the CAB's efforts to seize the various gang members' assets.

The next morning Bowden's detention period was due to expire at 6.30 a.m. It was decided to rearrest him under the Misuse of Drugs Act in light of the discovery at Greenmount. Tony Hickey had kept the DPP updated on developments across the weekend. There was ample evidence to charge Bowden with the sale and supply of drugs at Greenmount. A further charge of possession of firearms could be preferred at a later date. He could also be charged with being involved in the conspiracy to murder. Apart from his admissions, there was a wealth of hard evidence, including forensics, to convict him.

The next step was to corroborate what he had told them and then figure out how to use it against Gilligan and the rest of the mob. Crucially the ex-soldier had indicated that he was willing to testify in court. That presented a new set of unprecedented challenges which would have to be dealt with soon.

Early the next morning John O'Mahony and Bernie Hanley went with a search team to the old Jewish cemetery. Under a tombstone, bearing the name Miriam Norcup, they removed a flagstone and found the arsenal.

The cache included a Sten sub-machine gun, an Agram machine pistol, five Walther semi-automatic pistols, silencer barrels, spare magazines and 1,057 rounds of ammo. In Lucan, Bowden had been released and rearrested at 6.45 a.m. for questioning about the drugs and guns. He identified the property recovered in Greenmount and in the cemetery.

That afternoon he was brought, under tight security, to a special sitting at Kilmainham District Court. Bowden was remanded in custody on the drugs charges and held in Mountjoy Prison.

While the gardaí were watching the Ambassador Hotel, Paul Ward and Brian Meehan unwittingly avoided arrest when they decided to pick up the latest shipment themselves. Among Meehan, Mitchell and Ward, none was under surveillance. Despite being seriously concerned by the media reports on the charging of Bowden and the UK arrest of Gilligan, the greedy thugs were still determined to keep the drug operation rolling.

They collected the load of 380 kilos from Cork and brought it back to Dublin, avoiding the surveillance teams waiting at Greenmount and the Ambassador Hotel. It would be the last shipment the gang received from the Netherlands.

Meanwhile Gilligan refused to answer any questions during the two days he was held in London. The Dublin officers, however, gave HM Customs and the Crown Prosecution Service a full brief on the ongoing investigation in Ireland and the discovery of the gang's drug distribution centre the day before. They had the drugs and the guns, and the information from Russell Warren connecting Gilligan to the cash. The ink had also barely dried on Bowden's statement identifying Gilligan as the boss of a vast drug dealing operation. The information about cash transactions and his links with Rahman and Baltus had also arrived from the Netherlands.

On Tuesday 8 October, Gilligan was brought before Uxbridge Magistrates' Court under heavy armed guard. He was charged with an offence under Section 49 (1) of the Drug Trafficking Act 1994, laundering the proceeds of his drugs operation.

At the same hearing Roger Wilson was granted an application to hold on to the £330,000. He told the court that Gilligan couldn't offer a legitimate explanation for the source of the cash, that he was associated with two known English drug dealers and that he was linked with the seizure of drugs in Dublin.

Gilligan couldn't believe what was happening and was apoplectic with rage, claiming to be the victim of a conspiracy between the gardaí and HM Customs. The court remanded him to Belmarsh Prison in east London, a maximum-security jail where terrorists and other category 'A' class prisoners are held.

The mob boss couldn't bear his new surroundings in Belmarsh which had one of the strictest security regimes in Europe. He refused to acclimatize to his dramatic change of fortune and retained a legal team to immediately launch a series of challenges to his detention.

Gilligan could whine about his situation all he wanted – he was no longer controlling events. His days as a jet-setting drug baron were over.

Gilligan's imprisonment was a game changer. It dramatically increased the dismantling of his criminal empire. His cronies were not as scared of reprisals as they had been.

John Foy, a former member of the General's gang and a peripheral player in the Gilligan outfit, was located and watched. Bowden had indicated that Foy knew something about the motorbike and where the murder weapon had been disposed of. Having served time with

Gilligan, Ward and Meehan, Foy was a customer of the gang, turning over 30 kilos a week. Foy was believed to have helped Paul Ward cut up the motorbike in a lockup off Cromwellsfort Road, a place where Foy stored stolen cars.

In Lucan the order was sent out to put the other gang members under surveillance. The police strategy was to continue seeking out potential weak spots. They were aware from Bowden and other underworld informants that Shay Ward had been very upset since the murder. Perhaps he could lead them to the murder weapon. The investigators decided to arrest him on sight. But Meehan, Mitchell and the Wards had gone into hiding, moving between safe houses and hotels around Dublin, while they tried to find out who was talking.

Mitchell and Meehan met Julian Clohessy to quiz him about what he'd said while in custody. Meehan was beginning to panic after his boss was charged. Someone was talking somewhere. Bowden was in prison and he couldn't make contact with him. Meehan put the word out through the underworld network that anyone who agreed to co-operate with the investigation was dead.

On Tuesday night, 8 October, Paul 'Hippo' Ward was staying in a room in the Green Isle Hotel in Clondalkin when he was arrested at gunpoint on suspicion of being involved in an armed robbery. He was asleep when detectives burst into the room.

Hippo Ward was brought to Ronanstown garda station, where it was discovered that he was not the Ward they were looking for. The cops wanted to get their hands on Shay Ward. Hippo was released within the hour. The incident spooked the gang even more. It was time to leave Ireland.

Paul Ward, Meehan and Mitchell had already decided to get Shay Ward out before the cops got to him. He had a drug problem and was likely to buckle under interrogation. Shay was anxious that he was going to be lifted after Bowden's arrest. He had already warned the others that he was not going to take the murder rap.

The following evening Paul Ward met John 'Buffalo' O'Neill in a pub car park in Tallaght. Hippo, who was clearly anxious, had two passport forms and pictures of Shay Ward which he wanted O'Neill to stamp and sign in the station so he could obtain a passport in a false name.

By now the connection between the corrupt cop and Ward had been uncovered in Lucan. The telephone analysis showed that on one day alone Ward had called O'Neill fifty-five times. Hickey ordered a secret background check of O'Neill, aware that gardaí could potentially be on the gang's payroll.

Collators' reports showed that O'Neill had not been filing any information from his contacts with Ward. A discreet perusal of the cop's financial affairs showed that he had chronic problems. After repaying his various loans, O'Neill was left with a pittance each week but he clearly had plenty of cash. He was placed under surveillance.

The van used by Bowden and Shay Ward to deliver the drugs was also located and surveillance officers planted a tracking device on it to monitor its movements.

On Thursday afternoon Meehan called an associate and told him to get rid of the van. It was brought to a scrapyard in Dolphin's Barn in inner-city Dublin, which was being used as a front for dismantling stolen cars for spare parts. The NSU watched in astonishment as four men immediately set about destroying the dope mobile. To protect their anonymity surveillance teams do not make arrests unless it is a matter of life or death.

One of the undercover officers made an urgent call to Lucan, shouting: 'If ye don't get here soon, that van won't exist. They're swarming over it like ants.' The Lucan team members raced to the scene. When they arrived, they surrounded the yard and went in with guns drawn. The dismantlers were ordered to put their hands up and stand back.

The four men were arrested and taken in for questioning. The swoop on the yard led to a separate investigation by the Stolen Car

Squad. The four were subsequently convicted in relation to the stolen car scam and eleven of their victims were compensated.

That day a further seventeen searches were carried out throughout Dublin, including the home of Paul Ward. A warrant had been issued for his arrest. The following day he was spotted hiding drugs in a field near Tallaght but he again slipped through the net.

That afternoon another five associates of the gang were arrested in co-ordinated swoops. In the meantime Shay Ward was smuggled out of the country through Northern Ireland with the help of Brendan 'Speedy' Fegan. Speedy also organized false passports for Meehan, Mitchell and Paul Ward. Time was running out for the gang.

Meehan and Mitchell fled to the UK on 14 October. Meehan phoned John Dunne to inform him that there would be no more shipments for a number of weeks. The night before they ran the pair took out their frustration by beating up an off-duty cop outside a nightclub.

The previous evening Paul Ward had arranged to meet O'Neill in the car park of the Cuckoo's Nest pub in Tallaght. Ward gave the crooked cop four photographs of Meehan's girlfriend which he wanted stamped for a new passport.

A short distance away, Detective Sergeant Pat Keane was monitoring his colleague's meeting. There was now no doubt that O'Neill had gone bad. The same evening a man wanted in connection with the dodgy scrapyard investigation gave himself up. Detective Gardaí Sean O'Brien, Pat Walshe and Mick McElgunn were sent to collect him.

On the way back to Lucan the man appeared nervous. He had something to tell them but was afraid. The detectives said that he could talk freely to them. 'How can I, when I don't know who of you lot are working for Ward and Meehan?' the suspect exclaimed.

He went on tell the officers that he had been with the two gangsters when they were arranging passports with John O'Neill to flee the country. O'Brien reported the conversation to Todd O'Loughlin and Hickey.

Later that night O'Brien and McElgunn were called back to Lucan for a meeting. Todd O'Loughlin, Jerry O'Connell and Hickey were in a room on their own. Hickey filled them in on what was known about O'Neill. The normally cool and unflappable Kerryman could not contain his anger and fumed:

> This is fucking treason. If this happened a hundred years ago, a person would be hanged for it. Here we are breaking our backs, the whole force trying to catch these bastards, and one of our own is working for them trying to help them get away. It's nothing but fucking treachery.

The Buffalo's days as a policeman were numbered. Hickey swore everyone in the room to absolute secrecy.

By the time Meehan and Mitchell fled to the UK, Dutchy Holland had also departed. He popped up again in London where he stayed with some relatives. Within a few weeks the South East Regional Crime Squad found him and placed him under surveillance. With Shay Ward also gone, the only gang member left in Dublin was Paul 'Hippo' Ward.

All the indications were that Ward was seriously angry at being thrown into the middle of the murder. He was terrified of being linked to the crime. In Lucan it was calculated that Ward might even decide to come clean, but first they had to find him before he joined his pals on the run.

Ward was eventually tracked down a few days later. He was arrested with John Foy on 16 October. The order was also given to swoop on Ward's circle. Over the next few hours nine members of Ward's family were lifted, including his elderly parents and his girlfriend, Vanessa Meehan. Another twenty-two searches were carried out.

Ward was the second senior gang member to be arrested. He had also played a central role in the conspiracy and was a candidate for a murder charge. Hickey brought in experienced, veteran interrogators who had faced down the hardest men in the IRA to interrogate him. Vanessa Meehan and Ward's seventy-four-year-old mother, Elizabeth, were brought to see him in a bid to loosen him up. This move by the gardaí was later severely criticized by the judges in the Special Criminal Court.

Ward was subsequently alleged to have told the investigators: 'My part was to let them [Meehan and the hit man] use my house after the shooting. They came with the bike and the gun.'

Asked where he had hidden the murder weapon, Ward replied: 'Nobody will ever be killed by the gun where it is now.' Hippo was then asked where the gun came from. 'You know well where it came from. It was with the guns and ammunition you got in the graveyard.'

In other interviews Ward claimed his only role in the murder was the disposal of the gun and the bike. During his later trial in the Special Criminal Court these admissions were ruled inadmissible because they had allegedly been made under duress after the visits of Ward's mother and girlfriend. The court commented: 'Both meetings amounted to a conscious and deliberate disregard of the accused's basic constitutional right to fair procedures and treatment while in custody.'

The following day corrupt cop John O'Neill's home was raided and the nightclub manager who had introduced him to Ward was arrested. Underlining the seriousness of the situation Detective Inspectors Todd O'Loughlin and Jerry O'Connell went to the garda's home with four other officers. When he was shown the search warrant, O'Neill replied: 'Is this about my contact with the Wards?'

O'Neill then agreed to go to the Garda Dublin Metropolitan HQ at Harcourt Square, central Dublin, to be interviewed. He wasn't under arrest and was still a member of the gardaí when he confessed his dealings with Ward and Meehan. He also admitted to being on the payroll of two other well-known drug dealers, Tony Long and Derek 'Dee Dee' O'Driscoll, who were both from Ballyfermot. The two criminals were subsequently convicted for corruption and were also targeted by the CAB.

O'Neill was officially suspended from the gardaí. He then resigned from the force. Immediately after this he was arrested under Section 30 of the Offences Against the State Act and brought to Naas station in Kildare for questioning.

The arrest of O'Neill was a sad victory. It was a source of embarrassment to the police force, coming so soon after a murder which had challenged the public's faith in the keepers of law and order. However, it illustrated the depth of the cleanout that was under way.

Later O'Neill was brought to Lucan to confront Paul Ward. O'Neill told the murder suspect that he had told his police colleagues everything about their relationship. He encouraged Ward to 'tell the truth'.

Ward was angered by the visit and shouted at the officers who were interviewing him:

> Fuck off! There is no need to do that. He didn't tell me fuck all about the murder. The money is his fucking problem. I am saying nothing else to you.

The following day, 18 October, O'Neill was taken before the Dublin District Court where he was remanded on sixteen charges of accepting bribes. He was released on bail.

Later that evening Paul Ward was brought in a convoy of squad cars to the same court. He was formally charged with conspiracy to murder Veronica Guerin and was also charged with drug trafficking and remanded in custody.

The same day Russell and Debbie Warren were arrested for the second time, for questioning about the gang's arms stash. With Gilligan now safely locked up in the UK Russell Warren was more forthcoming. He described the events leading up to the murder, including being sent to Naas to look out for Veronica's car, but didn't admit that he had actually witnessed the shooting. In his second statement he claimed that after he left Naas he'd pulled off the dual carriageway and headed back to Tallaght on a back road. It was the following May before Warren finally admitted his full role in the crime.

On 25 October John Dunne was arrested when the cops pounced on the Cork end of the operation. His wife and the van drivers he paid to transport Gilligan's drugs to Dublin were also rounded up. Rather than use local garda stations the suspects were all driven the 250 kilometres back to Lucan station for questioning – the team was going for the maximum psychological effect.

At the same time the shipping company premises where Dunne worked was raided. Records were examined to get an estimate of the number of shipments that had come through from the Netherlands. What they discovered was staggering.

That evening one of the officers rang Chief Superintendent Fachtna Murphy at his office in the CAB and asked if he was sitting down. They had made a rough calculation of the amount of hash Gilligan had shipped through Cork. 'They've shipped in tons of the stuff, Chief, as far back as April 1994 – millions.'

Meanwhile Detective Inspector John O'Mahony, who had helped convince Charlie Bowden to unburden himself, had another breakthrough. On the journey to Dublin John Dunne readily agreed to tell all he knew. He was upfront and to the point. 'I was driven by pure greed and nothing more. After the murder I was too scared to get out,' he told O'Mahony.

Over the next two days Dunne gave a full account of his involvement with the Gilligan gang. He too was now a potential State witness against the killers. Dunne was later charged with the importation of illegal drugs.

Finally in early November John Gilligan's family and close personal associates, including his wife and children, were arrested in swoops. Traynor's group of associates were also lifted although he was still in hiding on the Continent. They were all later released without charge.

On 6 November the CAB used their new powers to begin hitting the gang. They seized vehicles belonging to Ward, Meehan and Mitchell and whatever money they had left behind. They also began the process of seizing all the properties owned by Traynor, Meehan, Mitchell and Paul Ward. And they continued building their case against Gilligan.

On 20 November the CAB arrived at Jessbrook with a large force of police and revenue officials. It was the first large-scale operation by the newly formed bureau. To protect their identities, the CAB officers covered their faces with scarves and the registration plates on their vans were removed.

Felix McKenna supervised the operation, which took most of a day. They seized horses, jeeps, horse trailers, stable and riding equipment, furniture, TVs and video players. Anything of value was taken. All that was left were personal effects and basic household equipment. The raid was in response to the Gilligans' refusal to pay the tax demand that had been issued in September.

Speaking to reporters at the gates of her home, where Veronica Guerin was beaten and her fate decided, Geraldine Gilligan said:

> I couldn't answer the tax assessment because the police have all my documents of returns and everything else, so I didn't have any documentation to answer with. My demand has gone from £882,000 to £1,292,000 [*sic*]. I can prove the source of any income.

Less than a year after the gang had languished on a beach in St Lucia and joked about crime paying, the swaggering mobsters had been reduced to the status of fugitives and prisoners.

CHAPTER TWENTY-THREE

BATTLELINES

Gilligan kept himself busy orchestrating a string of legal actions on both sides of the Irish Sea, as his first Christmas in an English prison approached. He was determined to beat the money laundering charges pending against him and to fight them every step of the way, using every legal technicality available to him. He was also instructing lawyers in Ireland to take on the CAB.

The mobster was still confident that he would beat the system – using legal and illegal means. He had a strong gang on the outside, led by Meehan and Holland, who could silence anyone who dared to speak to the police and testify against them. Even though they had fled Ireland Gilligan was sure they could still leverage plenty of influence there. Now that he was in one of Europe's most secure prisons, however, his ability to communicate with the outside world was severely curtailed. He could pass on instructions through his visitors and on the phone but in order to retain control he had to be back on the ground. Gilligan was desperate to get out.

The boss wasn't the only member of the gang who felt that way. Paul Ward was having a tough time in Mountjoy Prison. He told his visitors that he thought he was going out of his mind. Ward was frustrated and angry that he had been left to carry the can for the murder while his pals had apparently got away scot-free.

He once complained to another prisoner that he hadn't even pulled the trigger. Hippo had only got rid of the gun and motorbike because he had been told to. He had been pulled into this by Gilligan and the others and felt betrayed.

Meehan and Mitchell were off enjoying themselves in the sun and Ward knew, from his interviews in Lucan station, that Bowden had told detectives about the drugs. But he didn't know if the ex-soldier was going to testify against him. Hippo was about to explode.

Ward was being held in the prison's Separation Unit, or E Wing, and had been complaining about the living conditions since before Christmas. When he'd had a gripe about the regime in 1990 he and Meehan had led the riot which wrecked a wing of the prison.

On the evening of 4 January 1997 Ward was again in the news when he attempted another protest. At 6 p.m. the cells on E4 were unlocked to allow the prisoners free movement about the landing, which had a gym, a recreation hall and a shower room. Ward asked one of the officers if he would allow another prisoner, Stephen Galvin, to get out of his cell to go to the toilet. Galvin had been deprived of evening recreation for a disciplinary offence. Within seconds of being released, five prison officers were taken hostage. Ward and Galvin were the ringleaders.

The general alarm was raised and gardaí and trained negotiators were called in. Over the next two days the prison officers were put through a terrifying ordeal in which they had razors, knives and syringes held to their necks. One prison officer was placed on a chair and told he was about to be hanged. The hostages were told that they would be forced to drink AIDS- and HIV-infected blood. The prisoners walked around squirting blood from their syringes to illustrate the threat.

Ward emerged as the prisoners' spokesman, warning that if he didn't get access to a solicitor he was going to start breaking arms and legs. He threatened to cut off one of the officer's fingers if the hostage-takers were not transferred to another prison. Then he demanded that the media be told that he was protesting because 'I am innocent of the murder of Veronica Guerin.'

Members of the Army Ranger Wing were preparing to execute a forced entry, using explosives to blast the doors open, when a nun's intervention brought about a peaceful conclusion. She convinced them to release the hostages.

Ward and the other hostage-takers were removed to Portlaoise Prison, where they were placed in solitary confinement for several months. On 30 July 1999 Ward was sentenced to twelve years when he pleaded guilty to his involvement in the siege.

———

Meanwhile Brian Meehan and Peter Mitchell were wreaking havoc of another kind in Gran Canaria where they had been spending the Christmas holidays.

Over the previous months the pair had moved between the Netherlands, Belgium, France, Austria and Spain's Costa del Sol. Gardaí had little difficulty tracking the couple's movements. The pair of arrogant loudmouths hung around popular Irish haunts, making no effort to keep a low profile.

While in the Canaries, Meehan and Mitchell had approached a number of bar owners offering to invest in their businesses, but word of their reputations spread among the close-knit community and they failed to make a deal.

At one stage they ran into a number of gardaí from Dublin who were also on holiday in Playa del Inglés. Instead of maintaining a low profile, Meehan and Mitchell attempted to intimidate the guards, making shapes of guns with their hands. The officers had to seek alternative accommodation.

In a nightclub the pair encountered the Galway All-Ireland hurling team. Meehan began picking on the GAA men and attacked one of the team's brightest stars, Gregory Kennedy, breaking his ankle and potentially damaging his sports career. Mitchell ranted: 'Now do ye see what happens when you fuck with us?' On another occasion the pair gave a man a severe beating outside the same nightclub.

By the first week of February 1997 they had decided to leave the Canaries. Sticking together, they moved to mainland Europe, where they teamed up with John Traynor. The gang members were making every effort to regroup and resume their drug trafficking business. They were also desperate to find out what was happening in the Guerin investigation – and to silence anyone who talked.

Following the flurry of activity in October the investigation had gone quiet, but it was nothing more than a lull in the ongoing battle. The enquiry had entered a new phase.

Although it wasn't attracting the same level of media attention, the incident room was still the scene of intense activity as investigation files were prepared for the DPP on those who had so far been charged. They were also busily compiling investigation files on Gilligan and Meehan with a view to charging them in connection with the murder and drug trafficking.

On 22 January 1997 Gilligan and the rest of the gang got the first inkling of the extent of the State's case against them when he appeared at a pre-trial hearing in London. It was to decide on an application by Gilligan's lawyers that he should not be sent forward for trial on the money laundering charges.

During the week-long hearing officers from the CAB and the Lucan team gave evidence of his financial dealings in Ireland. It was the first time that details of the gang's drug operation were made public – along with the bombshell that a member of the gang had become a supergrass.

There were gasps of surprise when the Irish officers described how Gilligan had gambled almost £5.5 million (€10 million) in two and a half years and lost just over £600,000 (€1.2 million). Details were also given of his multitude of business-class flights between Dublin and Amsterdam.

In court Gilligan sat smiling and looking up at the ceiling, his arms draped across the bench where he was sitting. He would confidently wink across at the large group of Irish journalists covering the case. He was confident he was the Teflon Don.

But then the blood drained from Gilligan's face as John Dunne was brought to the witness stand. It was a development that he had not expected. He couldn't believe that anyone would dare to testify against him. The mobster's eyes narrowed and he made no effort to conceal the pure hatred he felt for the man who had come to betray him.

The former shipping manager, who was on bail for drug trafficking charges and under around-the-clock armed protection at his home in Cork, had been flown under guard to London for the hearing. He gave details of collecting and delivering the shipments of drugs on Gilligan's behalf although he claimed that he didn't know what was in the crates arriving from the Netherlands.

After Dunne's testimony the court threw out Gilligan's bid for freedom. But it was just the first of countless others.

Following his arrest in October 1996 Bowden spent six weeks locked up before being released on bail of £60,000 (€117,000). Meehan had provided a quarter of the bail money and the rest was raised among Bowden's family and friends. As soon as the quartermaster was released Meehan rang him, sounding agitated and dangerous.

He demanded to know what Paul Smullen and Julian Clohessy had told the police. Meehan was particularly worried about Clohessy because he had bragged to him about the murder. The Tosser's big mouth was catching up with him.

Meehan ordered Bowden to write a report of everything he and his friends had said while in custody. The reports were picked up and sent to Meehan. Then he issued instructions for Smullen and Clohessy to go to a criminal lawyer and swear affidavits to the effect that they had been forced to implicate him [Meehan] in the murder.

He wanted the pair to claim that the police had threatened to charge them with murder if they didn't agree. Meehan warned:

> If anyone who has made a statement against me doesn't sign an affidavit, I will have them taken care of. There's no way I'll let Clohessy get into the witness box. The guards won't be able to protect any witnesses because there is no witness protection programme in Ireland.

By the time Gilligan was facing John Dunne across a courtroom, Bowden and Warren were still not fully on board as State witnesses, although they had expressed their willingness to give evidence. Warren had not yet been charged with handling the drug money.

Tony Hickey and his colleagues were well aware of the huge security and legal challenges they would have to surmount before anyone gave evidence against Gilligan and his henchmen. The only way to beat the mob was to bring it down from the inside, through the testimony of their former associates and accomplices. This had been tried and tested especially in Mafia trials in Italy and the US, but never in the Republic of Ireland.

In return for their testimony Bowden and Warren would first have to be granted immunity from prosecution for the murder of Veronica Guerin. They and their families would also need protection, perhaps for the rest of their lives. Not for the first time the diminutive godfather was about to force fundamental changes in how Irish law enforcement operated.

In his discussions about the ongoing investigation with the DPP and the Department of Justice Tony Hickey informed them that a witness protection programme (WPP) was the only way to bring Gilligan to justice. It would take months before a decision was made.

In February 1997, when Paul Ward's charge was formally upgraded from conspiracy to murder to murder, Meehan phoned Bowden again. He told the quartermaster that it was now likely that he too would also be charged with conspiracy to murder. But Meehan had a plan. The Tosser suggested that he would get Charlie and Julie Bacon false passports and enough money to start a new life in Australia. It was gangland's equivalent of witness protection. Bowden agreed and sent passport photographs to Meehan through an intermediary.

In the absence of a deal with the State Bowden was seriously concerned about saving his own neck and was worried that he might be charged with the murder. The would-be hard man had never been in prison before and the six weeks he spent in custody were the toughest in his life. He was desperate to know if he was going to be granted immunity in exchange for his testimony against his former colleagues in crime. If not, he was likely to face a life sentence in prison based on his own admissions. But the gardaí couldn't answer Bowden's queries as Tony Hickey was still anxiously awaiting a response to his proposals from the Department of Justice and the DPP.

In a fit of panic Bowden absconded to England with Julie Bacon on 8 February. They stayed in a London guesthouse using false names. There was consternation when the team realized the ex-soldier had disappeared. But he wasn't missing for long.

On 20 February a surveillance team from the South East Regional Crime Squad watched as the couple met Dutchy Holland in central London. The gang's enforcer had arranged the meeting on Meehan's behalf.

Holland was fully aware that the police were likely to come looking for him soon. From his UK base he was also in the process of collecting drug money for Gilligan. His boss was owed about €1.9 million by customers who had taken advantage of his unexpected stay in Belmarsh Prison. Gilligan had promised Dutchy a 20 per cent commission.

The hit man told Bowden of his intention to organize a media campaign to win the right to have any interviews he did with the Lucan investigation videotaped. At the time the audio-visual recording of interviews with suspects had not yet been introduced in Ireland.

The source of Holland's anxiety was a front-page story in the *Sunday World* that featured his picture and revealed that he was the suspected hit man. He was not identified, and his eyes were blacked out, so the paper called him Dutchy to get around the legal niceties.

He quizzed Bowden about what he had told the police regarding his (Holland's) involvement in the murder plot. Bowden said he hadn't mentioned Dutchy's name in relation to the murder but had given a statement naming him in relation to the drugs operation. He admitted he had identified Holland on the list of customers, as the Wig. But Bowden made it clear that his statement could be withdrawn.

Holland then smiled and told Bowden not to worry:

> Everybody makes a statement but there are ways of dealing with people who do. They either don't get up in the witness box or, like you, they are given the option of running away. Or they could get popped.

He reminded the gang's quartermaster of the absence of an Irish witness protection programme. Before leaving the couple, Holland told Bowden to have a think about what he wanted to do.

The meeting terrified Bowden and Bacon. They felt isolated and vulnerable. Bowden knew that the gang could easily have him shot in the street.

Luckily for him, however, the covert police team had been listening to the conversation and later reported its content to Lucan. The gardaí sent a formal request to Scotland Yard seeking to have Bowden arrested as a fugitive.

The following morning the former soldier was feeling particularly paranoid while walking on the street and stood at a bus stop for ten minutes, watching to see if someone was following him.

His instincts proved to be correct. Suddenly both ends of the road were blocked by police cars as heavily armed officers ordered him to lie on the ground. He was arrested under the Prevention of Terrorism Act. Bacon was also arrested a short time later. When presented with an Irish extradition order he spoke to John O'Mahony on the phone. 'I want to come home. I want to co-operate,' he said. Bowden has nowhere else to run.

On 10 March Bowden and Bacon were escorted under armed guard to London City Airport. John O'Mahony and Bernie Hanley were waiting to accompany them home. Bowden was later brought before the courts for breach of his bail and returned to prison. For his own protection the ex-soldier was held in solitary confinement in Arbour Hill Prison, which is reserved for sex offenders. But by then Dutchy's ability to harm anyone was diminishing quickly.

In February sixteen officers from the CAB and Lucan swooped on Holland's luxury country house near Brittas Bay in Wicklow, arresting his wife, Angela, and a close family friend.

The CAB had obtained a High Court order freezing the property as a first step towards its full seizure. Holland was very upset when he heard of his wife's arrest which prompted him to go to the media. A friend set up a meeting for him with Dublin-based freelance reporter Ray Managh. The veteran journalist had been covering the courts for several years.

Holland wanted to give a newspaper and radio interview to plead his innocence. Pat Kenny, one of the country's most accomplished radio and television hosts, was interested when Managh tipped him off.

On 5 March Pat Kenny recorded an interview in a London hotel in which Dutchy denied any involvement in the murder of Veronica Guerin or that he was a hit man for hire. Holland, who had little difficulty killing a journalist, was now using the media in a bid to give himself a better image. He declared:

> I will be in Dublin in hours if the police give my legal representatives a written assurance the interview will be videotaped. I want to look Graham Turley in the eye and tell him: 'I did not kill your wife.' I want to tell her son: 'I did not kill your mother.'

Holland claimed that he had been forced to leave Ireland because of the *Sunday World* article. 'Where did the newspaper get my passport picture from?' he asked. 'Where did the information come from?'

He vowed that, despite his former criminal record, he had never been charged with violence or assault and he had never laid a hand on a woman. Although he had carried a gun in robberies, he had never used it.

In an interview with Ray Managh, which was published in the next morning's newspapers, Paddy Holland claimed:

> When I heard she had been killed, I didn't think much about it. I didn't follow it up. I didn't know the girl. All I knew was that she wrote articles. I'm not running the girl down. I heard she was dead. I didn't hear the details. It was later I found out it was in Clondalkin and that. I'm not saying it's right. I don't know anything. I just heard this girl got killed and I knew the name. I don't know details. I just got a news flash.

When the Pat Kenny interview was due to be aired, the Director General of RTÉ controversially intervened to block it. He told the furious host that the decision was based on the advice of the Garda Commissioner, who was afraid of prejudicing future investigations involving Holland.

Meanwhile Holland's solicitor contacted Detective Inspector Todd O'Loughlin to inform him that his client would be turning up voluntarily for an interview on 4 April. That later changed to 7 April when Holland still didn't appear.

The surveillance squad, however, which was keeping covert tabs on the killer had more accurate information. On 8 April they contacted Lucan to say that Holland was on his way to catch a late sailing from Holyhead to Dún Laoghaire. A team was sent to meet the boat.

Detectives posing as car checkers arrested Holland as he sat in the passenger seat of a car driven by a young woman with a child that had just rolled off the 5.45 a.m. ferry.

When he was taken to Lucan the assassin was searched and his clothes, shoes and socks were removed. He was given an overall suit to wear before being brought to an interview room. The SERC squad had observed him visiting a London store which specialized in providing high-tech bugging and surveillance equipment. There was reason to believe that Holland would be concealing a secret listening device at the interview.

At 8 a.m. Detective Sergeant Fergus Treanor and Detective Garda Sean O'Brien began interviewing Dutchy. As they did so an officer who was examining a Walkman found on Holland suddenly began hearing the voices of his colleagues in the next room, where Dutchy's shoes and other belongings were being kept.

Closer investigation revealed high-tech, James Bond-style bugs which had been built into the soles of the shoes. It was later discovered that he had paid the equivalent of €50,000 for the spy gear. A technical support team from Garda HQ discovered receiving and recording equipment in a guesthouse near the police station. In a follow-up investigation, packaging for the equipment was found in a rented room in a hotel near Tallaght garda station. An accomplice had planned to bug the interviews at Lucan in the elaborate plot to sabotage the whole investigation.

From then on the incident room and station house were regularly swept for bugging equipment, in addition to being protected against physical attack. When the equipment was found, Holland was asked to account for it. 'I am taking responsibility for it and all the rest of the equipment. I've been planning this for a couple of months, lads,' Holland replied amicably.

As the interview started, Holland refused to talk about the murder of Veronica Guerin, stating unequivocally: 'Gentlemen, I am not talking about that.'

He was more forthcoming about his involvement in the hash trade.

O'Brien: Paddy, the list which was found in Greenmount has you down for 34 kilos. Is that you, the Wig?

Holland: Yes.

O'Brien: What would you do with 34 kilos, Paddy?

Holland: Look, lads, I had my own customers. I am not going to implicate them. I have certain principles.

Later Detective Inspector John O'Mahony visited Holland in the interview room.

O'Mahony: You are admitting drug dealing. Is that correct?

Holland: Yes, only hash. The papers have us dealing in heroin and ecstasy. That's not true.

O'Mahony: Isn't it true that you were selling drugs for John Gilligan?

Holland: I'm not implicating anyone else. I'll speak for myself. I like John Gilligan. He is a nice fella.

After two days in detention, the DPP decided that there was enough evidence to charge Holland with drug trafficking offences, based both on his own admissions and the statement of Charlie Bowden.

On 11 April Holland was brought before Kilmainham District Court, south Dublin, in a convoy of squad cars, with blaring sirens and blue lights. There he was formally arraigned on the drug charges and remanded in custody to Portlaoise Prison.

The arrest of his feared assassin and enforcer was another serious blow to Gilligan's efforts to maintain his malign influence on events at home.

And he had legal problems of his own.

———————

John Gilligan was living up to Felix McKenna's prediction that in addition to intimidation, he would use every legal means possible to thwart the system. In the UK he had begun a series of challenges to every aspect of his detention and extradition. The legal battle would stretch out for almost four years, going as far as the House of Lords.

A week after Charlie Bowden was returned to custody in Ireland, Gilligan set out to have the hated Criminal Assets Bureau abolished. One of Gilligan's first legal battles with the State had been to argue that he was entitled to free legal aid, which he won. He then instructed his lawyers to go to the Dublin High Court to challenge the constitutionality of the Proceeds of Crime Act which gave the CAB its powers. After eight months in operation the Bureau had already won the admiration of international law enforcement. The British police had prepared a document for the British government on the operation of the Irish Proceeds of Crime Act with a view to adopting similar legislation. Other European police forces were also interested in the legislation and the powers it gave the gardaí.

Gilligan's assault was the first major test of the new legislation and the bureau's survival depended on the outcome. A lot was at stake. If Gilligan succeeded it would have serious consequences for the fight against organized crime.

During the four-day hearing, which opened on 18 March, the gangster's counsel, Brian Langwallner SC, claimed that the powers allowing gardaí to confiscate and dispose of an individual's assets were a 'slippery slope towards the creation of a police state'. He claimed the property seized from Gilligan had been bought with gambling money and a loan from a foreign businessman. He said:

> We are approaching a situation where a police officer can stop a man in the street and warn him that his property was being confiscated unless he could prove it was not the proceeds of crime. It is a slippery slope and it is not endorsed or acceptable in any civil jurisdiction.

Felix McKenna told the court that one of the effects of the Proceeds of Crime Act had been to 'force criminals above ground' and a lot of them had moved their money abroad. He said the public would become frustrated and disillusioned with the criminal justice system and be less likely to come forward as witnesses or informants if major criminals were not stopped.

Perhaps either due to coincidence or by design the High Court delivered its ruling on the landmark case on the first anniversary of Veronica Guerin's murder. Ms Justice Catherine McGuinness threw out Gilligan's challenge ruling that the Proceeds of Crime Act was indeed constitutional. She said the Act, and thus CAB itself, was a proportionate response to the kind of threat posed to society by organized crime.

In a direct reference to Gilligan she said the gardaí who had testified:

> ...painted a picture of an entirely new type of professional criminal who organized, rather than committed, crime and thereby rendered himself virtually immune to the ordinary procedures of criminal investigation and prosecution. Such persons are able to operate a reign of terror so as effectively to prevent the passing

on of information to the gardaí. At the same time their obvious wealth and power cause them to be respected by lesser criminals or would-be criminals.

In the meantime the Lucan Investigation Team, which was already battling with Gilligan and his gang in Dublin and London, opened up a third front in Europe.

Tony Hickey sent an operational team to the Continent to liaise with the Dutch and Belgian authorities. The objective was to follow up the source of the drugs and the guns. The enquiries by Detective Inspector Vincent Farrell and Detective Sergeants Pat Keane and Noel Browne would take almost a year to complete. CAB also sent liaison officers to follow the money trail to dovetail with enquiries conducted by HM Customs.

The DPP in Dublin sent an official request to the Dutch and Belgian authorities requesting assistance for the Irish financial and criminal investigations. The appeal included provision of the shipping records from the companies used by Rahman and Baltus.

Information was also sought from the bureaux de change, casinos and banks used by Gilligan and his bagmen. The Irish also wanted to interview the Gorsts, Simon Rahman, Johnny Wildhagen and Martin Baltus.

Despite exhaustive searches Johnny Wildhagen was never found, but in April Dutch police introduced the Irish detectives to Martin Baltus who agreed to co-operate. He had recently been released after serving a 150-day prison sentence for the counterfeit dollars scam which had caused a serious rift with Rahman.

Over the course of fifteen statements Baltus detailed his involvement with Gilligan including the names of the bogus companies used to ship the drugs, the quantities involved and the dates they were shipped. Baltus described packing the guns for the gang which included the distinctive Magnum .357 pistol used to murder the journalist. He also confirmed handling over £2.8 million (€5 million) of Gilligan's cash.

Baltus corroborated Bowden and Dunne's evidence in relation to the shipments of drugs and guns. He also corroborated Warren's admissions about delivering cash. Everything he said could be backed up with independent evidence. Baltus had cemented together the entire conspiracy of guns, drugs and money. It was an extraordinary breakthrough.

The Lucan detectives and their Dutch colleagues also visited Simon Rahman in a Dutch prison. They wanted to evaluate him as a potential witness against Gilligan. The imperious godfather listened with interest to the questions put to him and hinted that he might be prepared to testify if the price was right. The matter wasn't pursued any further.

In June the Irish officers, accompanied by Belgian police officers, met with Thomas Gorst and his wife Mariette in Antwerp. Thomas Gorst was not as forthcoming as Baltus had been. He admitted participating in the exchange of only £100,000 (€200,000) for Gilligan, for which he had been sentenced to six months' imprisonment.

Mariette Gorst was more informative and said that she knew Gilligan. She commented that she had rented a house for him and Carol Rooney shortly before the murder of Veronica Guerin. She told detectives:

> As far as John Gilligan is concerned, it now appears that I grossly misjudged his character. I only realized that I was dealing with a criminal when I saw an American newspaper and read an article about the arrest of John and four others. He was described as an important drugs trafficker, arms dealer and ex-member of the IRA. You may rest assured that I am quite prepared to assist in

the investigations and to provide all useful information which may provide evidence against Gilligan in Ireland. I am prepared to testify in court in Ireland if necessary.

Thomas Gorst also agreed to testify in Ireland but that particular breakthrough was short-lived. A few weeks later the couple left Belgium and went into hiding in Mexico. Before he disappeared, Gorst was holding over £800,000 (€1.5 million) of Gilligan's drug money. When they vanished, so did the money.

The following October Baltus was secretly brought to Dublin by his Dutch handlers amidst tight security. In Lucan he added another vital piece of the jigsaw when he identified the boxes and guns which he had organized and packed for Gilligan.

He also made a number of further detailed statements. Baltus told the Lucan detectives:

I have had many thoughts on this and I have given a number of interviews to the police of The Hague concerning these and other matters. I am here in Ireland freely and I acknowledge that I have been involved in bad things and I wish to put all this behind me in my life. I am prepared to travel to court here in Ireland and give the truth.

CHAPTER TWENTY-FOUR

SUPERGRASSES

When Gilligan heard that Charlie Bowden had returned voluntarily to Dublin after his arrest it confirmed the mobster's worst fears – that his quartermaster had turned traitor. From that moment Bowden was a marked man.

Around the same time the Lucan team submitted files to the DPP recommending that Gilligan and Meehan be charged with murder, possession of firearms and drug trafficking. The team's urgent priority was securing agreement from the DPP and the Department of Justice on granting Bowden and Warren immunity from prosecution in return for their testimony, and the establishment of a witness protection programme.

Time was running out. If they did not take action soon and implement the measures suggested by the gardaí, the State's case would fall apart. If any of the witnesses or their loved ones was attacked or murdered, it would be a disaster. Gilligan would walk and organized crime in Ireland would become stronger than ever.

Former Garda Commissioner Pat Byrne recalled:

I told the government that we could not allow Gilligan to get away with this [murder of Veronica] – we were not going to let that happen and if it required an unprecedented approach then so be it. Fighting crime is a very dirty business.

From his base in Europe Meehan made several urgent efforts to contact Julie Bacon. As Bacon was now co-operating and was prepared to testify a call was set up. Detectives attached a recording device to the public phone in the Hole in the Wall pub on Blackhorse Avenue in the hope that Meehan might say something incriminating that could be used in a criminal prosecution.

On the same day that Holland was charged, Meehan called the number at 4 p.m. Bacon answered nervously and tried to give the impression that Bowden was worried about an informant in the camp.

> Bacon: Charlie is going fucking mad. He wants to know what the fucking story is with Paddy Holland and how come Holland came home.

> Meehan: Paddy Holland came home to clear his name. He's innocent. It has nothing to do with Charlie.

> Bacon: He [Charlie] said they nicked him...He got told that someone ratted that he was coming on the boat, or else they said they had surveillance on the boats.

> Meehan: Holland has nothing to do with what Charlie got done for.

Bacon told Meehan that Bowden was being kept in a twenty-hour lockup in Arbour Hill, where he was 'going fucking mad...He went on hunger strike and everything, he did.' She said he had been put in Arbour Hill because he had hit one of the prison officers.

Meehan wasn't buying it.

Meehan: But the whole thing, Julie, like, tell me about what [*sic*] whole thing. Like, Holland has got nothing to do with what Charlie got done for.

Bacon: I know, he's just wondering, just worried what the story is, that's all.

Meehan: But it's nothing got to do with the murder and it's nothing. He's clear on the murder, Holland is, because they didn't do him with it, 'cause they've no evidence, right?

Meehan's tone then became more sinister and menacing.

Meehan: Now, listen to me and I'll tell you, 'cause I want to get things straight, 'cause things are looking very fucking fishy to me, right, and I'll tell you what, I'm after being good to everybody but I'm taking off my gloves now. If Charlie's going belly-up, if Charlie is going gammy, he better fuckin' think very strongly about what will happen.

Bacon: Are you threatening me, Brian?

Meehan: Threatening, Julie? You'll have no idea what I'm going to fucking do if he goes Turk. Now, I'm telling you. I'm his friend still, I'm helping youse every way I can, but I'm fucking starting to worry and worry and worry, 'cause I'll tell you who goes to Arbour Hill – rapists and fucking rats. I've done everything I fucking can to help him, everything, he has no worries against why Holland is home unless he made a statement against Holland, do you understand?

Bacon: He's going ballistic...he wants to know what the story is.

Meehan: I'll send someone to fucking kill you this fucking day, do you understand what I'm saying?

Bacon: What did you say?

Meehan: You are fucking hearing me. I'll send someone to kill you and everybody around you if he goes Turk. Now tell him I said that, right, and tell him I said I'm fucking considering doing him anyway, so he better not fucking think of going rat, right, that's the message now, right?

Bacon: You're a fucking knacker, that's all, you're a knacker.

Meehan: You're the fucking...and Charlie is a rat and if he rats on me, I'll fucking kill you.

Bacon: I don't fucking blame him if he does, you prick, you.

Meehan: Yeah, you fucking scumbag.

Bacon: You're a scumbag. Fuck off.

The conversation ended abruptly. Meehan's threat was taken seriously and Bacon was moved from her home to a safe house immediately. That night the house was fire-bombed. Chillingly, Gilligan sent word from Belmarsh that everything possible was to be done to silence the snout – at all costs.

———

In an urgent confidential memo to Garda Headquarters, sent just before Bacon's call with Meehan, Assistant Commissioner Hickey summed up the challenge he was now facing:

Intelligence indicates that the main players think that the absence of a witness protection programme in this country is to their advantage. There is no doubt that they will resort to murder to prevent witnesses giving damaging evidence in court...I think we should review the situation and if necessary set up a witness

protection programme, as all the vital witnesses will be under
severe threat if statements are served, and under prolonged threat
if and when they give evidence.

While a decision was awaited the police improvised. A special
squad of detectives from the anti-terrorist Special Detective Unit
was selected to protect the witnesses in the Guerin case. The ad hoc
formation later became known as the Witness Protection Unit.

Hickey and his team were aware that the gang was now focusing
all its efforts on silencing Bowden. Gilligan was not yet aware that
Warren had also made incriminating statements.

In an internal report Todd O'Loughlin noted:

> Confidential sources indicate that the principals in this murder
> who are still at large have concluded that the only way to stop
> the witnesses testifying against them, and to re-establish their
> control over these people, is to kill one or more of the witnesses...
> Attempts are now being made to find somebody who can kill him
> [Bowden] in prison.

Gilligan had pondered numerous options. At one stage he and
Meehan considered hiring a sniper to shoot Bowden, or launch
a rocket attack, when he was being driven from prison for court
appearances. A disused tower was consequently blocked up near the
prison. But the plan was dropped because no one would take the
contract.

Underworld informants also revealed how John Traynor had
offered someone £60,000 (€115,000) to put poison in Bowden's
food. As a precaution, all his food was specially prepared to prevent
such an attempt.

'Speedy' Fegan was instructed to take photographs of Bowden's
three children with a view to scaring him off. This plan, too, had to
be abandoned because the ex-soldier's family had been placed under

armed police protection at their home in Finglas by the time he turned up. Fegan was subsequently arrested about the incident. He said that the plan had been to send the pictures to Bowden to force him to withdraw his statements. As a result Bowden's children and his first wife were provided with bodyguards.

Fears for the safety of the State's witnesses were first publicly expressed by the police when they objected to Holland's application for bail on 22 July in the Special Criminal Court. Detective Inspector Todd O'Loughlin gave evidence that Holland was likely to interfere with and harm witnesses.

In support of this claim, O'Loughlin cited the meeting between Bowden and Holland in London, the phone call between Meehan and Bacon, and the arson attack on Bowden's house. Detective Garda Sean O'Brien said he had received confidential information that strongly suggested that Holland would try to kill witnesses if granted bail. Dutchy's application was refused.

The gang's lack of success in silencing the State's witnesses was reflected in their efforts to resume their drug business. By the early summer of 1997, the money was drying up. Meehan, Mitchell and Traynor desperately needed a major injection of funds.

On 7 May Meehan strolled into the Creditanstalt Bank in Vienna to withdraw his dirty money. But CAB had beaten him to it. After a delay, the manager explained to Meehan that his six accounts had been frozen by order of the Superior Court for Criminal Cases in Vienna, at the behest of the Irish authorities, on the grounds that the money was the proceeds of organized crime.

Meehan broke out in a sweat and began to scan the other customers in the large bank building. The bank's CCTV then showed him running from the bank to where Traynor and Mitchell were waiting nearby.

They were stunned by the development and fled the city as quickly as they had arrived. The gang never dreamt that the Irish cops could reach them across international borders. The world was closing in on the remnants of Gilligan's mob.

The same month the trio organized a 400-kilo shipment of hash which was smuggled through Northern Ireland to Dublin by Speedy Fegan. He had already moved smaller amounts for the gang. In early June the Northern Ireland newspapers reported that the RUC had seized a haul of 200 kilos of hash.

When the gangsters on the Continent read the article, they thought Fegan had stolen the other 200 kilos and tipped off the police about the remainder. Their assumption was correct.

Meehan phoned Fegan demanding an explanation. Speedy claimed that the other half of the shipment had been 'stolen'. Meehan threatened to kill him. 'Even if I have to go over there meself, I'll fuckin' kill you.' The falling-out meant the loss of the only supply route the gang had into the country. Fegan was subsequently shot dead for failing to pay the IRA protection money in May 1999.

The lack of money was creating tensions in the gang. Meehan turned on Traynor, telling him he was sick of giving him money. In Dublin, Meehan's father Kevin had to resort to collecting his son's debts.

Things were going from bad to worse for Gilligan and his protégé.

In June 1997 the DPP issued a secret directive to prefer charges against John Gilligan and Brian Meehan for the murder of Veronica Guerin. They were also to be charged with sixteen counts of having drugs for sale and supply and with possession of the firearms found in the Jewish cemetery.

Based on the level of threat the gangsters posed to a potential jury the DPP directed that the trials take place in the non-jury Special Criminal Court. Dutchy and Ward had also been returned to the court for the same reason.

In July and August the DPP also finally granted Charlie Bowden and Russell Warren immunity from prosecution for the murder of Veronica Guerin, clearing the way for them to agree to be State witnesses.

The Department of Justice also gave the go-ahead for the State's first witness protection programme (WPP) – another Gilligan legacy to law enforcement in Ireland. Eventually the WPP was drafted in law and a specific budget allocated. It was a huge undertaking that has continued to pay dividends. Over the past twenty-five years the WPP has been used to secure the convictions of several major gangland figures through the testimony of former associates.

The families and homes of the three main witnesses were also placed under full-time protection as part of the WPP. In their deal with the State Bowden, Warren and Dunne all agreed to plead guilty to the various charges for supplying drugs and money laundering. As the State's first supergrasses were each facing jail time the basement of Arbour Hill Prison was converted to house them together in one location.

Over the following months Hickey and Todd O'Loughlin attended two secret sittings of the Special Criminal Court to obtain extradition warrants for Gilligan and Meehan. The developments were kept a closely guarded secret known only to a handful of officers. Gilligan was in for a very unpleasant surprise.

On Monday 8 September, the mob boss expected his trial on the drug trafficking charges to begin in the courthouse adjoining Belmarsh Prison. That morning Hickey, Todd O'Loughlin and Jerry O'Connell travelled to London with eighteen extradition warrants for Gilligan.

In the days and weeks leading up to the event there had been high-level contacts between the DPP and the UK's Crown Prosecution Service (CPS). The two State law offices had agreed that the charges Gilligan faced in Ireland were much more serious than those in

England. The CPS consented to stand aside and let the extradition go ahead.

When he was informed of the extradition warrants and the individual charges were read to him, Gilligan had to be restrained.

The legal formalities involved him being first released from custody for the UK money laundering charges and then immediately re-arrested by the Metropolitan Police on the Irish warrants.

Gilligan was returned to Belmarsh Magistrates' Court for the first step in the extradition process. He refused to recognize the court. He sat looking at the ceiling and didn't answer any questions from the bench. Gilligan was shocked that three of his underlings had dared to betray him and were conspiring with the Irish authorities. This was the moment the narcissist finally realized that he had been cornered.

His counsel accused the UK and Irish authorities of an abuse of process. Gilligan was going to fight the extradition and use every line of appeal that was open to him. He was prepared to fight all the way through to the High Court of England and the House of Lords.

The longer he could drag out the proceedings in the UK the better in the hope that the delay would dampen the enthusiasm of his former minions. His priority now was to step up the intimidation of potential witnesses. That would be the responsibility of his trusted favourite, Meehan, to organize.

News of the extradition and confirmation that three former associates had turned State witnesses, however, sent Meehan into a panic. He went to ground with Mitchell and Traynor. He knew that it was highly likely that he too could face the same charges.

Meehan suspected that others like Cradden and Clohessy were also likely to testify in court. He found himself in a race against time to silence the informers before he was also lifted. By then he was already one of the most wanted criminals in Europe. As soon as the extradition warrants were issued in Dublin, Europol and Interpol circulated urgent alerts to police forces across the Continent to arrest Meehan on sight.

On 24 September Bowden affirmed his guilty pleas to the drugs and firearms charges. The security spectacle surrounding the court appearances of Bowden and the other defendants and suspects was unprecedented. It emphasized the level of threat organized crime posed to society. Sniffer dogs swept the building for suspect devices before Gilligan's quartermaster was ushered into court. He wore a bullet-proof vest and was surrounded by armed officers.

Detective Inspector John O'Mahony told the Dublin Circuit Criminal Court that Bowden was being kept in isolation in his cell in Arbour Hill Prison twenty-three hours a day and was permanently guarded by officers from the new WPP unit:

> His co-operation was given in the full knowledge of the risk to his own life and without any deal being offered to him. The more threats that are made against him, the more he is determined to give evidence against the rest of the gang.

On 8 October the Circuit Criminal Court sentenced Bowden to six years in prison. As he was taken from the court to begin his sentence snipers from the ERU kept watch from rooftops while a garda helicopter hovered overhead. Bowden, surrounded by armed officers and a protective, bullet-proof shield, was shepherded towards a line of high-powered jeeps and whisked back to prison.

The following month the scene was replicated when Russell Warren was sentenced to five years for money laundering. In January John Dunne also took up residence in Arbour Hill after he got three years for his role in Gilligan's operation. In each case the court was told that the defendant had agreed to testify.

On the same day that Bowden was sentenced the Lucan Investigation Team got another breakthrough. They had been tipped off that a nineteen-year-old hairdresser from Dublin's north inner city was planning to spend the following weekend with Meehan in Amsterdam.

The pair had been having a relationship behind his girlfriend's back, enjoying secret trysts in the Netherlands and Spain. The Tosser was besotted by the beautiful young woman. He also used her to convey messages to his criminal associates in Dublin.

The extradition warrants were sent to the Dutch authorities, with a request to intercept Meehan as soon as he showed up. On the following Friday afternoon, 10 October, the teenager boarded the Amsterdam flight under the watch of two officers from the NSU.

When Meehan's girlfriend arrived in Schiphol the detectives pointed her out and she was monitored by a large surveillance squad. She took the commuter train to Centraal Station, but there was still no sign of Meehan. However, a few anxious minutes after she stepped off the train Meehan and Traynor emerged from the throng of passengers around the station entrance.

It was a miserable, wet afternoon as the small Irish group walked through the leaf-strewn streets, chatting and avoiding trams. As they crossed Dam Square a police SWAT team suddenly descended on them with terrifying speed and force. In a flash the trio were pinned to the ground, hooded and their hands clasped behind their backs.

Traynor began to roar with fright and Meehan soiled his designer trousers. The cowardly Coach was still roaring as the squad manhandled each of them into the back of vans which appeared out of nowhere.

They were taken to police HQ, where the liaison officers from the Lucan team officially identified the man they wanted – Brian Meehan. Traynor, who was still in shock, was told he was free to go as there were no charges against him. The Coach had made sure there was no evidence directly linking him to any of the crimes, including the murder. The hairdresser was also released.

Meehan was given clean clothes before being informed that he had been arrested on foot of an Irish extradition warrant to face murder, drugs and firearms charges. He was too stunned to reply. Eight hours later he was still trembling, ashen-faced and staring at the wall of his cell. Reportedly he looked like a zombie.

The following day, Traynor's instinct for self-preservation kicked in. He phoned the Irish liaison officers and met them in a downtown bar. He wanted to know what the prospects were of doing a 'deal' with the State in return for his assistance. His offer was turned down.

Traynor suddenly found himself in the gangland equivalent of limbo. His main sources of cash, Gilligan and Meehan, were locked up in maximum-security prisons. His partners in crime, such as Mitchell, were keeping a safe distance from him, and the cops weren't interested.

Ironically, the sudden and violent arrest of Meehan was a blessing in disguise for the Coach. The gardaí later received information that Meehan and Mitchell had been plotting to have Traynor murdered.

The arrest of Meehan, his most trusted associate, was another devastating blow to John Gilligan. It was the final nail in the coffin of his drugs empire. With Meehan in prison the efforts by the remaining free members of the gang to use intimidation to silence the witnesses had been greatly diminished. It meant that Gilligan's only avenue to freedom was by continuing to use and abuse the law.

A month later there was more bad news for the godfather. On 18 November Holland was the first member of the Gilligan crime gang to stand trial. Senior Counsel Peter Charleton, who would lead the prosecution in all the Gilligan gang trials, opened the State's case by establishing a link between Holland's prosecution and the Guerin murder. It was, he said, the journalist's death which prompted a major garda investigation which led to the discovery of the massive drugs distribution operation in which Holland had been a central figure. He stated: 'The entire operation was motivated by greed and motivated by profit at the expense of the people of Ireland and Patrick Holland was part of it.'

The prosecutor said that 47 kilos of cannabis had been recovered at the gang's lockup in Greenmount. A search of Holland's house had produced two blank driver's licences which were linked to similar licences found in the warehouse. He maintained that the State would show that Holland had made up to £3,000 (€6,000) a week from this enterprise and that his name had been found on a list of the gang's customers.

Detective Garda Marion Cusack, who arrested Dutchy, was asked to point out the man she knew to be Patrick Holland. She pointed up at the hit man in the dock, who smiled and gave the detective a little wave.

A minute later Cusack wiped the smile off Holland's face when she told the court why she had arrested him for questioning:

> I had formed the opinion that Patrick Holland was the man who shot dead Veronica Guerin on 26 June 1996. When I saw him coming through the port, I was of the view that he had murdered Veronica Guerin and, as a result, I arrested him.

There was insufficient evidence to charge him for Veronica Guerin's murder but the case on the drugs offences was strong. There had been much anticipation of the appearance of the State's first supergrass, Bowden, who seemed relaxed and confident as he testified about Holland's involvement in the drug enterprise.

After two weeks of evidence, on 27 November, the court convicted Holland of the drug charges. The court accepted Bowden's evidence as it had been corroborated by the Wig's own admissions.

The assassin, who had got away with murder, was then sentenced to twenty years' imprisonment for the drugs charges. It was subsequently reduced on appeal to twelve years.

The verdict sent a chill through the rest of the Gilligan gang.

CHAPTER TWENTY-FIVE

—

FACING JUSTICE

The conviction of Dutchy Holland impelled Gilligan to step up his legal strategy of delaying his extradition with a string of challenges and appeals in London. His objective was to stretch the process out until the supergrasses were released from their prison sentences in Ireland. Gilligan hoped that once they were free Warren and Bowden would leave the country and refuse to return to testify against him. But as each legal challenge was rejected in turn by the English courts, and his appeals on these decisions were also rejected, Gilligan knew that time was running out.

Russell Warren, who could link him to the murder, had become his main focus. Out of desperation Gilligan decided to put pen to paper to convince his former bagman to shut his mouth. He wanted to reassure Warren that he was not in danger and could safely withdraw his evidence. But he had to be extremely careful in how he worded the documents which he knew would be seen by the authorities.

In the first of a series of letters sent from his prison cell, Gilligan wrote:

> I hope you are doing OK and I'm sorry for the shit you and your wife
> and family went through but I could do nothing as I did nothing

wrong but I have a big, big fight on my hands. I will say good night and God bless. Please take care and I wish you all the best.

Gilligan continued the crude attempt at psychological manipulation with more letters which were sent over a period of several weeks. In one he sought to reassure Warren that there was no need for his family to be worried about 'people trying to get at them'. Gilligan told him that 'me, Brian and Paul [Ward] aren't even thinking like that'.

He wrote that there was no need for Warren and his family to leave Dublin and all he wanted was for the bagman to 'tell the truth' in court, 'It should not be lies.' He ended the note:

> Letting you know I only need the truth to come out in court. If that be the case, the witnesses I have in court, I will not need to call them. It's not too much to ask. My life is in your hands when you tell lies.

In another letter, he wrote: 'Please tell your friends to stop taking notice of all the shit in the newspapers. Believe me, I wish I could help your families.' It was signed: 'Your friend, John Gilligan.'

Gilligan's last communication ended with a thinly disguised threat which betrayed his growing sense of desperation:

> You don't need to leave your country over me, say what you like in court. Run away. You have a home and family now and your new child may well want to come back to where he was born. You have my word on it. No one is after you. The papers are mad. Anything to sell them. God bless and take care and I wish you all the luck in the world. Your friend, John G.

Gilligan eventually got a response to his correspondence when his former bagman pleaded guilty to charges of money laundering. In court it was also revealed that Russell Warren had agreed to testify against the gang.

In the meantime Brian Meehan had already exhausted every legal avenue open to him in the Dutch courts to fight his extradition. On 3 September 1998 the Tosser was returned to Ireland to face justice. The dangerous criminal, hooded and handcuffed, was handed over to Detective Inspector O'Loughlin and other members of the Lucan team at Eindhoven military air base. He was flown home on board an Irish military aircraft.

When it touched down at the Air Corps base in Baldonnel Meehan was formally arrested and it took O'Loughlin almost an hour to read him the eighteen charges. He was then whisked away to the Special Criminal Court in a convoy of garda vans, jeeps and motorbikes, watched over by a police helicopter. Meehan was arraigned and remanded in custody.

A half-hour later the once swaggering gangster was brought to Portlaoise Prison under military escort. He was reunited with Dutchy Holland and Paul Ward on E1 wing, where they had first formed their unholy alliance with John Gilligan.

A month later, on 6 October 1998, Paul Ward stood trial for murder in the Special Criminal Court. In his opening remarks State prosecutor Peter Charleton SC said Ward had been 'complicit' in the crime.

While it was accepted he was not one of the two men on board the motorbike on 26 June 1996, it was the State's contention that he had taken part in discussions and had given comfort to the killers by aiding their escape and disposing of the vehicle and the gun. The evidence was grounded in the testimony of Bowden and Ward's admissions while in custody in Lucan.

Ward's trial was the first time that the Irish public heard the full harrowing details of the journalist's murder, as seen through the eyes of the witnesses who were sitting in traffic on the Naas Road that day.

Nurses Michelle Wall and Brenda Grogan described finding the journalist slumped over the passenger seat of her car, bleeding heavily.

Grogan explained she had checked for a pulse but found none.

Truck driver Michael Dunne saw the motorbike pillion passenger pull alongside the car and smash the driver's window. 'I saw Veronica just slumped across the seats, her whole chest was blood and gunshot wounds,' he recalled.

During the marathon thirty-one-day trial Bowden was subjected to some of the most robust cross-examination ever seen in an Irish court at the hands of the legendary defence barrister Senior Counsel Paddy McEntee.

McEntee, who labelled Bowden a liar at every opportunity, asked why the former soldier had converted from conspirator to confessor. Bowden admitted that his original intention was to lie to the gardaí but when he saw the photographs of the journalist lying dead in her car, he changed his mind. He recalled:

> It was unreal. I could detach myself from it and my role in it. When I saw those photos of the girl lying in the car shot, I went to pieces. I just couldn't handle it. My wife and my children were going to suffer from my giving this evidence, for me talking to the police. By the same token I wanted to tell the police exactly what my role was.

In his own evidence to the court Paul Ward described Bowden as 'more of an associate than a friend'. Ward admitted that he had been involved in crime but denied that he had any part in Guerin's murder. He stormed:

> I am accusing Charlie Bowden of telling lies and implicating me in something that I had nothing to do with whatsoever. Mr Bowden is the one I blame. He is the man who told those guards this and he convinced them.
>
> That man should be in the dock. I was asked to do the same thing that that man did and I refused because I knew nothing about

Ms Guerin's murder. I am a victim of being accused of this. Mr Bowden is the main man, the main person who has me here. I know the guards have to do their job. I am not making myself out to be a saint – far from it. I don't blame the guards. I blame Mr Bowden for the lies he said about me and he is after convincing the guards. He is putting poison in the guards' minds, saying that I was involved in that woman's murder. I wasn't.

Amazingly, however, in his testimony Ward corroborated much of Bowden's evidence regarding the drugs business. He admitted that he had personally made £300,000 (€590,000) from selling drugs. Ward said that the members of the gang would pay Gilligan £2,000 per kilo of hash. Any margin above this was kept for themselves. Ward admitted that he had collected around £3 million (€5.9 million) from the sale of the hash on Gilligan's behalf.

Hippo even talked candidly about the trip to St Lucia in March 1996, a video of which the Lucan team had seized. He recalled lounging about the hotel pool talking about the journalist and the assault.

The woman's [Guerin's] name was brought up and they [Mitchell and Meehan] were laughing at Gilligan. He was convinced he would get off the charge. It was funny that they were slagging Gilligan and winding him up. They were slagging him about what happened. He was laughing back and saying he didn't think he would go to jail.

Ward commented on the murder:

I felt it was terrible. It never entered my head why that lady was killed. I think it would be crazy for anyone to kill a woman to save themselves from going down for six months.

He believed she had been shot because she had threatened the continuation of a 'multi-million drugs empire'.

On Friday 27 November, the three judges of the Special Criminal Court found Ward guilty of the murder of Veronica Guerin. It was to prove a landmark judgment. Paul Ward, drug dealer and killer, was on his way to prison with a life sentence. Mr Justice Barr said Bowden was by his own admission an accomplice and the court felt he was 'a self-serving liar'. The court, however, found that his account of Ward's involvement was accurate and credible. Bowden had no vested interest in trying to shift responsibility for his own actions on to Ward. Mr Justice Barr stated:

> Having reviewed the relevant evidence in this trial with meticulous care – and in particular that of Charles Bowden and the accused – the court is satisfied beyond reasonable doubt that the accused, Paul Ward, was an accessory before the fact to the murder of Veronica Guerin on 26 June 1996, and therefore is guilty of the offence charged in the indictment.

Mr Justice Barr was withering in his criticism of the way the Lucan team had handled aspects of Ward's arrest and questioning. The court viewed the involvement of Ward's girlfriend and his elderly mother as being designed to put undue pressure on Ward. His lawyers informed the court that they intended lodging an appeal against the conviction.

As a result of his open admissions during the trial about the gang's drug business and the St Lucia trip, relations between Ward and Meehan deteriorated. For a time after that Hippo was isolated from Meehan and the other criminals on E1 in Portlaoise for his own protection.

—————

Carol Rooney had watched developments closely from her base in Australia. It had been over two and a half years since she'd fled more than 15,000 km to get away from her ex-lover and his cohorts. In

March 1999, happy in the knowledge that Gilligan, Holland and the other key gang members were locked up, she felt that it would be safe for her to return home for a short visit to see her elderly grandmother.

But if Gilligan's mistress thought that she had been forgotten she was very much mistaken. Rooney had planned to stay in Dublin for a few days with her parents and her grandmother who lived in Ballyfermot. However, the Lucan team soon discovered she was back. Rooney was arrested on 29 March and taken to Lucan station by Detective Sergeant John O'Driscoll.

As soon as she was taken in Rooney began talking and didn't stop until she had related everything she had seen and heard with Gilligan. Her evidence was the lynchpin which pulled the whole case together and corroborated vital parts of the information being offered by the other supergrasses. The only problem was that she was too terrified to testify. She refused an offer for herself and her family to join the witness protection programme. Hickey's officers could only take her statements and then let her go, in the hope that she might change her mind. After her release Rooney immediately left the country and returned to Australia.

Word of her arrest had leaked out into the media. Gilligan was concerned that his former girlfriend had forgotten his earlier warnings and sent word to an associate in Dublin to have it sorted. Rooney's family was approached and warned that their lives were in danger. In one incident a condolence card was sent to her parents' home with a sock in it – to remind them all to put a sock in it and remain silent. It had the desired effect. Rooney was determined to stay away from the witness box.

Brian Meehan's trial for murder, drugs and firearms offences opened before the Special Criminal Court on 3 June 1999 and lasted for over six weeks. This was the first case where all the State witnesses – Bowden, Bacon, Warren, John Dunne and Julian Clohessy – gave evidence. Meehan's defence team dismissed them as 'a gallery of rogues and convicts whose evidence is laced with implausibility and pockmarked by contradiction and inconsistency'.

Much of the evidence was a rerun of that given in the Ward trial. Julian Clohessy, a former sales assistant in a menswear shop, recalled the conversation in which Meehan bragged about the murder. Clohessy claimed:

> Meehan looked at me in a way that I could not forget. He said he was there, he said he was involved. He led me to believe that he was there at Veronica Guerin's murder and he was involved in Veronica Guerin's murder. I remember what he said to me.

He also recalled how Meehan had attempted to intimidate him after Clohessy's arrest in 1996.

John Dunne, the shipping manager, told how he had started working for John Gilligan in 1994 and gave details of how the gang's import/export system worked. He pointed to Brian Meehan in the dock as the man who had been identified to him by Gilligan as 'Joe'.

On 5 July, as Meehan's trial was ongoing, Russell Warren's parents, sister and brother-in-law were jailed for money laundering offences having all pleaded guilty. Patrick and Yvette Warren, both aged sixty-nine, were given eighteen months each, while his sister Nicola was sentenced to a year and her husband, Brian Cummins, got eight months.

It was a severe blow to Russell that his previously law-abiding family had not received suspended sentences. Meehan hoped it would unsettle the bagman and he would retract his evidence. The Tosser was disappointed.

In his testimony Warren described his work collecting and counting the drug money, and delivering it to Belgium, the Netherlands and the UK. He agreed with Peter Charleton's description of his job as 'a bagman, money counter and sometimes chauffeur' for John Gilligan.

Warren detailed his involvement in preparing the motorbike and being sent to stalk Veronica. He described what he saw on the Naas Road:

> He [hit man]) shot once, then he shot twice. He moved to look into the car and he fired three consecutive shots. I froze. I went to get out of the van as if I could help. I just stopped. It was like slow motion. I realized then what I was after doing.

Warren said that he continued collecting, counting and delivering cash for Gilligan after the murder out of fear:

> The activity became more intense after the murder. I was afraid not to continue working for the gang. If I had left or had tried to leave, I don't think I'd be sitting here today. You can't say no.

Charlie Bowden was put through the most intensive cross-examination he had yet encountered in his new career as a supergrass. Meehan's defence barristers were determined to punch holes in Bowden's testimony to discredit him.

Julie Bacon, who by now had married Bowden in a prison ceremony, gave her evidence of the threatening phone call she had received from Meehan. The court also heard extensive evidence on the series of calls between Meehan's mobile phone and those of his co-conspirators on 26 June.

The prosecution's closing speech began on 20 July. That night Meehan's father, Kevin, was shot at the door of his home in Crumlin. He was rushed to hospital but was found not to have been seriously injured. He was released a day later and returned to court in a show of solidarity with his son. It was claimed at the time that the attack had been carried out by the IRA.

On Thursday 29 July 1999, Brian Meehan was convicted of murder. He was also convicted on the drug charges and possession of firearms for an illegal purpose. This time the court refused to accept the evidence of either Bowden or that of Bacon in relation to the murder charge, describing it as unreliable. It found that Bacon had lied on a number of occasions during her testimony and accused Bowden of being prepared to lie under oath. In particular the court noted how Bowden had denied that he had bolstered his evidence so that he could eventually write a book. The court said that despite denying this in 'explicit terms' the defence had produced a letter Bowden wrote to this writer exploring the possibility of telling his story. When this was exposed Bowden admitted to the court that he had lied.

Mr Justice Freddie Morris said, however, the court was prepared to accept his evidence, which was corroborated, regarding Meehan's involvement in drug trafficking and the importation of firearms.

The court fully accepted Russell Warren's testimony that he had supplied the motorbike used in the murder to Meehan and that he was sent to stalk Veronica Guerin on the day of the assassination. The judge said:

> The court is satisfied that this evidence leads to only one conclusion, namely that the accused was a fundamental part of the conspiracy or plot to murder Veronica Guerin, that he participated fully in the event.

Meehan showed no emotion as the verdict was read. In addition to being sentenced to life for the murder charge, Meehan was given concurrent sentences of twenty and twelve years for the drug offences. He also received concurrent sentences of five and ten years for possessing firearms for an illegal purpose.

Meehan and his mentor Gilligan had reckoned that they would literally get away with murder. Three years and one month later

Meehan was the third member of the gang to take the one-way journey to Portlaoise Prison.

John Gilligan was shattered when he heard the news. He had been monitoring the case on a daily basis through his associates, lawyers and from daily press cuttings which were delivered to him in Belmarsh. The mob boss knew his own day of reckoning was looming.

———————

After holding up the system for four years Gilligan could no longer stave off the day he dreaded most – his extradition to Ireland to finally face justice. In October the final block on his extradition was removed when the law lords threw out Gilligan's appeal seeking to have the extradition ruled as unlawful. But just as arrangements were being made to bring him back for Christmas, the mob boss pulled another legal stroke at the eleventh hour. This time he submitted a writ of *habeas corpus* to the High Court in London, on the grounds that his detention in the UK had been illegal. It delayed any moves to extradite him at least until the New Year.

Gilligan was becoming more agitated and desperate as each day passed. True to form he had to take it out on someone. He was transferred from Belmarsh to High Down Prison in Surrey after violently attacking prison officers.

From his new prison cell he wrote letters to Bowden and Warren, enquiring how they were and insinuating that they should retract their evidence against him on the grounds that the police had forced them to lie. The letters were ignored.

Gilligan's legal circus finally came to an end on Thursday 3 February 2000, when the UK High Court threw out his *habeas corpus* application. The court ruled that it was nothing more than an abuse of process by the gangster. It had been one of the longest and hardest-fought extradition battles ever staged in the UK legal system.

Detective Inspector Todd O'Loughlin and Detective Garda Mick Murray from the Lucan team had been in London for three days awaiting the decision of the High Court. Back at base, Tony Hickey had decided that as soon as the London court issued its ruling they would bring Gilligan home immediately.

That morning the same Air Corps aircraft that had picked up Brian Meehan was dispatched to retrieve another fugitive. On board were key members of the team who had worked to make this moment possible.

The aircraft touched down at RAF Northolt in Hillingdon, which was close to High Down Prison, where O'Loughlin and Murray were waiting.

At 2.30 p.m. O'Loughlin and the other officers watched as a convoy of police cars and vans sped up to the plane. Gilligan was taken from a van and escorted onto the plane by one of the British officers and officially handed over to Detective Inspector O'Loughlin.

The diminutive thug looked comical in bright green and yellow prison overalls. He resembled 'Laa-Laa', from the *Teletubbies* children's TV show – earning him the nickname 'Laa-Laa Gilligan' for a while. It was a humiliating denouement to his reign of terror.

The aircraft was barely in the air when Gilligan started making demands to be allowed to change into his normal clothes. O'Loughlin insisted that Gilligan stay put in his seat with his handcuffs on. When the plane touched down at 4.30 p.m. Gilligan was furious to see photographers and cameramen waiting for him at the Baldonnel Air Corps base for the long-anticipated perp walk.

Gilligan was filmed as he stepped off the plane, covering his face with his hand and keeping his head down. Footage was shown that night of the comical-looking John Gilligan – Public Enemy Number One. It made people wonder how such an insignificant-looking individual could have caused so much grief to so many lives.

When Todd O'Loughlin finished reading the charges to Gilligan he was taken in a convoy of garda vans, escorted by heavily armed troops, to the Special Criminal Court for his arraignment. The State was taking no chances of the mob boss escaping. On the way the convoy passed the location where Veronica Guerin was murdered.

After arriving in the court building Gilligan refused to go into the dock for his arraignment until he had changed his clothes. He was allowed to put on a blue blazer over his jumpsuit, making him look even more comical.

He stepped up into the elevated dock, flanked by prison officers. As he did so he smirked and winked at the large pack of reporters in the body of the court.

The last time he had stood there, Gilligan was a little-known gangster who had been sentenced to four years for the theft of hardware goods. Now he was back as the most notorious crime boss in Irish criminal history and the head of a multi-million-euro drug empire.

Detective Inspector Todd O'Loughlin gave evidence of Gilligan's arrest. The presiding judge, Mr Justice Richard Johnson, asked Gilligan if he was legally represented. 'No, Your Honour,' he replied, 'I'm representing meself.'

Gilligan then stood tapping his fingers on legal papers and staring up at the ceiling as the list of murder, drugs and gun charges was read out at the arraignment.

The mob boss was then told that he could apply for bail. But he smirked down at the three judges from the dock. 'I think bail would be out of the question, wouldn't it?'

After that Gilligan was transported to Portlaoise Prison in a convoy of military and police vehicles. In 1993 he had vowed never to return. It was brutally ironic that his determination to avoid prison had resulted in him possibly spending most of his life there.

On 3 April Gilligan returned to the Special Criminal Court where he made submissions about the book of evidence. Mr Justice Kevin O'Higgins, the presiding judge, asked Gilligan to move out of the dock and stand in the benches normally reserved for defence counsel. Gilligan looked chuffed.

During fifty minutes of often rambling and disjointed submissions the barrack-room lawyer requested that the murder charge and the drugs charges be dealt with separately. 'I don't think I can handle it all together,' Gilligan told the court.

He demanded full disclosure of all evidence that the gardaí had against him. He even objected to use of the non-jury court declaring that it was neither independent, nor impartial, and in breach of his human rights.

Gilligan used the opportunity to publicly plead his innocence. He cited the prosecution's claim that his motivation for the murder had to do with his fear of being jailed if convicted on the assault charge and denied ever assaulting Veronica Guerin. The forensic evidence in the possession of the gardaí, he incorrectly claimed, showed there was no damage to the journalist's blouse or jacket. He maintained, on that basis, that he would not have been convicted in Kilcock District Court:

> From fear of going to prison for six months, I had that lady murdered, which is not true. The evidence was that I was supposed to have struck Veronica Guerin all around her body, which I didn't. She got more boxes than Tyson [Mike Tyson, boxing champion] could give a man, in her statement. I had no fear of Kilcock. I wasn't going to get convicted.

Then Gilligan appeared to use his monologue, which he knew would get widespread publicity, to send a message to the State witnesses. He denied making threats against them and said he had not ordered a 'price' on their heads. He disingenuously commented:

> I have no problem with any person giving evidence against me. Them people up in Arbour Hill, they have gone through enough.

> They have nothing to fear from me. I ordered nothing. The only thing I ordered is a cappuccino. It's all rubbish.

After his long-winded attempt at advocacy, the godfather told the three judges he was nervous about representing himself:

> I don't do this every day. I am not too sure of myself. I thought I'd be able to handle this case. I certainly can't handle it. I'd like to apply for legal aid. I haven't a penny.

CHAPTER TWENTY-SIX

GILLIGAN'S LAST STAND

From his new base in Portlaoise Prison Gilligan launched a series of challenges to the Irish legal process in a bid to delay his trial as long as possible. He objected to the presence of two of the three judges initially assigned to hear the case and they discharged themselves. He also hired and then fired two legal teams. It was a delaying tactic later adopted by other criminals.

One of the most anticipated criminal trials in Irish legal history finally began on 4 December 2000. Gilligan stood in the dock as each individual charge was read to him. To each count he was asked: 'How do you plead? Guilty or not guilty?'

Gilligan replied to each charge: 'Not guilty.' When the last count was read out to Gilligan, he added a contemptuous grin: 'And my final answer is not guilty.'

From the start Gilligan's very able defence barrister, Michael O'Higgins SC, made a number of applications to have the case thrown out and the trial abandoned. The motions were rejected by the court.

Opening the case for the prosecution Peter Charleton SC laid out his stall. The murder conspiracy, which had exposed Gilligan's drug business, had begun when Veronica Guerin had visited Jessbrook and he assaulted her. Charleton said this was the incident which provoked Gilligan and was ultimately responsible for her murder. On 25 June 1996 Gilligan 'deliberately left the jurisdiction having put in place the elements whereby Veronica Guerin was to be murdered and from abroad he directed that murder'.

Charleton said that Gilligan had inspired the murder because he wanted to protect his drugs empire and to ensure that he stayed out of jail at a time when he was making a great deal of money. Gilligan, he said, was the 'controlling mind' behind the criminal gang which he 'cloaked in secrecy and terror'.

The murder was arranged on his instruction, through agents who were members of his gang. It was the prosecution's contention that Gilligan and his gang had imported thousands of kilos of cannabis and a small amount of cocaine, as well as some firearms and ammunition. 'The motivation for the murder of Veronica Guerin was the protection of that empire and the protection of the lie that he was not involved in these offences,' said Charleton, as he charted Gilligan's career trajectory in the narcotics trade from his release from prison in 1993.

He mentioned Gilligan's contacts in the Netherlands. Chief among them was Martin Baltus who, he said, would testify for the prosecution about his extensive dealings with Gilligan on behalf of his boss Simon Rahman. The evidence included details of the packing and shipping of drugs and guns which were routed through Cork labelled as machine parts.

Charleton described Gilligan's dealings with Russell Warren in relation to the motorbike used in the murder. He also repeated Gilligan's comments to detectives outside Kilcock District Court the day before the murder when he'd said: 'She's a fucking stupid bitch. This case will never get off the ground.'

The prosecutor also referred to evidence of telephone records between Gilligan and the members of his gang on 26 June 1996. He said when the Lucan Investigation Team arrested Russell Warren it 'was the beginning of the end of the criminal gang based in Greenmount and controlled by John Gilligan'.

The trial was to last forty-three days. Throughout the proceedings Gilligan spent much of his time smirking and gazing at the skylight above him. In between he scribbled notes which were then handed by prison guards to his legal counsel.

Whenever the State's protected witnesses – Bowden, Warren and Dunne – were mentioned in the opening address to the court, Gilligan's gaze dropped from the skylight into the body of the court and he gave a dismissive smile. And when each of the supergrasses took the witness stand Gilligan fixed them with a cold, contemptuous stare as if trying to psych them out.

Veronica's husband, Graham, and her brother, Jimmy, attended every day of the trial, sitting in the body of the court under Gilligan's gaze.

Over 200 witnesses were called to testify, including eyewitnesses to the murder, forensic experts, telecommunications specialists and gardaí. Gilligan's legal team interrogated every witness and forensically reviewed all the evidence. They followed a similar strategy to that deployed in Meehan's trial, taking turns grilling the former gang members and their garda handlers in cross-examination. They highlighted inconsistencies, lies and contradictions in the statements and evidence of the key witnesses. The defence focused on the arrangements between the witnesses and the State regarding their immunity from prosecution and the witness protection programme. They wanted to show the court that the gang members had been incentivized to give evidence against Gilligan. Their case was that Bowden and Warren in particular had told a pack of lies and were trying to shove their own culpability onto Gilligan's shoulders.

One of the first witnesses was Felix McEnroy SC who had heard Gilligan's threatening phone call to Veronica Guerin the day after the assault. He said when he met the journalist that day she had the appearance of someone who had been in a fight. McEnroy said he could hear Gilligan, in a controlled voice, threaten to kill Veronica and to kidnap and rape her son.

'Especially the reference to the child,' recalled McEnroy. 'No one in their right mind could forget it. The imprint is still on my mind.' McEnroy then gave an unexpected insight into the personality of the gang boss whom he had represented in 1989:

> Mr Gilligan does not have much in the way of social conversation. When he speaks, he knows what he wants to say and, more importantly, he wants you to listen. He has what I would call a Dublin city, a working-class accent. He is somebody who, when he speaks, knows what he is about. He has good diction and is well capable of expressing himself. He is very direct in the way he expresses himself. This man is unusual. He is quiet but when he speaks, he speaks with a level of intensity that immediately grips you. You will know he is talking to you. When I heard that outburst on the phone, I had seen this before and I knew who it was because I had seen that outburst before.

McEnroy said that he had told Veronica Guerin to stop the telephone conversation at once and made it clear that she should make a statement to the gardaí.

After just over a week of evidence the trial was adjourned for the Christmas recess on 13 December until 11 January 2001. Gilligan was glad of the break. There was important work to be done over the festive season if he was to guarantee his acquittal.

Gilligan was confident that the State's witnesses could be discredited, as long as others remained silent and did not appear in court to corroborate their evidence. He wasn't worried about his former mistress. Despite repeated attempts by Tony Hickey's detectives Carol Rooney had steadfastly refused to change her mind. Before the trial commenced the State had paid for her to fly back to Belgium to meet members of the investigation team. She was given cast-iron assurances of her safety, and that of her family, but she was still too terrified to do the right thing. She returned to her overseas hideout. Rooney was determined to remain in Australia until Gilligan's trial was over.

With her out of the way Martin Baltus was Gilligan's biggest fear. From reading his statements in the book of evidence Gilligan knew that Baltus could corroborate vital parts of the evidence of the three supergrasses. The mob boss sent word to Fatso Mitchell and John Traynor to resolve the issue.

It would not be easy. Baltus was receiving police protection. The previous September Detective Inspector O'Loughlin had received intelligence that serious efforts would be made to prevent Baltus from testifying. O'Loughlin had passed on the information to the police in The Hague who began patrolling the area near Baltus's home where he lived with his wife and son. When his police handlers discussed his security with him, Baltus said that no one had attempted to intimidate him and he was still determined to appear in the Special Criminal Court in January.

A few days into the New Year O'Loughlin and Tony Hickey were informed by their Dutch colleagues that over Christmas Baltus's older daughter had been abducted from another location in the Netherlands. She had been held against her will overnight until her father had a change of heart. Baltus was now refusing to testify, citing fear for his family.

O'Loughlin immediately flew over in a bid to get Baltus back on side. The Dutch offered to place the former bagman in the equivalent of a witness protection programme but Baltus refused. Nothing would convince him to travel.

Gilligan's time-honoured tactic of using fear and intimidation had thwarted the State yet again. O'Loughlin returned to Dublin empty-handed. And there was nothing anyone could do about it.

When the trial resumed John Dunne was the first former accomplice to testify. He related how he had been recruited by Gilligan and detailed his function in the gang's drug trafficking operation. Bowden also returned to tell what he knew.

Between them the three former gang members, particularly Bowden and Warren, spent several days being pummelled in the witness box by the defence who set out to shred their credibility. At one stage Russell Warren broke down in tears when he was being cross-examined about the day of the murder and the court took a break until he regained his composure.

'I drove the woman to her death...I only sent the woman to her death,' he said, after explaining that he had kept in telephone contact with Meehan and Gilligan about Guerin's movements on the day of the murder.

When the court finally retired to consider its verdict on Friday 9 March Gilligan believed that he was home and dry. He was so confident that he organized a farewell party for his chums on E1 wing, the night before the court was due to deliver its verdict.

On Friday 15 March, as he was leaving Portlaoise, he told a prison officer: 'I won't be back. I'll never be back in this kip again.'

A large crowd of journalists queued outside the Special Criminal Court from early that morning. After nearly five years the finale of John Gilligan's case was major news.

Mr Justice Diarmuid O'Donovan, the presiding judge, took almost two hours to read the judgment in which, unlike a jury trial, the court explained its interpretation of the evidence and the rationale used to reach its verdict.

Gilligan smirked and gazed up at the skylight as he listened. The court made it clear that the uncorroborated evidence of an accomplice witness could not be sufficient to secure a criminal conviction in this State. While the court expressed its suspicions about the truthfulness of Bowden and Warren it said it was satisfied with the evidence they offered in relation to the drugs importation because it had been corroborated independently.

> It is the view of the court that under cross-examination, he [Bowden] was exposed as a self-serving liar in a variety of different ways, so much so that the court was compelled to conclude that, in the interests of justice, it would be unsafe to rely on any evidence which Charles Bowden gave unless it was supported by circumstantial evidence.

Bowden's evidence in relation to the collection of cartons of cannabis from the Ambassador Hotel and their transportation to the Greenmount lockup, however, was plausible.

The court was particularly comfortable with the testimony of John Dunne, who was described as 'a credible witness'. His account of the importation of hundreds of consignments of drugs was supported by senior executives in shipping and importation companies in Cork.

Bowden's claim that John Gilligan was the controlling force was consistent with the testimony of Dunne and it also tallied with independent evidence gathered by the gardaí, including the March 1996 wedding video in St Lucia. Gilligan's loud-mouthed behaviour had come back to haunt him.

Judge O'Donovan said there was a reasonable inference to be drawn from such evidence that Gilligan was responsible for importing cannabis and was the 'largest beneficiary'. He commented:

> That would suggest that he was the supreme authority among the members of the gang but in the view of the court, the evidence falls short of establishing that Mr Gilligan played an active role in the day-to-day activities of the gang.

Then the judge turned his attention to Warren:

Mr Warren was a self-confessed perjurer, a proven self-serving liar [under cross-examination, he specifically conceded that telling lies did not worry him as he said, 'If you can get away with lies, you would.'] and a person who, apparently, did not care who he hurt, if by doing so there was some benefit to himself.

Despite the court's scepticism, it was prepared to use parts of Warren's account which could be corroborated. In particular the letters he received from Gilligan while in jail supported other evidence of the existence of a gang and of Gilligan's position in it.

The court was therefore satisfied that Gilligan was guilty of the eleven drugs offences of which he was charged. The mob boss continued staring and smiling at the roof above at this statement.

The court then acquitted Gilligan of the firearms charges as it said there was too much doubt hanging over the prosecution's claim that he was in possession or control of firearms and ammunition. Bowden's evidence was being relied on by the prosecution but it could not be corroborated. Gilligan shifted his gaze from the ceiling to the court at these words. He began to look even more confident.

The judge then turned to the murder charge, commenting that the main grounds for the prosecution lay in the testimony of Russell Warren, which the court described as inconsistent and uncorroborated.

Judge O'Donovan explained the standard of proof required to assess whether John Gilligan had killed Veronica Guerin. He said that if it could be shown that Gilligan was in control or command of the murderers, he would be judged to be every bit as guilty as the man who had pulled the trigger. The fact that Bowden and Warren were granted immunity from prosecution in relation to the Guerin murder would indicate that their testimony wasn't necessarily unreliable. As the judge said:

No matter what evidence these two men gave at whatever trials they chose to give evidence on behalf of the prosecution, including this trial, they can never be prosecuted for the murder of Veronica Guerin and, therefore, is there sense or logic in their giving perjured evidence? The court thinks not.

But attempts by the prosecution to draw Gilligan into the murder by highlighting his links with the gang were not enough:

The court is invited to draw the inference that although he was not present at the time, John Gilligan, because he had a history of associating with all of these men at one time or another, must be deemed to be a party to the plan to kill Veronica Guerin. In the view of the court, that would be guilt by association and that alone, which is not a concept recognized in our criminal jurisprudence.

The court was particularly scathing of Russell Warren's evidence about events on 26 June 1996. If his version was true, the court said, it would have little difficulty in concluding that Gilligan had played 'a pivotal role' in the murder of Veronica Guerin, but his story was not credible.

Of significance was the fact that he did not tell the gardaí anything about the phone contact with Gilligan on the day until officers had returned money to him that had been previously seized. This was capable of being seen as an incentive to confess, something which the gardaí had vehemently denied. In addition there was no evidence from telephone records to support Warren's claim that he rang Gilligan after he allegedly saw Guerin leaving Naas.

Although the court had no way of knowing it at the time, Carol Rooney and Martin Baltus could have provided the vital corroboration to fill in the gaps in the testimony of Warren and Bowden.

Judge O'Donovan explained:

As there was no evidence whatsoever to corroborate the events involving Mr Gilligan which Mr Warren said had occurred

in the days preceding Ms Guerin's murder, and no evidence
to corroborate his testimony that he had been in Naas on the
morning of that day, the court could not but have a doubt about
all of those matters.

While this court has grave suspicions that John Gilligan was
complicit in the murder of the late Veronica Guerin, the court has
not been persuaded beyond all reasonable doubt by the evidence
which has been adduced by the prosecution that that is so and,
therefore, the court is required by law to acquit the accused on
that charge.

As he listened to the judgment the customary smirk on Gilligan's
face broke into a broad grin. He had won a monumental victory
over the law and the police. He had literally got away with murder.

After the judgment was read, the court adjourned for lunch. In the
afternoon it would sit again to pass sentence for the drugs offences. It
gave everyone a chance to absorb the implications of what they had
heard. The ruling was a bitter blow to Hickey and his team especially
as they were aware of Gilligan's machinations to undermine the trial.

Gilligan could hardly contain his joy as he sat in the holding cell
beneath the Special Criminal Court, eating fish and chips for lunch,
washed down with a can of Coke. That evening he expected to be
eating the finest steak and drinking champagne as a free man.

He phoned Geraldine, who had been busily redecorating Jessbrook
for her husband's return. Their unending string of vexatious legal
challenges against the CAB's right to seize the property would ensure
they could continue living there for years to come.

Gilligan told her to arrange a car to collect him after the trial.
He was unconcerned about the drug trafficking conviction or the
sentence he would get in the afternoon. Gilligan expected to be
released based on the four years and five months that he had been in
custody. He was in for a shock.

After 2 p.m. Gilligan was led back to the dock to hear his fate. He stood with his hands clasped in front of him, gazing once again at the skylight. Mr Justice Diarmuid O'Donovan looked sternly at Gilligan. He said the court had no doubt that Gilligan had 'reaped staggering profits' from the drugs racket and was a man of insatiable greed:

> The court is at a loss to find words to express its revulsion for what you have done. You have been responsible for an avalanche of drugs. Never in the history of Irish criminal jurisprudence has one person been presumed to have caused so much wretchedness to so many.

He commented that he hoped that the CAB would find Gilligan's hidden fortune and confiscate it. He then sentenced Gilligan to a total of twenty-eight years of imprisonment on the drug charges. Gasps of surprise could be heard throughout the courtroom.

It was the longest sentence ever handed down in Ireland for drug trafficking. The blood drained from Gilligan's face and his smirk disappeared. He was stunned.

Before he left the court to begin his prison term Gilligan instructed his legal team to immediately launch an appeal against his conviction and sentence. He could not believe that he had received the equivalent of a life sentence for selling dope.

Later that afternoon Tony Hickey and, his then boss, Commissioner Pat Byrne participated in a press conference at Garda Headquarters in the Phoenix Park. Byrne described the outcome of the case as 'satisfying'. In reality it was a deeply disappointing outcome for the years of hard work by the Lucan team. The only consolation was that Gilligan would be in prison for a very long time. Byrne was upbeat and supportive of his officers:

> We [gardaí] cannot take this on a personal basis. We are professionals and we are tasked to investigate crime, get the

evidence and prepare it for the Director of Public Prosecutions. We have dealt a serious blow to organized crime and to a particular group of people in organized crime. But we won't rest on our laurels and we know we have a long way to go.

CHAPTER TWENTY-SEVEN

BACK INSIDE

Gilligan was still in a state of shock as the convoy of police and military vehicles arrived at Portlaoise Prison. When it wore off he ranted and raved about the severity of the sentence to the prison officers who would have to endure his presence for a long time to come.

It was beyond the mobster's comprehension. He had got away with murder but left the court with what amounted to a life sentence. Like most narcissists he was oblivious to his culpability and saw himself as a victim of injustice. He couldn't grasp that he had brought about his own downfall. In many ways Gilligan shared most of the less appealing attributes of former US President Donald Trump: he had no respect for the truth and simply could not accept defeat. Gilligan was never wrong.

The reality, however, slowly sank in. Even if the sentence was reduced on appeal, he was still facing the prospect of spending at least another decade behind bars. Gilligan was fuming that he was back in Portlaoise Prison, even though he had been reunited with many of his old friends on E1. He had to take out his irritation on someone – and in the process earned himself even more time inside.

Ten days after being sentenced Gilligan and Meehan had a meeting with their lawyers in Portlaoise to discuss their respective appeals.

Gilligan then demanded that Assistant Chief Officer (ACO) Martin Ryan make arrangements to open the E1 tuck shop especially for him. He wanted to buy sweets and cans of Coke to take back to his cell. When he was told no, Gilligan flew into a rage and began hurling abuse at the ACO.

The mobster was incapable of learning from past mistakes, especially the consequences of assaulting prison officers as he had done before in Portlaoise in 1992 and while being detained in Belmarsh. As Brian Meehan struggled to restrain him, Gilligan punched Ryan on the side of his head. The officer was later treated in hospital and put on sick leave. Following the incident, in accordance with prison rules, the prison officers tried to strip search Gilligan.

He screamed at Ryan and his colleague, Declan O'Reilly:

> I will see that you're fucking killed for this. I will prove that I am not bluffing. I will see that you are got at while going from work. You better bear in mind that I will get your families as well.

He was brought before the deputy governor who ordered that he be placed in isolation for a period of two months. Gilligan was told that he would be confined to his cell for twenty-three hours a day for three days. He would lose fourteen days of remission of his sentence and his privileges, including visits, letters, tuck shop and telephone calls, were to be revoked for two months. True to form, Gilligan wasn't prepared to accept his punishment and sent his lawyers to the High Court to apply to have it declared unconstitutional.

In throwing out the claim, Mr Justice McKechnie clarified that Gilligan '...could be "Joe Bloggs" instead of John Gilligan. It is entirely immaterial to me. His presence in Portlaoise is of relevance only in that he is a prisoner and in lawful detention pursuant to due process.' He ruled that Gilligan 'must accept discipline and accommodate himself to prison life and understand that prison is a recognized form of punishment'.

The threats Gilligan made to kill the two prison officers were taken very seriously. They were removed from duty on E1 and they and their families received armed police protection. In January 2002 Gilligan was charged with assault and making threats to kill the officers.

———

Within a few weeks of the end of Gilligan's trial, Charlie Bowden and Russell Warren were freed from prison. They were relocated outside the State as part of the witness protection programme, with new identities and new lives. The rest of their families remained under protection back in Ireland for a number of years. Neither Warren, Bowden or their partners have been heard of in the last twenty-five years.

In the meantime the Criminal Assets Bureau stepped up its investigations to locate Gilligan's hidden fortune. By that time it had successfully stripped the other gang members of their cash, properties and vehicles, all which had been auctioned off. But their boss wasn't giving up so easily.

In December 2001 the Special Criminal Court began hearing the CAB's application to appoint a receiver to realize Gilligan's identifiable assets, including Jessbrook and his children's houses. The CAB estimated the entire portfolio of assets to be worth €24.5 million.

While Gilligan mounted legal battles with the State on numerous fronts, he was also attempting to deploy more physical ways of regaining his freedom by targeting John Dunne. The former shipping manager was the only one of the three supergrasses who had refused the offer of relocation outside the country as part of the WPP. After serving his sentence he had returned to live in Cork where he and his family were protected by armed detectives. It was an error of judgment that almost cost him his life.

Acting on Gilligan's instructions Dinny Meredith made contact with Dunne and convinced him to meet away from his police minders. At a rendezvous in Cork, on 3 March 2002, Meredith advised his former friend to swear an affidavit retracting his evidence against Gilligan and Meehan. Dunne was told that he would be approached by two men who would make him a proposition. Meredith urged him to listen to what they had to say.

Sometime later, two men with strong Northern Ireland accents, believed to be members of the INLA, 'advised' Dunne to swear a similar affidavit to the one sworn by Martin Baltus during Gilligan's trial, in which he officially withdrew his allegations about his dealings with the mobster.

Dunne was terrified by the menacing approaches. He contacted his garda handlers and agreed to enter the witness protection programme with his family. Dunne also gave a detailed statement about the incident to the Lucan team.

Meredith was arrested and questioned about the episode. Detective Inspector Todd O'Loughlin also arrested Gilligan at Portlaoise Prison and questioned him about the intimidation attempt. A file was sent to the DPP but no charges were preferred on the grounds that Dunne was now embedded in the WPP.

Three weeks after Dunne was approached in Cork the Court of Criminal Appeal overturned Paul Ward's conviction for murder which was good news for Gilligan. Ward's legal team had filed thirty-two grounds of appeal, the vast majority of which challenged the evidence given at the trial by Charlie Bowden.

The three-judge appeal court found that the State's evidence showed that Ward did not participate in the planning of 'this atrocious crime' and that there was no evidence to support the finding that Ward's role was to dispose of the murder weapon and motorbike used.

The Special Criminal Court appeared to have been misled by 'confusing evidence and voluminous documentation'. The appeal court said it was 'questionable whether one could be confident of eliminating all the factors that would motivate and encourage liars, such as Bowden, so as to justify a belief beyond all reasonable doubt in any evidence given by him'.

The judges said that the Special Criminal Court had found, and Bowden himself admitted, that he was an inveterate liar. Cross-examination had exposed errors and inaccuracies in Bowden's evidence against Ward. Bowden's credibility was further compromised, as he had been an accomplice in the murder.

Ward was delighted with the result but he still wasn't going to be leaving prison anytime soon. He was returned to serve the remainder of the twelve-year sentence for his involvement in the Mountjoy Prison siege in 1997.

The ruling came as a major blow to the gardaí. Assistant Commissioner Tony Hickey, however, commented: 'The point is, no matter what happens at this stage, we set out to dismantle a particular gang and we have done that.'

Ward's once close pal and fellow gang member Brian Meehan did not fare as well – he lost a series of appeals against his conviction. In the summer of 2021 it was revealed that the prison authorities were preparing to move Meehan to Shelton Abbey, an open prison in County Wicklow. The move is a first step towards his full release after spending most of over twenty-three years in maximum security.

On the same day that Ward's conviction was overturned, John Gilligan received less welcome news when the Special Criminal Court ordered him to pay over €21 million to the CAB within twelve months based on his profits from the drug trade. Gilligan had no intention of settling or paying anything. He would continue battling the CAB for another fifteen years.

A few months later Gilligan stood trial in the Special Criminal Court for the assault and death threats made against the two prison officers. Martin Ryan told the court:

Prisoner Gilligan threatened me and told me I was nothing only a cunt and a fucking scumbag. He also struck me a blow on the left jaw with his clenched fist.

It emerged that Ryan and his family had been forced to move to a new home as a result of the threats.

Gilligan was convicted of threatening the prison officers on 25 June 2002, the eve of the sixth anniversary of Veronica Guerin's murder. He was sentenced to two concurrent five-year jail terms which were to run consecutive to his drug trafficking sentence.

Mr Justice Johnson said that the court took 'very seriously' the threats uttered by Gilligan:

They came from the accused, a person described by his own counsel, Mr Michael O'Higgins, as a notorious and dangerous criminal... Threats of the nature to have been uttered by a person such as John Gilligan are of the most serious kind.

After receiving his sentence, Gilligan grinned and said: 'Keep it clean.' Within a week he had instructed his legal team to appeal the decision. The sentence was subsequently reduced to two years. In an ironic twist, that same day Carol Rooney came out of hiding and returned to live in the UK where she later married. Gilligan no longer posed a threat to her life as she had refused to testify. Rooney had decided it was safe to move on.

———— · ————

The CAB mounted an international investigation to find Gilligan's secret wealth. The bureau estimated that he had successfully spirited away millions which, to this day, have never been located.

The investigation homed in on Liam Judge, a drug trafficker and the owner of a transport company from Allenwood in County

Kildare. Judge had been the logistics manager for George 'the Penguin' Mitchell for several years and also worked with other gangs including Gilligan. On top of that he was a police informant.

While Gilligan was fighting his extradition from the UK, Judge began a relationship with Tracey Gilligan. He left his wife and family and moved to live with the mobster's daughter in Alicante on the Spanish Costa Brava.

Judge was suspected of laundering Gilligan's money by buying property and investing in various legitimate businesses. The portfolio included plant hire companies and a pub in Torrevieja called the Judge's Chambers. Since Gilligan's arrest Judge had also been running a new drug smuggling operation on his behalf between Spain and Ireland.

On 15 September 2002 Judge's estranged wife was kidnapped from her home in County Kildare in a bid to force him to pay a large ransom demand. The incident was the result of a row between Gilligan and Judge and another drug gang. She was released after two days.

Gilligan, however, made no secret of the fact that he had involved himself in the matter. He sent a message to the kidnappers in an interview in the *Sunday Business Post*, speaking from an illegal mobile phone in his prison cell.

> This will be sorted. I am not leaving this go. I will go to whatever lengths are necessary. The people who did this will be dealt with. We've done our homework. We know who did it. And they know we know. And they know it's not finished. Even if they give us €250,000 compensation, it's not over. If they want to dance, let's dance...If they want to go to war, let's go to war.

In December 2003 the police listened in as Gilligan threatened Judge saying that he would have him shot in a row over drug money. Gilligan ranted and raved telling Judge that he would put several bullets in him. 'Remember I fucking own Spain,' Gilligan declared.

Gilligan never got a chance to realize the threat. A few weeks later fifty-year-old Judge died from a massive heart attack brought on by his fondness for cocaine and booze.

His death caused the mob boss a major headache as the Spanish properties were legally held in Judge's name. A bitter row erupted between the Gilligan family and Judge's widow when her lawyers indicated that she wanted to sell off her late husband's business interests.

Geraldine and Tracey Gilligan claimed that they were part-owners in the businesses and were owed money. But there was no legally binding written agreement between the parties. Gardaí believe that the Judge family was threatened as the matter went quiet shortly afterwards. The CAB has never been able to establish what kind of settlement arrangement was agreed.

In any event legislation regarding the seizure of the proceeds of crime had still not been enacted in Spain at that stage, which blocked the CAB moving to have Judge's properties seized. Gilligan had thwarted the law again.

In Portlaoise Gilligan continued to be involved in the drug trade. In 2004 garda intelligence sources confirmed that they believed he was running his business from his jail cell. The authorities had deliberately turned a blind eye to criminals like Gilligan having mobile phones which they then bugged. It provided a rich vein of highly valuable intelligence which would cost him dearly.

As a result of the information gleaned the Garda National Drug Unit and their Spanish colleagues busted several members of Gilligan's gang in Spain and Dublin and seized cocaine with street values running into millions of euro. It was more bad news for Gilligan who by then knew that he would not be getting out of prison for a long time.

Gilligan's appeal against his conviction opened in the Court of Criminal Appeal on 1 July 2003 and was heard over seven days amid tight security.

In another twist of irony the hearing coincided with Gilligan's biggest claim to international infamy yet – featuring as the real-life bad guy in the Hollywood movie *Veronica Guerin*, which premiered in Dublin on 8 July. Directed by Joel Schumacher and with Cate Blanchett as the eponymous heroine, Gilligan was played by Irish actor Gerry McSorley who did a masterful job of portraying the godfather's malevolence.

A month later the Court of Criminal Appeal delivered its decision to uphold his conviction. Gilligan then launched an appeal against the severity of his sentence in the same court which proved to be more successful. The following November the court ruled that the twenty-eight-year prison sentence had been disproportionate and implied that he had been effectively sentenced for the murder he had been cleared of. The sentence was reduced by eight years.

Gilligan's legal team then made an application to the court to have points of law arising from the case referred to the Supreme Court on the grounds that they were of exceptional public importance. They included the operation of the WPP and the evidence of the supergrasses.

The highest court in the land threw out his appeal in November 2005. Gilligan was guaranteed to spend up to eight more years behind bars.

In April 2006 Patrick 'Dutchy' Holland was released from prison and launched a brief, but unsuccessful, publicity campaign to clear his name. Now sixty-seven the old-age pensioner then went back to crime. Less than two years after his release the killer was convicted of conspiracy to kidnap a businessman in London and was sentenced to eight years. Holland died in his sleep in Parkhurst Prison on the Isle of Wight in 2009.

In the meantime his former boss continued his war of attrition with the law. In May 2007 Gilligan fought a bid by HM Customs to officially confiscate the £330,000 (€640,000) seized from him at Heathrow Airport in 1996.

Gilligan was giving nothing up without a fight.

He attended the two-day hearing via video link from Portlaoise where he was again in isolation for threatening prison officers. This time the source of his anger was the seizure of his mobile phones and a flat screen TV from his cell in a clampdown by the authorities. It followed an extraordinary incident when his cell mate, armed robber John Daly, phoned Joe Duffy's Radio One show to berate this writer live on air.

At Uxbridge Magistrates' Court Gilligan loomed over the proceedings, on two large TV monitors. Behind him a prison officer sat under the official crest of Portlaoise Prison. It was symbolic of the shadow Gilligan still cast across gangland.

Derek Baker, his former bagman, had been sent to Uxbridge to give evidence on Gilligan's behalf. The one-time bookie told the court that Gilligan derived his money from gambling.

Garda intelligence later learned that Baker had at first refused to go to court but was then threatened by Dessie O'Hare and Dutchy Holland who explained the likely consequences if he didn't appear. Baker later confirmed that he was there under duress from Gilligan. He told this writer:

> I'm only here because I was put under pressure. What could I do? I got a call to meet two fellahs in a car park. They said: 'Whatever you were told to do just do it.' Jaysus all I am trying to do is get my fucking life back. I regret the day that I ever met John Gilligan. I could be whacked over this.

Baker was obviously uncomfortable with the situation he found himself in. The former bagman had no more dealings with Gilligan after that.

Gilligan's legal war with the State began with his original arrest and continued for two decades. It cost the Irish taxpayer millions of euro as he used his entitlement to free legal aid. No criminal has ever played the system as adroitly or with such obduracy as the little man.

Analysis of his myriad legal actions against the CAB alone show that he and his family mounted seven separate legal challenges in the High Court and Supreme Court. There were a further eighty-eight separate applications, leading to fourteen separate judgments and twenty-nine appeals.

In one of those hearings, in 2008, Gilligan sacked his legal team so that he could personally address the court – and pull a publicity stunt. He used the occasion to publicly claim that John Traynor 'had Veronica Guerin murdered' but he [Gilligan] had 'nothing to do with it'.

In an hour-long address to the High Court, in which he was opposing a bid by the CAB to have a receiver appointed to his properties, Gilligan said the only reason he was facing the receivership action was because of the killing of the journalist in June 1996.

'That was a horrible thing that happened to her, but I had nothing to do with it,' the fifty-five-year-old claimed despite being repeatedly told by Mr Justice Kevin Feeney to stick to the case before the court. Gilligan ignored him. 'He [Traynor] said to me he stole Brian Meehan's telephone...', but the mobster was again interrupted by the judge and told not to go into the criminal case against him.

The calls made and received by Meehan's mobile phone on the day of the killing had been crucial to his conviction. Gilligan, who was deeply resentful that the much cleverer Traynor had got away so easily, wanted the world to believe that it had been the Coach using Meehan's phone on the day of the murder. The mobster was delighted with his publicity coup.

But while Traynor seemed to have escaped any real consequences for his involvement in the gang and the murder of Veronica Guerin, his past did eventually catch up with him.

Following the smashing of Gilligan's gang, Traynor and Peter 'Fatso' Mitchell had continued to be partners in the drug business, operating between the Netherlands, Spain and the UK. By 2008 they were involved in a major international drug trafficking syndicate with Dutch and UK criminals.

The organized crime grouping was running multi-million-euro drug shipments primarily supplying the UK market. One of their partners was a London gangster called Noel Cunningham, one of Britain's most wanted criminals. The forty-seven-year-old and his fellow armed robber, Clifford Hobbs, had been sprung from a prison van in 2003 as it brought them from Brixton Prison to the Old Bailey in London. They were facing charges relating to a foiled Stg£1.25 million security van heist.

As a result a major joint Dutch–UK police investigation was launched in 2009 to target the drug syndicate. Cunningham was arrested by the Dutch later that year and returned to the UK.

On 23 August 2010 an undercover Dutch police team was monitoring the premises being used by the gang in Amsterdam. They watched as a man and woman exited and got into a car which was connected with another gang member from Liverpool.

When police stopped the vehicle, the driver gave his name as Paul Joseph Reilly and produced an Irish driving licence. When 'Reilly' was asked to confirm his date of birth he had to refer to the document and became nervous. He then admitted that his real name was John Traynor. The woman in his company was his long-time mistress, Irish woman Marie Kiernan, who was the registered owner of a pub in Amsterdam. It was suspected that the business was being used to launder money for Traynor and Peter Mitchell. Traynor was arrested and taken in for questioning.

In a follow-up operation the cops searched Traynor's residence where they found Mitchell who was also living there. The police did not have grounds to arrest Fatso who promptly fled the country the next day. Mitchell, who continued to operate as a mid-level drug trafficker, was never charged with any offence connected to the Guerin murder. Shay Ward also escaped capture. After his brother Paul was released from prison he too has maintained a low profile although he is still believed to be mixed up in organized crime. In the past twenty-five years he has been operating between the Netherlands and Spain and is classified as a business associate of the Kinahan crime cartel.

When the Dutch checked with their UK colleagues they discovered that Traynor had been unlawfully at large since absconding from prison in 1992. He had another five years to serve for receiving stolen bearer bonds.

The Coach was placed in custody and was voluntarily extradited to the UK in November 2010. He was released from prison in September 2012. He later set up a second-hand car business in Kent where he continues to live.

His former partner in crime, who had been in custody for sixteen years since his initial arrest in London, should have been eligible for release with remission around the same time. But Gilligan still had to serve an additional two years for threatening the prison officers. He had also received another six months after being found with a mobile phone in his cell.

John Joseph Gilligan's release date was set for October 2013.

CHAPTER TWENTY-EIGHT

_____

FREEDOM AND PAIN

The seventeen years spent in prison had neither rehabilitated nor mellowed John Gilligan. Despite reaching the age of sixty-one he still had not realized where it had all gone wrong. His defining characteristics of hubris, arrogance and obstinacy had not softened over time.

When he was released from Portlaoise Prison on 15 October 2013 he was confident of reclaiming his rightful place in the hierarchy of organized crime. Even though he had no gang infrastructure he was determined to pick up where he'd left off. To him age was not a barrier – his fearsome reputation as a criminal godfather would earn him respect from the young Turks. His naïve assumptions would prove to be a huge mistake.

The mobster was also determined to continue his fight against the CAB. In anticipation of the intense media attention that would inevitably focus on his return to freedom, Gilligan issued a tongue-in-cheek statement in advance through his lawyers asking for privacy.

In a demonstration of his legendary chutzpah the man who had ordered the murder of a journalist wanted her colleagues to know that even if they offered him '€1 million' he would not be giving any interviews. The statement read:

As of now, and continuing upon his release, he is engaged in litigation with various authorities in the Republic of Ireland. For this, and other reasons, neither he, nor any member of his family, will be speaking to the media concerning any of his plans or intentions with regard to his future, nor any other subject. In particular Mr Gilligan wishes to stress that offers of money or any other reward for media interviews or comments will not sway him from the position set out above.

On the morning of his release a large group of journalists were waiting as he emerged through the gates of Portlaoise Prison clutching his belongings. He made no effort to hide his face as he smiled and waved for the cameras.

As the car driven by his brother, Thomas, took him away, Gilligan pressed his face, wearing his customary sneer, up to the rear window. His first port of call was a welcome home party at the house of one of his siblings in Clondalkin.

But the media weren't letting him off the hook. Michael O'Toole, the intrepid crime editor of the *Star* newspaper, called to the door. Instead of abuse, Gilligan decided to give him an impromptu scoop. He denied being involved in Veronica Guerin's murder and retracted previous admissions that he had threatened to rape her son, commenting:

> This girl [Veronica], God rest her, she never wrote one word about me. I don't accept I assaulted her. People said I admitted it – I did no such thing. She did call to Jessbrook. I'm after being on trial and [it's] been proved nothing ever happened.

Gilligan made a point of telling the world – including the criminal fraternity – that he had no intention of going to ground. He told O'Toole:

I'm after being decent enough, respectful enough. I didn't duck and dive. I could have come out of the prison and hid. I won't be hiding from nobody. I have no problem with anybody...My plans are to have another beer. I'm delighted to be out of prison. I feel great.

Gilligan didn't mention that his plans included returning to a life of crime. As soon as his hangover wore off the following day he set about rebuilding his lost empire. But he needed start-up capital to get back in the game.

Gilligan seemed to be broke despite the fact that most of the fortune he'd made in the 1990s has never been traced. It is one of the abiding mysteries of Gilligan's story – where did all the money go? In the weeks after the Guerin murder he had bragged about having made £15 million (€29 million). The enquiries conducted by the CAB and the Lucan team confirmed that he was actually telling the truth. Only the man himself can know what happened to it.

Vital to his plans of restoring his dominance of gangland was Stephen Dougie Moran, his new enforcer, bodyguard and partner in crime. The forty-six-year-old member of the travelling community was a widely feared senior figure in the notorious McCarthy/Dundon crime family from Limerick, dubbed 'Murder Inc.'.

Moran had been directly connected to several killings in Murder Inc.'s terrifying campaign of violence which raged in Limerick for over a decade, claiming more than twenty lives. The innocent victims included Sean Poland, Brian Fitzgerald, Roy Collins and Shane Geoghegan.

The enforcer was regarded as a violent and clever criminal with close associations to dissident republican gangs, the INLA and the Continuity IRA. Moran used a security company as a front for his activities which included drug trafficking and the supply of firearms and hit men to other gangs. He was an ideal companion for Gilligan.

Within days Moran was driving Gilligan around Dublin in his armour-plated jeep. It was an unambiguous message to the rest of the underworld that the boss was back in town and had plenty of muscle behind him.

Blinded by narcissism and a sense of invincibility, Gilligan could not see how much the underworld had changed during his seventeen-year absence. The gangland that he had helped to pioneer had been transformed beyond recognition. He was about to find out the hard way that this was not a country for old crime lords.

A new generation of criminals had emerged to feed the country's burgeoning love affair with cocaine which by 2004 had become a billion-euro industry. Gilligan had even cashed in on it for a time while inside, before falling out with his partners on the outside.

The millions involved created a climate of greed and paranoia which in turn fuelled an unprecedented rise in gangland violence. As others rushed to fill the void left by the demise of the Gilligan organization, there was a proliferation of drug gangs. Criminals feuded over money and turf as the phenomenon of gangland assassinations became the norm.

By 1996 there had been less than twenty gangland killings recorded since organized crime first emerged in the early 1970s. In the years since that seminal event the murder rate had increased exponentially. Between 2000 and Gilligan's release in 2013 there were over 150 gangland slayings in Ireland. At one stage in the noughties it had the highest per capita rates of gun crime in Western Europe. One of the bloodiest years on record was 2006, the tenth anniversary of the Guerin murder, when twenty-two people were gunned down in the madness.

The new breed of gangster was heavily armed and routinely killed anyone who crossed them, including a so-called gangland celebrity like Gilligan. In many ways it was Gilligan who had helped usher in this new era of savagery – it was his legacy.

More importantly the balance of power had shifted dramatically within the underworld hierarchy. The Irish drug trade was now controlled by Gilligan's old friends, Christy Kinahan and John Cunningham, operating from a base on the Costa del Sol in Spain.

In the years that Gilligan spent on E1, the Kinahan cartel had grown into one of the most powerful criminal organizations in Europe. It was a highly sophisticated billion-euro global business. The cartel dealt in multi-ton loads of narcotics, especially cannabis and cocaine, and also supplied weaponry. At the other end it employed an elaborate money laundering system investing in property and other business ventures in several countries.

In Ireland the Kinahan syndicate was a seamless alliance of major organized crime groups including the family of Gerry Hutch, the Monk, and the Byrne clan in Crumlin, south-west Dublin. It was easy to see how Gilligan's attempts to muscle in became an instant irritant.

Gilligan, with Moran at his side, began pushing his weight around to extort what he called 'welcome home money' from other criminals. In one incident a dealer in west Dublin was beaten up and told he would be shot if he didn't pay up. The problem was that the gangster worked for the Kinahans.

Worse still Gilligan started putting pressure on his lifelong friend John Cunningham, for money he claimed he was owed. Factory John wanted repayment for helping to smuggle the kidnapper out of the country in 1996 and for providing seed money to get him started in the drug trade with Kinahan, who at that time was still a relatively small player. Gilligan was now a potential threat to a hugely successful operation.

The little man would later deny that he had flexed his muscles with Cunningham. In a taped interview with the former godfather that was obtained by the *Irish Mirror* in 2017, Gilligan said that he had asked Cunningham for a 'favour'. He stressed:

> But there was no such thing as 'Give us this, give us that'. I
> know him all me life. A lifelong friend. Closer to me than some
> of me brothers. I hadn't hassled anybody for money [including
> Cunningham].

Gilligan also pointed out that he and Kinahan had been good friends. Kinahan had served a sentence for fraud on E1 in Portlaoise with Gilligan in the late 1990s.

While the Cunningham episode remains wrapped up in gangland's code of *omerta*, Gilligan's innate sense of entitlement would not allow him to play second fiddle to anyone, especially the friend he had helped to set up in the drug business. In Gilligan's mind Cunningham owed him big time. He made no secret that he was intent on muscling in for a chunk of the market. Once he got re-established the drug gangs would have to come to him for their supplies. Factory John thought he could use his famous bullyboy tactics to reclaim his crown but he was greatly mistaken. It was, like with the murder of Veronica Guerin, a monumental miscalculation.

In the new underworld order Gilligan's insufferable arrogance was a source of intense irritation and he brought unnecessary trouble wherever he went. Cunningham and Kinahan knew him well enough to realize that he would become a major problem for them in the future. The only way of dealing with Gilligan was to have him neutralized – permanently. It was, to paraphrase an old Mafia line, as much business as it was personal.

The cartel had a small army of loyal assassins who were willing and able to do the job. Such was the cartel's power, its bosses literally decided who lived and who died. Shortly after Gilligan's release gardaí picked up intelligence that there was a plot to kill him and officially informed him that his life was in danger. He wasn't told who was behind the plot but officers advised him to review his personal security. Gilligan laughed it off. Who would dare fuck with him?

On the evening of 3 December 2013 Gilligan and Moran arrived at the Lucan Spa Hotel for a meeting. The pair sat at the hotel bar and, according to garda intelligence sources, Gilligan appeared to be anxious about the arrival of another individual. 'This fella is a good lad and he is never late,' Moran was overheard reassuring him.

About forty minutes later they were joined by James Quinn, a member of the Kinahan cartel and a killer for hire. Quinn was connected to a string of killings which had been ordered by Christy Kinahan and his son Daniel. He was subsequently convicted of the murder in 2015 of Gary Hutch, the nephew of Gerry 'the Monk' Hutch, which ultimately sparked the deadly Kinahan–Hutch feud a year later.

Quinn handed Gilligan an envelope containing several untraceable, encrypted mobile phones. The cartel used the phones to avoid law enforcement agencies listening in and also sold them to other drug gangs. Quinn spoke to Gilligan and Moran for a short while before the group left.

When they learned of the meeting gardaí were anxious to establish what was afoot. It was speculated that, apart from picking up special phones, Gilligan and Moran may have been hiring Quinn to carry out a hit on their behalf. As they began investigating, Gilligan found himself in the cross hairs of a would-be assassin.

Two days later Gilligan was drinking in the Hole in the Wall pub on Blackhorse Avenue near the Phoenix Park. At the same time a masked man stormed into the Halfway House pub in Ashtown, a short distance away. He ran around the bar waving a handgun shouting: 'Where's Gilligan?' When he couldn't locate his target, the shooter left on the back of a waiting motorbike.

The would-be assassins were chased by gardaí and threw the weapon away before making their escape. Minutes later Gilligan received a phone call from an associate informing him of what had happened. He was driven off in Moran's bullet-proof jeep. It was a close call. Some years later Gilligan claimed that his psychic abilities had saved him from the grim reaper. He had intended going to the Halfway House that evening but had a premonition and went to the other pub instead.

The attempted hit on the notorious gang boss, coming so soon after his release from prison, was big news. The following morning Gilligan turned up at the Dublin High Court as part of his ongoing battle with the CAB. He was determined to put on a brave sneering face. When RTÉ's crime correspondent, Paul Reynolds, asked him about the incident he shrugged it off.

> I haven't a clue. Halloween prank too late...I've no problem with anybody and I've no fear of anybody. I've no enemies.

When asked why anyone would want to kill him, he scoffed:

> I haven't got a clue. Halloween. Kids making mistakes.

In the weeks after the murder bid Gilligan and Moran placed a contract on the prime suspect for the incident. The dangerous criminal from north Dublin was a gun for hire and connected to the Kinahan cartel. He was subsequently informed by gardaí of a threat to his life. But Gilligan's threat of reprisals wasn't going to scare off anyone.

On 1 March 2014 Gilligan was attending a christening party at his brother Thomas's house in Clondalkin when the shooters came back to finish the job. Shortly after 7 p.m. two armed and masked men knocked on the door. When it was answered, they ran in and cornered John Gilligan in the hallway shooting him six times. The mob boss was hit in the nose, upper chest, stomach, hip and leg. Another round grazed his forehead. The assassins fled in a waiting getaway car which was later found burned out.

Gilligan miraculously survived the shooting. He was rushed to hospital where he underwent emergency surgery and that night was described as being in a stable condition. The attack showed that he was no longer untouchable or feared in the new gangland. He was a pariah in civilized society and a nobody in the world he'd once dominated.

In the taped interview obtained by the *Irish Mirror* Gilligan was heard describing how playing dead saved his life:

> I lay on the floor – I just played dead. I thought I was a goner for sure. If I hadn't done that, I wouldn't be here to tell the tale now.

Gilligan was kept in hospital under armed guard while he underwent a number of surgical procedures. The protection was put in place to prevent the assassins striking again while he was there. As he was recuperating Dougie Moran and his associates geared up for a revenge attack. But the cartel was not finished yet.

On Saturday 15 March, exactly two weeks to the hour since the assassination attempt on Gilligan, the hit man stuck again. Dougie Moran returned to his home at Earlsfort View in Lucan around 7.30 p.m. His house was festooned with CCTV cameras and was fortified with bullet-proof glass and a reinforced front door. The property was also protected behind railings and electric gates. It took him about ten seconds to get from his jeep to the safety of the house. The years of involvement in gangland murders had taught Moran to be security conscious.

Moran got out of the bullet-proof jeep and was headed for the front door when a hit man appeared from the shadows. His timing was perfect. Gilligan's enforcer was shot several times with a handgun and died almost instantly.

When he got word about the murder a short time later Gilligan was reportedly terrified. His enemies would stop at nothing until they closed his eyes – permanently. He was no longer a man of respect or power in gangland. Gilligan had been reduced to nothing more than a problem that needed eradicating.

With Moran dead and many of his Murder Inc. henchmen gone into hiding for fear of further attacks, Gilligan was left with no protection and was extremely vulnerable. He had good reason to believe that the cartel would kill him as soon as he left the hospital.

For the first time in his long criminal career Gilligan was running for his life. He would only survive if he left the country – fast. The pain from his wounds had been replaced with raw panic and fear. Gilligan told the cops protecting him: 'I have to get out of here.'

The next morning, despite his still serious injuries and the fact that he required a wheelchair to move around, Gilligan made hurried arrangements for his escape. He wasn't prepared to give the hit man a second opportunity to earn the bounty on his head.

Around 11.30 p.m. on Sunday 16 March, Gilligan discharged himself from James Connolly Memorial hospital. Armed gardaí escorted the mob boss as he was taken by wheelchair to a waiting car, driven by a friend. Gilligan was a pitiable figure as he was pushed through the hospital doors to the waiting car. He was a shadow of his former blustering self as he sat huddled up in an overcoat, with a black cap pulled down on his head, clutching a plastic bag containing his belongings. The image, taken by a photographer from the *Irish Independent*, captured the ignominious fall of a gangster who had changed the face of Irish organized crime.

The face that once struck terror into his enemies was now gaunt and full of fear, as his eyes darted nervously, watching for danger in the shadows of the car park. The arrogance and the trademark sneer had vanished. John Gilligan was a frightened old man being forced to flee for his life under the cover of darkness. The former godfather had been reduced to the grandfather that no one wanted. For those of us who had followed the exploits of the hated mobster for decades, this was his just deserts. It was justice of the poetic kind – it was karma.

Gilligan was driven under garda escort to the ferry terminal at the North Wall where his friend's car boarded the ferry for the 2.15 a.m. sailing to Holyhead. In the UK arrangements were made to admit Gilligan to a private hospital to resume his recuperation. After that he was reportedly living incognito with Moran's relatives in the travelling community, moving between camps around England.

For over two years after his late-night flight to safety Gilligan was neither seen nor heard of again. Then in a calculated gesture the sixty-four-year-old returned to Dublin in 2016 shortly after the twentieth anniversary of Veronica Guerin's murder.

By then the Kinahan cartel had unleashed an unprecedented cycle of violence against the Monk, his family and friends, which brought terror and death to the streets of Dublin's north inner city.

The conflagration had ignited in February when Gerry Hutch orchestrated an audacious attack at a boxing weigh-in at the Regency Hotel in Dublin. A five-man hit team – three of whom were dressed in garda SWAT uniforms and brandishing AK-47s – stormed the building, intent on wiping out Daniel Kinahan and his top lieutenants.

The attack came as a timely reminder that two decades after the last seminal event in gangland history, organized crime was more pernicious than ever. Just as Gilligan had done in 1996, the Kinahans and the Hutches were demonstrating to the world that they too had no fear of the law and could do what they liked. And like the diminutive mobster, their actions would prove to be a spectacular miscalculation.

It was probably as a result of that brutal gang war that Gilligan considered it safe to return home. Garda intelligence sources revealed that the fallen mobster had brokered some sort of deal with the Kinahans. Either the cartel was no longer interested in killing him or it was simply too busy executing others in the bloody feud. Either way the mob boss felt safe enough to resurface.

Gilligan quietly returned to live in the family home at Jessbrook. He kept a low profile, steering clear of his former partners in crime. He appeared to have been reduced to penury and was living on the charity of family members.

By now the CAB had sold off most of the Jessbrook estate, including the show jumping arena and the adjoining 80 acres of land, after Gilligan's myriad appeals and challenges had finally failed in 2015. But, through his wife Geraldine, he was still fighting a last-ditch challenge in the Supreme Court over the ownership of the family home on the estate where she still lived.

It was a fight that he was not prepared to give up. In any event it was costing him nothing – Irish taxpayers were still paying for his battle with the State.

Around the same time that Gilligan returned this writer was involved in making a documentary series, *State of Fear*, with Tile Films for TV3 (now Virgin Media), to mark the anniversary of Veronica's murder and assess how organized crime had developed over the two decades that had elapsed. A retrospective overview of the horrific crime that shook the nation, it was also an analysis of Ireland's gangland in 2016. Coming face to face with John Gilligan wasn't in the script.

The afternoon of 8 November was cold and wet when we arrived at Jessbrook Equestrian Centre. I and my producer/director Richard Stearn were there, by kind permission of the new legitimate owner, on a reconnaissance mission in preparation for filming the closing sequence for the series. The property had been sold by the CAB earlier in the year.

Standing there in the middle of the impressive edifice that had remained unused for two decades was an emotional experience. The physical structure was a permanent reminder of why Veronica Guerin had been gunned down without mercy. This was where the story had begun and ended.

We had been tipped off that Gilligan could regularly be seen cutting bushes and fixing fences around the house he had built with drug money. He acted, we were told, as if he was still the rightful owner of the property and showed no intention of leaving.

Having been warned by our lawyers not to 'trespass' on the grounds of the house I was filming with my mobile phone along the boundary fence when I spotted a figure walking on the other side of the tree line.

Gilligan, wearing a wax hat and matching coat, was carrying shears on his way to cut bushes. And then he was standing in front of me. In that second I felt a rage that had been simmering inside me for twenty years. The story of Gilligan for many crime journalists was every bit as personal as it was business. The very fact that he was still here after all that time was a grotesque insult to the memory of a brave colleague who was doomed to death because she came here to ask him a question.

As he was about to open the gate to enter the field I was standing in, I walked up to Gilligan and said, 'Hello, John, it's Paul Williams...' In that moment I expected to have a testy confrontation that might even become physical. The film shows how Gilligan paused for a second, looking startled, before immediately turning and walking away without a word.

'I have always wanted to meet you again, you scumbag...what are you doing back here?' I shouted without thinking. As Gilligan scurried away, I yelled: 'Come back, I don't have a gun.'

It was not the Gilligan of old. There was no sign of the bullish image he had always projected to the world. In the days before the hit men targeted him, he would have at least responded with some glib remark or even threats.

It was further evidence of how the tables had turned and the mob boss had ultimately received justice. The once sneering brute was a broken man running away from Veronica's colleagues.

When the documentary was broadcast a few weeks later the public was shocked that the notorious crime boss had successfully staved off eviction for twenty years. It was seen as a smack in the face to the many thousands of citizens who had lost their homes following the economic crash. For them there had been no free legal aid to pay for myriad court challenges and appeals to the highest courts in the land. But then they weren't criminals who knew how to play the system.

In February 2017 the Supreme Court threw out Gilligan's final appeal. He was given until the following June to hand over the keys of the former family home at Jessbrook which he duly did. But, true to form, he then appealed his case to the European Court of Justice and applied to the local authority to be housed. In 2021 that court also threw out his claim, describing his marathon legal battle with the State as nothing more than a series of vexatious challenges and appeals to stall the seizure of his assets. All his identifiable assets have since been sold off by the CAB with the last property, the house he bought for his daughter Tracey, being sold in December 2019 – twenty-three years after the murder of Veronica Guerin and the establishment of the revolutionary bureau.

In 2018 Gilligan reached retirement age, turning sixty-six, and became eligible for an old-age pension and a travel pass. He could also have a free TV licence. Despite all that he had been through he continued to dabble in the drug trade, spending his time between a house in County Roscommon and a villa in Alicante, Spain. His new approach, however, was remarkably low-key and non-confrontational.

On Thursday 23 August 2018, Gilligan was about to board a flight to Alicante at Belfast International Airport when he was stopped by border guards. When his bag was searched it was found to contain €23,000 in cash and he was arrested on suspicion of money laundering.

The UK's National Crime Agency believed the cash was the proceeds of an operation involving the smuggling of an anti-insomnia prescription medication called Zopiclone from Spain into the UK and Ireland. It was sold on to drug addicts at an average profit margin of eight times its original price. The next day Gilligan appeared at Coleraine Magistrates' Court in County Derry where he was charged with money laundering offences.

The veteran gangster was heading back to prison once again after being remanded in custody at Maghaberry Prison, Lisburn. Just less than five years after his release from Portlaoise Gilligan again found himself locked in a battle with the authorities over what he claimed was his unfair incarceration. His lawyers argued that he was a marked man in Ireland and the money he was carrying came from family and friends to help him start a new life in Spain. Despite making a number of bail applications to the Belfast High Court Gilligan spent Christmas behind bars. The National Crime Agency claimed that he was a suspected drug trafficker who was likely to abscond if granted bail.

Gilligan's efforts eventually paid off, however, when he was given bail in January 2019 after spending another five months of his life inside. The conditions of his release were that he remain in Belfast until his trial. This was later amended and he was allowed to travel outside the jurisdiction.

Eventually, on 29 October that year, the Crown Prosecution Service dropped the charges and Gilligan was free to go. The five months that he had spent in custody were the equivalent of a ten-month sentence. The offence with which he had been charged carried a maximum of six months. For once Gilligan decided that it wasn't worth complaining and headed for Spain again.

The experience did not derail his ambitions in the drug business. It wasn't long before he was again the subject of a major international investigation involving police in Ireland, the UK and Spain. While he was out on bail in Belfast, Gilligan had continued quietly building a modest drug trafficking operation.

On 20 October 2020 he hit the international headlines again when he was one of six people arrested when Spanish police swooped on his new gang in Alicante. The Spanish force was investigating what they said was an Irish-led gang engaged in using the postal service to traffic guns and drugs into the UK and Ireland. Four kilos of marijuana, 15,000 pills, four handguns, two cars, ten mobile phones and documentation were also seized in the series of searches.

The Spanish National Police's dramatic raid on the villa where Gilligan was living in Torrevieja was recorded and uploaded to its official Twitter account. It showed Gilligan being forced to lie on the ground and then being led away in handcuffs.

When they stormed the premises the mob boss was in the process of preparing thousands of Zopilcone or 'Zimmo' pills for postage to Ireland. But it was the discovery by the police of an unusual Colt Python, a .357 Magnum revolver, found buried in Gilligan's garden that ensured that the bust made international news.

In a press statement shortly after the arrest the Spanish detectives caused a sensation when they highlighted the fact that the weapon could have been the one used to murder Veronica Guerin. It was the same make and model used by Dutchy Holland over twenty-four years earlier.

The revelation led to speculation that somehow Gilligan had kept it as a souvenir. In Ireland the hypothesis, while well intentioned, didn't carry much credit among the cops who knew Gilligan best. He wasn't that stupid.

While the Spanish National Police force did not name Gilligan it was clearly pointing the finger at him. He was still being haunted by the sins of the past. In a statement the police said:

> Investigators managed to intercept four postal deliveries in Spain in which four kilos of marijuana and 15,000 pills had been hidden. The well-known Irish criminal who allegedly headed the organization was sentenced to twenty-eight years in prison in 2001 and served seventeen years. Irish investigators linked his organization to the murder of the Irish journalist.

It added:

The revolver that has been found is the same mark and model as the one used in the assassination of an Irish journalist in Dublin in 1996. Spanish officers are working with the Irish police to determine if it's the same gun used to end her life.

Ballistics tests later ruled it out as the murder weapon.

Gilligan meanwhile was arrested and remanded in custody. The sixty-eight-year-old grandfather of organized crime was released on bail just before Christmas 2020. His passport was confiscated and he was barred from leaving Spain. He was also ordered to sign on every fortnight at a court in Alicante.

In February 2021, as part of the ongoing investigation, the Spanish police arrested four more members of Gilligan's gang when they raided a number of properties in Alicante, including a cannabis grow house. In a statement the police said that it had arrested the remaining members of the crime group which it described as an 'Irish organization dependent on the arrested leader'.

At the time of writing, Gilligan is still the subject of the ongoing judge-led criminal investigation. It is understood that the joint Irish, UK and Spanish probe has uncovered extensive evidence of the drug trafficking operation and the supply of firearms to criminals in Ireland and the UK. If convicted Gilligan faces the prospect of five more years in prison.

———

On 26 June 2021 the twenty-fifth anniversary of the murder of Veronica Guerin was commemorated by her family, former colleagues, members of the Lucan Investigation Team and a large section of the Irish population who still remember where they were when they heard the news on that fateful day in 1996.

The reaction illustrated how John Gilligan and the actions of his gang have never been forgotten: he is still as reviled and notorious as ever.

But then it seems that he doesn't want to be forgotten for his horrific crime. On the eve of the anniversary, Friday 25 June, a video was posted on social media showing Gilligan partying with a group of Irish pals at the poolside bar in the Doña Monse Hotel in Torrevieja, Spain.

One member of the entourage boasted how Gilligan had bought two rounds of drinks, blathering: 'It's not often you get two drinks off him!' As the camera turns to Gilligan he is laughing and smiling as others in the background chant: 'He didn't do it.' The video, which was clearly intended to coincide with the anniversary, went viral.

Ireland's most hated crime figure wants the world to know that he hasn't gone away. The final chapter in his life has yet to be written.

ACKNOWLEDGMENTS

This book tells the story of the life and crimes of John Gilligan, Ireland's reviled public enemy number one, whose dark presence has loomed over gangland for decades. It is the culmination of over 25 years spent chronicling the deeds of the man who pioneered the modern drug trade – and murdered a journalist colleague to protect his empire. In many ways it is as much personal as it is business. Much of the material is based on first-hand accounts from the main players in this dramatic story: cops, criminals, victims and associates of Gilligan. I thank them for their generosity and trust along the way – understandably they would prefer to remain anonymous for obvious reasons.

My gratitude and thanks to the indefatigable Charlie Collins of the Collins Photographic Agency for the use of his pictures, including the front cover and to my colleagues at the *Irish Independent* for others. The rest of the photographs were sourced by the author. My gratitude to *Irish Independent* editor Cormac Bourke, head of news Kevin Doyle and news editor Gareth Morgan for kindly allowing me use of the pictures and serialising the book.

As always my deepest thanks to my extremely talented, and patient, editor Aoife Barrett, of Barrett Editing, who has worked on most of my books, making the manuscript both legible and understandable.

And to Ireland's top libel lawyer and my dear friend Kieran Kelly – the Consiglieri – of Flynn O'Driscoll Lawyers who has always been a rock of strength and moral support in the toughest of times.

Thanks also to the doyen of Irish publishing Jonathan Williams of the Jonathan Williams Literary Agency, for his wisdom and impeccable advice. I would also like to thank my publisher, Will Atkinson the MD of Atlantic Books and Atlantic's group associate publisher, Clare Drysdale, who also published my previous bestseller, *The Monk*.

Finally, as always, my love and gratitude to Anne, Jake, Irena, Archie and 'Bunny' for putting up with me.

INDEX